FATAL CHARGE AT GALLIPOLI

FATAL CHARGE AT GALLIPOLI

The Story of One of the Bravest,
and Most Futile,
Actions of the Dardanelles Campaign;
The Light Horse at The Nek, August 1915

John Hamilton

FRONTLINE BOOKS

FATAL CHARGE AT GALLIPOLI
The Story of one of the Bravest, and Most Futile, Actions of
the Dardanelles Campaign
This edition published in 2015 by Frontline Books,
an imprint of Pen & Sword Books Ltd,
47 Church Street, Barnsley, South Yorkshire, S70 2AS

ISBN: 978-1-84832-902-7

First published as *Goodbye Gobber, God Bless You*
by Pan Macmillan Australia Pty Ltd., 2004

CIP data records for this title are available from the British Library

Printed and bound by CPI Group (UK) Ltd, Croydon, CR0 4YY
Typeset in 10.5/12.5 Palatino

For more information on our books, please email: info@frontline-books.com,
write to us at the above address, or visit:
www.frontline-books.com

To all the men who lived and died
in the Gallipoli campaign of 1915.
Lest we forget.

Contents

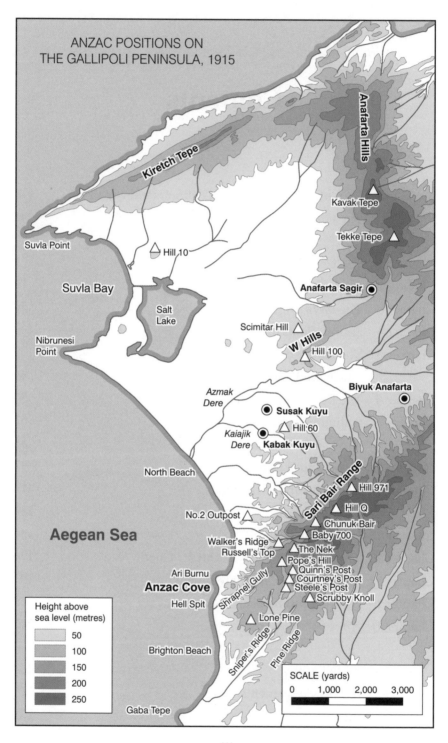

ANZAC POSITIONS ON
THE GALLIPOLI PENINSULA, 1915

Kiretch Tepe

Anafarta Hills

Kavak Tepe

Tekke Tepe

Suvla Point

Hill 10

Suvla Bay

Salt
Lake

Anafarta Sagir

Nibrunesi
Point

Scimitar Hill

W Hills

Hill 100

Biyuk Anafarta

Azmak
Dere

Susak Kuyu

Hill 60

Kaiajik
Dere

Kabak Kuyu

North Beach

Sari Bair Range

Hill 971

No.2 Outpost

Hill Q

Aegean Sea

Chunuk Bair

Baby 700

Walker's Ridge
Russell's Top

The Nek

Pope's Hill

Ari Burnu

Quinn's Post
Courtney's Post

Anzac Cove

Shrapnel Gully

Steele's Post

Hell Spit

Scrubby Knoll

Lone Pine

Height above
sea level (metres)

50

Sniper's Ridge

Pine Ridge

100

Brighton Beach

150

200

SCALE (yards)

250

0   1,000   2,000   3,000

Gaba Tepe

viii

8th Light Horse

By Cuthbert Flynn

Lengthening shadows on lonely graves, blistering bones in the sun,
And I work here at a dreary desk, with a pen instead of a gun.

And yet I belonged to the 8th Light Horse, of the 3rd Light Horse Brigade,
You remember us clattering through the streets, the workmanlike show we
    made;
And don't you remember the waving flags, and the crowd, and the storm of
    cheers,
The women that laughed, and prayed, and wept – the maidens who smiled
    through tears;
And I rode then, with Peter and Ben, their knees pressed hard to mine,
Pete never came back from bloody Anzac, Ben died at Lonesome Pine.

And the shadows lengthen on Peter's grave; Ben's bones bleach in the sun,
And I sit here, with a pen in my ear, while they fall one by one.
I wonder how many are left of the men, of the 3rd Light Horse Brigade,
How many have fallen of those brave chaps, who fought as hard as they
    played,
It's not so long since we laughed at the men who plugged along per boot,
But the 8th Light Horse wouldn't stay behind when the guns began to shoot.
With scarcely a thought for the horses they brought, they went on board with
    a cheer,
They blazed their track at grim Anzac – and I sit lonely here.

Out of six hundred and fifty men, answered the roll-call a score,
The horses may wait on the lines awhile, their riders will come no more.

Tiny and Lofty, Peter and Mick, all of us comrades true,
We lived and loved, and worked and played, and quarrelled as comrades do.
And I remember how Lofty laughed, and the way Mick brushed his hair;
They all of them fell in that one mad rush – bar me, and I wasn't there.
I'll bet they were first in that frenzied burst when the 8th Light Horse went
    down
In a hail of shell, and a blast from hell, that won them a hero's crown.

Lofty lies broken on Turkish soil, Mick's eyes stare at the sun;
And Tiny has gone to his last account, with his fingers clutching his gun.

The skies are blue, and the air is clear, and the sun shines overhead,
But I could choke when I think of the smokes I've borrowed from men who
    are dead.
The dearest mates that a man could have, are numbered among the slain.
The men that turned out to 'stables' with me will never do 'stables' again.
No more will 'reveille' awake Jim McNally – he too is gone with them all;
'Tis easy to die, do you wonder that I was silent at duty's call?

But the shadows still lengthen on lonely graves, the bones still bleach in the
    sun,
And I sit here at a dreary desk, with a pen instead of a gun.

So shed me a tear for the gallant 8th, of the 3rd Light Horse Brigade,
Who went to their death with as steady a nerve as they rode out on parade,
And if they discarded a few odd clothes – if they didn't look pretty well,
They sewed a patch on the back of their shirts, and they charged like the
    hammers of hell.
They didn't hang back, on the slopes of Anzac – through a solid wall of lead;
They dashed and then they died like men – God rest their gallant dead.

And I wonder whatever they think of me, in their shallow graves in the sand,
That I didn't charge with them at grim Anzac,
That the tears of a woman held me back,
And the clutch of a baby's hand.

Introduction:

The Hill of Valour

High above Anzac Cove on the Gallipoli peninsula is a place where few visitors stop because there is so little to see: a tiny war cemetery called The Nek at Russell's Top, up Walker's Ridge.

Most Australians and New Zealanders knew of the bloodstained Walker's Ridge once. It was as famous and familiar in battlefield despatches as the Dardanelles campaign itself.

Today you don't have to climb the ridge to get to The Nek. You can drive there, taking a small turn-off from the road that now snakes its way along the front lines between the battlefields halfway up the Sari Bair Range.

You can walk much of this road in less than an hour. Famous names like Lone Pine and Quinn's Post are marked, other stop-off points, and you stride on from them, up the hill past The Nek, to the bushy bumps known as Baby 700 and Battleship Hill, and then on further up to the commanding hump of Chunuk Bair. Everything is so close here. Chunuk Bair is only a few kilometres from where the first Australians landed at the Cove on 25 April 1915, way down there below the wrinkled crevices and to the left.

The Anzacs' front line here was reached from North Beach below by the long and dangerous climb up this rough and jagged spur. Men toiled up and down here constantly with food, ammunition and water. Or they waited it out, simply existing in shallow burrows and on ledges on the sides of Walker's Ridge. They were under constant threat by snipers hidden in the crags around them and by sudden, vicious bursts of exploding shrapnel, as they waited their turn to go up, yet again, and fill the trenches facing the Turks only a matter of metres away at the top.

At the end of that first day, 25 April, there were 2,000 men dead or wounded, and on the beach the gravel and the rocks were slippery with their blood.

By the end of eight-and-a-half months of the Gallipoli campaign, nearly 60,000 men would have lived on the heights, the slopes and the valleys here, like rodents, scuttling along the maze of trenches and saps, with the flies forming a constant blue-green spread on their food to match the colour of the swollen corpses in No Man's Land. A trench life of bullets and bombs, snipers and shrapnel, blood and bayonets, diarrhoea and enteric fever.

When you're here alone, it is not hard to feel you are with the spirits of the Anzacs on Gallipoli. Walk the battlefields, climb the ravines, scramble up the crumbling gullies ... then stop.

Sometimes you feel there is someone walking beside or behind you. You look around – nobody.

Yellow gorse blazes. There is the smell of wild thyme. Tiny birds twitter in the prickly undergrowth. A hawk hovers over the nearby Sphinx.

Nobody.

Then silence again, deep brooding silence. And sadness. It envelops you like a blanket.

Once there was chatter and chiacking, laughter here too, 90 years ago. Along with the shriek of shellfire, the stutter of rifle fire, the snicker of machine-guns, the thud of homemade bombs. The screams and cries for help of the dying and wounded. Now only stillness.

The first thing that strikes any new visitor to Gallipoli is how very small and rugged the whole killing ground is. English names have been given to all these gullies, ledges, dips and valleys – Turkish features so insignificant to farmers and fishermen until war came here.

Walker's Ridge, for instance, should really be Serce Tepesi, which means 'Sparrow Hill', after the little birds that again dart and chatter uninterrupted in the bushes growing over the holes that were once dugouts and the furrows that were trenches.

Here on top of Sari Bair, part of the Kocacimen Tepe range that joins a spine along part of the peninsula, the distance between the Australian and Turkish trenches was little more than today's two-lane stretch of winding bitumen. Easy then for a quick throw of a handmade jam-tin bomb or a pot shot by a sniper with a spotter looking over the parapet through a hand-held periscope. The cemetery at The Nek is built over this short corridor – No Man's Land, as it was 90 years ago. It measures only 25 metres by 33 metres. There are only ten raised grave markers in its springy turf, set in two clumps of five, separated by the grass where a few small wild mauve anemones glow in the spring sunshine.

A low stone wall surrounds the cemetery. Its raised and simple main memorial is common to all 31 cemeteries here, made from clean Turkish limestone, carved with a cross and the words 'Their Name Liveth For

Evermore'. Around the cemetery are carefully planted flowerbeds with purple irises bursting out of bud, and there is the scent of wild thyme and rosemary in the air. The soil is crumbly, brownish yellow, half clay with small round pebbles. There is a glorious view to the north, over the prickly oak bushes that cover the ridge, down to the blue Aegean Sea and a flat white shimmering salt lake that points the way to Suvla. To the left and right of this narrow cemetery the land falls away down steep and wild razorbacks, places where only goats could carefully pick their way without falling.

There are no clues in the grave markers to tell us what happened here. Five of the graves honour those who are known to be buried in this cemetery; the other five mark special memorials to those only believed to be buried here. Only one grave has an epitaph:

TROOPER H.E. STANLEY 8LH. AGE 20
ANOTHER HERO'S PART IS DONE
ANOTHER SOUL GONE WEST

Trooper 857 Stanley. Young Bert Stanley was only nineteen years and three months old when he enlisted in 1914, riding away from the property called 'Mount Cole' near Ararat in far-western Victoria, where he worked as a farm labourer and orchardist. His enlistment papers show he was nearly 5 feet 9 inches tall, weighed 151 pounds, and had light brown hair, a fair complexion and grey eyes.

Bert's father was dead so, on 9 November 1914, it was his mother, Janet, who scrawled in ink on a piece of lined note paper: 'I freely give my consent for my son Herbert Stanley to volunteer for service.' Almost exactly a year later Janet would begin receiving a pension of £1 a week from a grateful nation, in recognition of her son's death, and in 1921, she was given a memorial scroll and a message from King George V.

Then, on Anzac Day 1922, a message was sent from Australia House in London to the Department of Defence in Melbourne. Bert Stanley's identity disc had been picked up outside The Nek Cemetery, Anzac, 'separate from any remains with which it might have been connected', and the Imperial War Graves Commission (as the Commonwealth War Graves Commission was then known) had 'intimated that it is their intention to add Tpr. Stanley's name to the "presumed to be buried roll" for the cemetery'. His mother received the worn identity disc two months later. His grave could now be marked with the epitaph that she chose.

And so Bert Stanley lies up here beyond Walker's Ridge on top of a scrubby peak in Turkey, the only Australian light horse trooper really personally remembered here.

Behind the cemetery's main memorial is a grove of pine trees where the wind sighs. Beneath the tree nearest to the road is a bronze plaque, modelled and placed there by an Australian called Ross Bastiaan, who has dedicated himself to remember the fallen in foreign fields. But the plaque is now weathered dull by the severe Gallipoli winters and the harsh summer sun, so much so that the words (in both English and Turkish) are sometimes hard to make out. 'The Nek', reads the heading, almost half covered by pine needles and crusted with bird droppings. Below it there is the following inscription:

> This key position defended vigorously by both sides saw repeated attacks across this narrow ridge. The Anzac trenches were located close to the cemetery. The Turkish trenches originated near the bare raised memorial stone on your right and went in 8 tiers to the top of the next hill (Baby 700).
>
> A courageous but futile attack by the Australians was made on August 7, 1915 when over 300 men were killed immediately in front of you.

In fact, 326 soldiers of the British Empire, some from earlier fighting, lie here, in six rows under the turf, from a battlefield area that could be covered by just three tennis courts. Most are the men of the 3rd Australian Light Horse Brigade.

Just after dawn on that day in August 1915, some 600 men charged across this tiny space in four lines that followed one after another, 150 men at a time. They did not hesitate as they ran to their deaths wearing ragged shorts and worn flannel shirts, with roughly stitched white patches on the back and white armbands – for the purpose of recognition during the expected hand-to-hand fighting with the Turks.

The Australians were armed with rifles, but with no bullets in the breech. Only fixed bayonets. And they were mown down like wheat before a combine harvester. Flattened by the hailstorm of enemy rifle fire and the torrents of lead from machine-guns that hosed this tiny battlefield, back and forth, back and forth, from the eight tiers of trenches on the rising hillock of Baby 700 ahead. It was a massacre.

The Turks had also charged down this hill and across the same piece of ground, just five weeks earlier, in another feat of heroic madness. They'd lost at least as many soldiers, probably many more. The Turks now call this place Cesarit Tepe ('Hill of Valour').

Their memorial is half hidden in the pine grove, where their trenches began, almost discreetly veiled away from the bare Australian plot.

Here each March they celebrate the Battle of Çannakale, the glorious victory of 1915 when Mustafa Kemal – later the legendary Atatürk, creator of modern, secular Turkey – took on the might of the invading Allies, sunk half their navy and, after a long and bitter land battle, forced the invaders to abandon the peninsula and go home.

It cost the Allies over 141,000 casualties, but the Turks nearly 214,000 men, including 86,000 dead or missing.

Most of their fallen have no known graves. In fact, there are very few Turkish burial grounds, the majority of the dead having tumbled into abandoned trenches and tunnels or over cliffs. The bone shards are still washed to the surface after the winter rains, brittle as teacher's chalk or crumbly like feta cheese. Turk or Australian, New Zealander, Briton or Frenchman, there is no difference when the bones are washed up. It is not hard to find them.

And with the bone shards comes the detritus of battle. A brass bullet casing now verdigris green, the firing-pin imprint still marking a definite full stop on the detonator cap; squares of shell casing like Scrabble tiles; thin Turkish bullets and fatter Australian bullets lying like sullen lead slugs in the yellow-brown dirt; wafer-thin rusty slivers of bully beef cans; brown shards of shattered stone rum jars; and, occasionally, uniform buttons that still gleam when washed and polished.

During the eight-and-a-half months of the Gallipoli campaign, about 1,000,000 men from both sides fought here. Between one-third and a half of that figure became casualties.

Some 60,000 Australians, the majority of them very young, came to fight on Gallipoli against an enemy that most had never heard of when they rushed to join up eight months before. A total 8,709 were to be killed in action or died of wounds.

The dead – the *identifiable* dead – were buried in the 31 cemeteries that sprinkle the beaches, the valleys, the ridges and the plains, with their flat, identical concrete markers pushing up through the well-tended turf like orderly rows of flat grey mushrooms. So many of the dead were never identified.

The remains of those who died on No Man's Land that dreadful day on The Nek were not found until 1919, when the ridge was visited by the Australian Historical Mission and the Imperial War Graves Commission.

'We found the low scrub there literally strewn with their relics,' wrote Australia's official war historian C.E.W. Bean in his account of the mission's work. His companion, artist George Lambert, insisted on going back there one morning so he could feel the atmosphere, and to draw in the dawn light in which the charge at The Nek had been made. The famous painting that resulted now hangs in the Australian War Memorial in Canberra. Below it, there are display cabinets full of pieces they collected: a water bottle pock-sieved with bullet holes, a frayed dark-stained canvas fragment, a pile of sharp-pointed, spent bullets …

'Very cold, bleak and lonely,' wrote Lambert in his diary, 'the jackals, damn them, were chorusing their hate, the bones showed up white even in the faint dawn and I felt rotten … the worst feature of this after battle work is that the silent hills and valleys sit stern and unmoved, callous of the human, and busy only in growing bush and sliding earth to cover the scars left by the war-disease.'

The silent hills and valleys still sit stern and unmoved today. The scars are still there, zigzag depressions under the prickle bush where men once lived and died in the trenches.

The bodies of some of those who died at The Nek on 7 August, those who died of their wounds in the trenches or whose bodies were hauled in by grappling hooks thrown out afterwards, are buried elsewhere. The epitaphs of these men were supplied by their loved ones and added to the markers when the Imperial War Graves Commission had finished its work. They scream out today across the decades, rage against the sadness and futility of war.

Just a short stroll from The Nek is another small cemetery on Walker's Ridge, where a further 92 men are buried or remembered. The graves are separated into two plots by an old trench line that runs through the middle.

There in the second row, grave C4, lies Trooper Harold Rush, aged 23, of the 10th Light Horse. He was originally an apprentice clothier, born in Suffolk, England, who sailed off to Australia to start a new life, free of class distinction, as a farmer in Western Australia. He would have spoken with the soft singing burr of the English countryside, yet he spoke in the words of an Australian.

Trooper Rush died at The Nek. Back in Britain, his father, in service at Broome Hall (the large country house later to be the seat of the descendants of Lord Kitchener), chose the epitaph etched on his son's headstone:

> HIS LAST WORDS
> 'GOODBYE COBBER
> GOD BLESS YOU'

Each year, growing numbers of pilgrims come to this remote peninsula over 300 kilometres from the great city of Istanbul with its ancient mosques, minarets and sultans' palaces. They come here for Anzac Day, the anniversary of that moment in time – 4.18 am on Sunday, 25 April 1915 – when the first boats grounded in Anzac Cove and the struggle began. It is commemorated each year by the thousands of people who shiver for hours wrapped in sleeping bags and flags, awaiting the dawn service. They pause and they cry as they read the words of Kemal Atatürk on the massive concrete memorial erected here by the Turks:

> Those heroes that shed their blood
> And lost their lives …
> You are now lying in the soil of a friendly country.
> Therefore rest in peace.
> There is no difference between the
> Johnnies
> And the Mehmets to us where they lie side
> By side
> Here in this country of ours …
> You, the mothers,
> Who sent their sons from far away
> Countries
> Wipe away your tears,
> Yours sons are now lying in our bosom
> And are in peace.
> After having lost their lives on this land
> They have
> Become our sons as well.

The pilgrims today are mostly young. They have established a new tradition. The first real pilgrimage back here was in 1925, when 400 survivors and relatives came aboard the *Ormonde* for the unveiling of the New Zealand Memorial on Chunuk Bair.

A year later *Stella d'Italia* sailed in with 300 passengers. From 1936, however, the peninsula became a Turkish military zone again and for 30 years visitors were required to have formal permission to enter, with a military escort.

Then things began to change. Film-maker Peter Weir visited in 1976, discovered relics in Shrapnel Valley, and said he 'felt like an archaeologist wandering through the ruins of some earlier Australian civilisation'. He was inspired to make the moving film *Gallipoli*, which created enormous interest – a yearning, even – especially in the young, to see the peninsula for themselves. Interest was boosted further in 1990 when a specially equipped Qantas Boeing 747 flew the last remaining

100 Anzacs to Turkey for the seventy-fifth anniversary of the landing, and again in 2000 when 10,000 Australians came to Gallipoli to commemorate the eighty-fifth anniversary with Prime Minister John Howard.

Today, visiting Gallipoli at this time has become an established rite of passage. Australians and New Zealanders make their way to their own Mecca, trying to explore their own kind of national legacy, the hard-to-explain words of the Anzac legend, the mystery of its mantra: fortitude, friendship, kindness, humour and irreverence.

Who were these Anzacs exactly? Why did they come here? What happened to them? Again and again the questions are asked as the young roam the cemeteries before and after the Anzac Day ceremonies, reading the family inscriptions, absorbing the grief, learning of an age altogether foreign to Australia today. It was an age when men went off to war to fight for God, King and Empire; when Australians were British. But it does relate to today because the men who fought were the same ages as many of today's pilgrims, and they left mothers, sweethearts, wives and families back in their remote island home so very far away.

The Anzacs came here as part of a large Allied expeditionary force that was landed on the Gallipoli peninsula in the second year of the First World War as a strategy to break the trench-warfare deadlock on Europe's western front. The aim was to secure the important straits of the Dardanelles, cause a Turkish surrender at Constantinople (present-day Istanbul), and then open up a new southern front against Germany and its allies.

But the Gallipoli campaign was ill-planned and an almost total shambles from start to finish, soon getting itself bogged down itself into a stalemate interrupted by desperate hand-to-hand fighting in the trenches. The only real success occurred when the Allies were eventually forced to evacuate, and the top-secret withdrawal operation resulted in just a handful of casualties.

In between the landing and the evacuation was the August Offensive, when a series of co-ordinated actions were launched to try to break out of the impasse. Although it was only one of a number of failed actions at that time, there was nothing sadder or more futile than the charge of the 8th and 10th regiments of the 3rd Australian Light Horse Brigade at The Nek. It was heroic but it could have been stopped. In the words of Lieutenant Colonel Noel Brazier, commanding officer of the 10th, it was sheer bloody murder as well.

The regiments were completely shattered. Those who did survive were affected for the rest of their lives. Few wanted to talk about it, even to their loved ones. Those responsible closed ranks and later blamed each other. Reports of the action were censored or held up. Officialdom rather hoped that The Nek would go away and be forgotten. It was all a ghastly mistake, a tragedy, a failure, to be eclipsed in historical memory by the lasting glory and the nobility of the seven Victoria Crosses won in the victorious action at Lone Pine, which had begun the previous evening at a place across from Walker's Ridge.

On 15 August 1915, eight days after the charge at The Nek, Charles Bean, official correspondent with the Australian Expeditionary Force (and later official historian, of course), filed a despatch back home reconstructing what had happened at The Nek. Under the headline 'Gallant Australians', the report only appeared in *The Argus* on 28 September.

> There are no Victoria Crosses, there are no Birthday Honours; but for sheer self-sacrificing heroism there was never a deed in history that surpassed the charge which two Australian Light Horse regiments made in the first light of Saturday, August 7, in order to help their comrades in a critical moment of a great battle.
>
> And as for the boys – the single-minded, loyal, Australian country lads who left their trenches in the grey light of that morning to bivouac in the scrub that evening the shades of evening found them lying in the scrub with the wide sky above them.

No official list of the total casualties at The Nek has yet been found. The official war historian's best estimate compiled from several sources says that the 8th Light Horse suffered 234 casualties – including 154 dead – out of 300 men. In the confusion before and afterwards, there could have been more.

The 10th suffered 138 casualties including 80 dead. Like the 8th, they were the flower of their state's manhood, cut down in their prime and scattered on this godforsaken ridge like dead weeds.

This book is an account of some of the men, mostly from the 8th and the 10th regiments, and their great adventure as they set out from Australia into the unknown, to fight for King and Country. It is offered, humbly, to their immortal memory.

Chapter 1

The Coming of War

On Sunday, 2 August 1914, Phillip Frederick Edward Schuler, a 25-year-old reporter with *The Age* newspaper, was a guest at a suburban tennis party in Melbourne. He was affectionately known to his many friends as 'Peter' and he never forgot the impact of that day. Within a year he would be the newspaper's correspondent on Gallipoli.

As the gathering storm began to break, Schuler wrote of an army friend hastily being summoned to leave that winter tennis party:

> When I went to see him at Victoria Barracks the same night, I found the whole place a glare of lights from end to end of the grim, grey stone building. It was the same the next and the next night and for weeks, and so on into the months.
>
> But even when the Governor General, Sir Ronald Munro-Ferguson, sent to the Prime Minister, Mr Joseph Cook, the telegram bearing the announcement that we all knew could no longer be withheld, the strain seemed unlifted.
>
> 'England has declared war on Germany' was the brief but terrible message quickly transferred to the broadsheets that the newspapers printed at lightning speed and circulated while the crowds in the street cheered and cheered again as the message was posted on the display boards.

Outside the office of *The Age*, there was now almost always a permanent crowd as the crisis unfolded. They sang *Rule Britannia*, *Soldiers of the King* and *Sons of the Sea* over and over again. People who waved Union Jacks were raised shoulder high. There were frequent choruses of *God Save the King*, men and women standing to attention. If any man forgot to remove his hat, he was soundly abused.

'That night the streets were thronged,' wrote Schuler, 'as they were for weeks to follow and there was a series of riots, quickly subdued by the police, where raids had been made on German premises. Feeling was extraordinarily bitter considering the remoteness of the Dominion ...'

The crisis had developed with extraordinary speed since 28 June, the day that a seemingly obscure event took place in far-off Europe: the assassination of the heir to the Austrian throne by a Serbian nationalist. Most Australians, on their farms and their stations, or in their shops and their factories, would have been very hard put to find either nation on an atlas of the world.

European nations now jostled into alliances. On 30 July, Australians read that Austria-Hungary had declared war on Serbia, and Russia was mobilising to help its fellow Slavs in Serbia. Germany had then issued Russia with a warning; and if Germany declared war on Russia then France would be called in to help its ally, Russia. The dominoes were ready to fall.

If France was brought in, the expectation was that Britain would be pushed in also, as there existed an informal agreement between the two countries to support each other if attacked. And if Britain entered the war, Australia would be there.

On 30 July 1914, a coded cablegram sent the day before from the British Government arrived at Government House in Melbourne, the seat of the Commonwealth Government. The gracious white Victorian mansion, reached by a long carriageway and surrounded by sweeping lawns, with the Royal Botanic Gardens as its backyard, was a rich copy of Queen Victoria's country house on the Isle of Wight, complete with a ballroom and a gilded throne. And here resided the newly arrived representative of the King, Governor-General Sir Ronald Craufurd Munro-Ferguson, heir to a Scottish estate.

The secret cable warned the government of the imminent danger of war and that it was time, if the government thought fit, to bring into force the 'precautionary stage' of a secret defence scheme – the mobilisation of Australian men for the armed forces. The cable was relayed to Sir Ronald, who was in Sydney on 30 July, as was the Minister for Defence, Senator Mullen. But the Prime Minister, Joseph Cook, was in Melbourne, albeit somewhat distracted by the federal election campaign then under way against Andrew Fisher, the Leader of the Opposition.

There was some scrambling and muddle initially, therefore. The only concrete action for the next couple of days was when Minister for Defence Mullen requested that the acting chief of the military staff travel up by train from Melbourne and meet him in Sydney, thus leaving Australia's military headquarters at Victoria Barracks without a leader.

Rather than call an immediate cabinet meeting, the Prime Minister was busy preparing for an important speech at Colac in Victoria, while the rest of his ministers were scattered throughout Australia. (One received an urgent telegram in the country but there was nobody with him who could decode it.)

On 31 July the Governor-General, still in Sydney, put the pressure on from London. He sent a telegram to Cook: 'Would it not be well in view of the latest news from Europe, that ministers should meet in order that Imperial Government may know what support to expect from Australia?'

That night the Minister for Defence issued a statement: 'If necessity arises, Australia will recognise she is not merely a fair-weather partner of the Empire, but a component part in all circumstances.'

The same night, Andrew Fisher, 'a man of translucent honesty and high purpose' who would go on to win the election and become Prime Minister on 5 September, stood in a hall in Colac and declared famously: 'Should the worst happen, after everything has been done that honour will permit, Australia will stand by the mother country to our last man and our last shilling.' The sentiment was echoed by Prime Minister Cook, speaking the night after Fisher, in the same hall: 'If there is to be a war, you and I shall be in it. We must be in it. If the old country is at war, so are we.'

The die was cast. On the afternoon of 3 August, Cook convened a special cabinet meeting, after which a cable was sent immediately to London:

> In the event of war the Government is prepared to place the vessels of the Australian Navy under the control of the British Admiralty when desired. It is further prepared to despatch an expeditionary force of 20,000 men of any suggested composition to any destination desired by the Home Government, the force to be at the complete disposal of the Home Government. The cost of despatch and maintenance will be borne by this [Australian] Government.

So Australia had committed itself to sending troops even before war had been declared. Cook announced the offer to the press after leaving cabinet and the news was published in the British press the next day. The Imperial Government responded that while there was no immediate need for the force, 'it would be wise to take steps in case the necessity arose.'

War was declared on the night of 4 August in London (9 am on 5 August in eastern Australia) but already men had started to appear at military headquarters in both Sydney and Melbourne, begging to enlist. On 5 August a staff was set up at Victoria Barracks to register their names. That same day the Governor-General cabled London: 'There is indescribable enthusiasm and entire unanimity throughout Australia in support of all that tends to provide for the security of empire at war.' The day afterwards, the Secretary of State for the Colonies telegraphed that the British Government 'gratefully accepted the offer ... to send a force of 20,000 men and would be glad if it could be despatched as soon as possible'.

'A tremendous wave of enthusiasm swept over the land,' wrote Schuler, 'and the acceptance by the Home Government of the offer was the occasion of great outbursts of cheering by the crowds that thronged the streets of the great cities and eagerly scanned the news sheets and official announcements posted outside the newspaper offices. Recruiting began without delay.'

In fact, recruiting for the Australian Expeditionary Force did not begin until 12 August, although many men had offered their names before war had even begun, of course. Initially the force was to comprise of a complete division (a full British division at the time comprised 18,000 men) and a brigade of the light horse. The initial offer was for 2,226 men and 2,315 horses.

The origins of the Australian light horse go back well before Federation. In the early 1800s the number of British forces stationed in the Australian colonies began to decline, and the colonies were told to raise volunteers to fill the gaps. The Crimean War of 1853-56 proved to be a catalyst and 1854 saw the formation of the Victorian Volunteer Yeomanry Corps, the Adelaide Mounted Rifles and the New South Wales Cavalry Troop. Five years later there were other volunteer mounted detachments in New South Wales, Queensland, Western Australia and Victoria.

In Victoria by 1861 there were a number of independent mounted troops, who wore extravagant uniforms of their own devising and took their names from local towns – such as the Castlemaine Dragoons and the Kyneton Mounted Rifles. Eventually the Victorian independents were amalgamated under the title of 'the Royal Victorian Cavalry Regiment', with each troop being distinguished by the name of the town from which it was raised. They were also granted the prefix 'Prince of Wales' in honour of the marriage of the heir apparent to the British throne.

In 1876 General Sir William Jervois was appointed as governor of South Australia – and commissioner of defences for all colonies except for Western Australia. He recommended that the best way of ensuring a volunteer force was to introduce partial pay for militia units. As Australia was a country of vast distances where horses and horse-drawn vehicles were essential, it was natural that the numbers and importance of mounted troops would continue to grow. The Darling Downs Mounted Infantry in Queensland, the Victorian Mounted Rifles and the Tasmanian First Light Cavalry Corps, were all birthplaces of the Australian light horse and there were many more. By 1900 Australia could muster 18 mounted regiments and 29 infantry regiments.

Three months before the Boer War broke out in 1899, Queensland offered 250 mounted troops to the British Government, an offer that was soon followed by bushmen on horse from the other states.

The recruiting standards were advertised in the press and state gazettes: 'Men to be good shots and proficient swordsmen, of superior physique, not under 5ft 6in or 34 in chest, good riders and bushmen accustomed to find their way about in strange country.'

The Australian horsemen who went into action in southern Africa were attached to British regiments, fighting in what was an empire army. They learned a great deal about the art of soldiering from the British and, conversely, the British soon became impressed by this colonial force, which easily adapted to fighting a guerrilla war with the Boers over countryside that was remarkably similar to parts of Australia.

The Australian bushmen had grown up in the saddle and were used to living rough in tough conditions and extremes of climate. They could make do with little food and water, and knew how to use a gun to live off the land. Being on their own did not worry them. Joining together with others for big jobs like mustering on stations meant they could also come together and work as a team: they could rely on their mates. Translated into military life, this meant that the light horseman could operate effectively as a fighting unit on his own or mesh in with a section, troop, squadron or regiment, as needed.

By the end of the Boer War in June 1902, Australia had sent 16,175 mounted men and 16,314 horses. The reputation of the Australian light horse had been made and the experience of these men, many of whom would later join the light horse again and serve as veterans on Gallipoli, would be invaluable. As observed by one British general, who had once commanded a section of mounted Australians on the veldt: 'The Australian Light Horseman combines with a splendid physique, a restless activity of mind … on every variety of ground – mountain, plain, desert, swamp or jungle – the Australian Light Horseman has proved himself equal to the best.'

Similarly impressed was Lord Kitchener, who visited Australia a few years later as a guest of the new Commonwealth Government. The

British field marshal made an inspection and pronounced that the light horse were 'the pick of the bunch'. They were less disciplined than British cavalry, he said, but capable of showing more initiative; in short, they were 'real thrusters'.

By 1914 there were 23 light horse regiments throughout the country, made up of 456 officers and 6,508 men of other ranks. Most owned or bred the horses on which they did their few weeks of compulsory annual training.

Despite the fact that the Australian Military Forces (as the home service was called) had some 45,000 militia at their disposal by August 1914, Australia had decided to send an entirely new force to the service of the empire. The majority of this militia were aged between nineteen and 21, and Australia could not send away an army of boys, however willing. As large numbers were required for what was generally accepted as a short-term engagement, it was decided to raise a separate army, which would have its own commander, headquarters and staff.

As for a name for this new force, its recently appointed commander, General William Thorsby Bridges, had firm views: 'I want a name that will sound well when they call us by our initials. That's how they will speak of us.' And so he decided on 'the Australian Imperial Force' and, sure enough, the initials 'AIF' would never be forgotten by history.

The scheme for the new army went ahead with breakneck speed. The proposed date for embarkation was 10 September. By 8 August, General Bridges had decided that the force would be drawn largely from men who had undergone some training. Half would be those then serving in the citizen army, mainly youngsters; the other half was to be made up of men not then in the forces but who had once been in the militia or had served in the Boer or other wars. The units would be connected with the different states and were to be definitely local and territorial. The infantry and light horse regiments would continue to be recruited from their own states throughout the war.

Pay was decided. A private would get 5 shillings a day active pay and 1 shilling a day deferred (to be paid on discharge). The 'six bob a day' soldiers were getting more than a private in any other army: the New Zealander got 5 shillings, the American 4 shillings and 7 pence, the British Tommy only 1 shilling a day at the beginning of the war. The Australian officers, though, were not to be particularly well paid. A lieutenant would get £1 1 shilling a day while abroad; a captain £1 6 shillings. Even a brigadier general only £2 12 shillings and 6 pence.

The majority of the men and officers were not in it for the money. Some who had been officers in the militia entered the AIF as privates, and some who could have had a commission enlisted in the ranks to be alongside a mate. Brothers often joined to be together in the same unit – one could be an officer, the other a private. 'For the most part the wealthy, the educated, the rough and the case-hardened, poor Australians, rich Australians, went into the ranks together unconscious of any distinction,' wrote Bean. 'When they came into an atmosphere of class difference later in the war, they stoutly and rebelliously resented it.'

The recruiting tables were set up around the country on 11 August and the rush to enlist began the following morning. There were 1,000 waiting outside the gates of Victoria Barracks in Melbourne an hour before the first man signed up. Across Australia there were extraordinary stories of men riding 3,000 kilometres or more to a recruiting centre or walking hundreds of kilometres to answer the call.

Recruits like Harold Brentnall and George Fish did not have so far to travel. Harold had just turned nineteen and was training to be a dental mechanic. Leaving his Nicholson Street home in the inner-Melbourne suburb of Brunswick, he would have taken the cable car that ran past his front door, past the Our Lady Help of Christians red-brick church on the hill, with its gold statue of the Madonna, on into the city. A short walk across Princes Bridge and then it was up to the bluestone barracks on St Kilda Road.

Harold didn't know George Fish then. They were to meet at the Broadmeadows Army Camp to the north of Melbourne. George was just 23 years and five months old, a salesman with Felton, Grimwade and Company, the big manufacturing chemists. He left for the war from a neat Victorian cottage in Mackay Street, Essendon, which stands to this day, with its wrought-iron, cream picket fence and pale rose bushes in the front garden.

George's sister, Jessie, went to visit her brother at Broadmeadows after he had been accepted. That's where she met Harold Brentnall. A hundred letters later, she would marry Harold when he came back from the war.

A dental mechanic and a chemical salesman – sufficient qualifications for both to be accepted for the 2nd Field Ambulance, First AIF. One year later they would be on Gallipoli as stretcher-bearers, carrying the shattered remains of the light horse regiments down from the heights, down the crumbly brown banks of Walker's Ridge, as the snipers' bullets zipped and the shrapnel shredded, and they washed the blood off the canvas in Anzac Cove.

There had been enormous enthusiasm to join the light horse across Australia and soon the original plans were expanded to admit more volunteers. They became part of a well-organised mobile army.

The *Australian Light Horse Training Manual* of 1910 had set out plans for wartime establishment and elaborate training procedures. Specifically, the light horse mounted forces were to be organised into brigades and then broken down progressively into smaller, flexible groups, as follows:

- A brigade (between 1,500 and 1,700 men) consisted of three regiments of light horsemen.
- At the outbreak of war, each regiment had an establishment figure of some 25 officers and 497 troopers.
- The regiment was broken down into three squadrons – A, B and C – often with a four-man machine-gun section attached.
- Each squadron was then divided into six troops, each consisting of approximately 32 men and their horses.
- Each troop was then broken down further into sections, four men to a section.

The first light horse brigade to be raised was made up of the 1st Australian Light Horse Regiment (drawn from New South Wales), the 2nd (from Queensland) and the 3rd (jointly from South Australia and Tasmania). A further regiment, the 4th, was raised in Victoria, to go with the infantry initially as its 'divisional cavalry'.

So many men from the bush, the towns and the cities were coming forward that a second light horse brigade was offered. It was made up of the 5th Regiment (from Queensland) and the 6th and 7th (both from New South Wales). But still the rush continued, and before the end of September it was found that many experienced horsemen were being forced to enlist in the infantry – because the mounted corps were full. Added to this there was added pressure from the Western Australian Government, which felt that the state's own horsemen should be taking part in the call to arms.

So the decision was made to raise a third light horse brigade. This would comprise: the 8th Light Horse Regiment (from Victoria), the 9th (made up of two squadrons from South Australia and one squadron from Victoria) and the 10th (from Western Australia). Like the other two light horse brigades, it also had its own attached signal troops, light horse field ambulances and brigade trains, but no horse artillery or field engineers.

Before the 3rd Light Horse Brigade was formed, Harold Brentnall, George Fish and the other first army recruits in Victoria were heading towards Broadmeadows, the name bestowed, perhaps by some early

8

property developer with a poetic imagination, on a sometimes dusty, sometimes muddy stretch of ground on the northern outskirts of Melbourne. The city had earned itself the sobriquet 'Marvellous Melbourne' after the gold rushes of the 1850s, and now Victoria's capital was caught up in the new fever of the recruiting rush.

The Broadmeadows Army Camp (or 'Concentration Camp' as it was termed on maps of the day!) opened on 14 August 1914. The army had moved fast.

One of the first to start organising the training camp was Ernest Albert Smith, a 44-year-old clerk in the Education Department. He had served as a bombardier previously in the old Victorian Permanent Artillery, when General Bridges was an instructor – and the commanding officer of the First AIF knew his man. Ernest enlisted on the first day of recruiting and was immediately promoted to sergeant; on 17 August he was placed in charge of the advance party at Broadmeadows to prepare the camp for the volunteers. This advance party consisted of thirteen men in makeshift uniforms who, posing for a photograph at the camp, christened themselves 'the Cheerful Idiots'. The camp would eventually stretch over 3 kilometres wide by nearly 2 kilometres deep.

The Argus newspaper gave a breathless preview of what was expected to happen when the rest of the first volunteers set off for Broadmeadows two days later:

> The first of the main body will march through the city streets passing the Town Hall shortly after 11 am and the public will have the opportunity of forming an opinion of the splendid material from which the expeditionary force is to be moulded ... The nucleus of the four battalions numbering 1,500 men will be paraded at Victoria Barracks and accompanied by three bands will pass through the city and up the Sydney Road to Broadmeadows. Colonel M'Cay [Colonel James Whiteside M'Cay had been appointed to command the first brigade raised in Victoria] intends taking no risks of his troops developing sore feet in the initial stages of their work but as a precautionary measure he is anxious to have on hand a stock of Vaseline or any soothing ointment equal to treating 1,000 cases a day ... The need might recommend itself for the attention of those public spirited citizens who are anxious to do something for the young soldiers.

Men who had been medically examined, many of whom had signed up at other places, assembled at Victoria Barracks on 19 August 1914. At 9.30 am, 2,500 men set out to march to Broadmeadows. Some were in

Citizen Military Force uniforms; the majority were in civilian clothes. After a number of rest stops en route, the men reached the camp at 5 pm and went under canvas.

Phillip Schuler of *The Age* witnessed the march and would write of it later:

> [A] band of cheerful youths ... headed by a band of Highland pipes and bugles that had volunteered to lead them, swinging with irregular broken step along the main streets. Their pride swelled in their veins as they waved brown felt hats, straw deckers, and bowlers to their mates watching from office windows and roofs.
>
> It was the first sight of the reality of war that had come to really grip the hearts of the people, and they cheered these pioneers and the recklessness of their spirits.
>
> There were men in good boots and bad boots, in brown and tan shoes, in hardly any boots at all; in sack suits and old clothes and smart-cut suits from the well lined drawers of a fashionable home; there were workers and loafers, students and idlers, men of professions and men just workers, who formed that force.
>
> But they were all fighters, stickers, men with some grit (they got more as they went on), and men with a love of adventure. So they marched out to their camp at Broadmeadows – a good ten-mile tramp.

On 21 August, an *Argus* correspondent reported from the camp itself. 'The rows and rows of tents looked most impressive in the sunlight,' he wrote. 'In the paddock nearest to the road as one walks from the railway station are camped the field artillery. Further west lie the long lines of the infantry battalions and still further to the east is the Light Horse.'

Meanwhile, on the night the men marched into Broadmeadows, a Patriotic Meeting had been held in Melbourne Town Hall, attended by Prime Minister Joseph Cook and the Victorian Premier, Sir Alexander Peacock. After *God Save the King* had been sung, there were splendid speeches, during which Cook told the gathering that one of his sons had joined up. The Prime Minister added: 'I trust this war will teach the world a lesson and that is – war is a terrible thing and a thing to be avoided wherever possible. Australia will do her part.'

Sir Alexander echoed the frenzied patriotic fervour of the occasion. 'Britain is proud of her colonies and the colonies are fiercely proud of Britain,' he announced. 'Let outsiders flout the Motherland and they will find her cubs from all parts of the world will come to her rescue.'

The following Sunday was the first visitors' day at Broadmeadows Army Camp. At 10 am the men assembled in a three-sided square for a church parade, with a gun limber covered by a large Union Jack serving as a pulpit. The very first units of the light horse formed the left of the square as they all sang the *Old Hundredth* hymn and *Onward, Christian Soldiers*. There was a short sermon before the men again sang *God Save the King* and marched back to their tents.

At 3 pm the visitors came. Twenty thousand came that first Sunday, many more the following weekend. Broadmeadows Camp was soon the wonder of the time.

For the official inspection, in the second week of September, a vice-regal motorcade arrived from the city carrying both the Governor-General Sir Ronald Munro-Ferguson and his wife, Lady Helen, and the Governor of Victoria, Sir Arthur Stanley, and his wife.

The party inspected the lines of tents, visited the kitchens and watched 'the infantrymen drilling in their countless squads in the large paddocks which form the parade ground'. They also visited a vast ordnance store, where they saw the light horse saddles and harnesses 'gleam in all the glory of their newly polished leather'.

Phillip Schuler reported on progress in the camp:

> Every morning ... they were doing exercises with rifle and bayonet and the drab black of their clothing changed to khaki uniforms; and as rapidly as this change came so the earth was worn more brown with the constant treading of thousands of feet and the grass disappeared altogether from the camp and the roads became rutted.
>
> More men and still more men crowded in and filled the vacant tents till other lines had to be pitched. The horses began to arrive and motor-lorries with immense loads thundered across the paddocks to the stores where huge tarpaulins covered masses of equipment and marquees tons of meat and bread.
>
> From four thousand the army grew to ten; for fresh contingents were offered, accepted and sent into training.
>
> Tents peeped from between pine trees that enclosed a field and guns began to rumble in and were parked in neat rows. They waited for the horses, which the gunners were busily lashing into control ...
>
> All around the hills were green still. Each day they were covered with lines of moving troops. Infantry passed the guns on the road and the Light Horse passed the infantry and wheeled in through the same break in the panelled fence.

The Lord Mayor of Melbourne also made a run out to Broadmeadows and was impressed by the YMCA tent, which 'with its piano, its papers and its pens and paper is such a boon and a blessing to the soldier at

Broadmeadows'. He promised to do a costing to provide another amenities tent so that the troops could write more letters home.

Letters were arriving for the soldiers, too. A little girl wrote to headquarters: 'Dear Soldiers. I am glad to know that you are so brave. And we know that you will come back to good old Australia again. And don't forget that in the country you are going to there are little girls like me. And I know that you will treat them like little Australian children.'

Chapter 2

Bugle Calls

As Harold Brentall, George Fish and the other city dwellers rushed to join the march to Broadmeadows and be in the first contingent of the AIF, war fever had already spread across the countryside, on across the flatlands to the west of Melbourne, to the fabled Western District, home of the squattocracy farming some of the richest grazing country in Australia. This would be one of the major collection areas for the men who joined the 8th Light Horse Regiment and the town of Hamilton was its capital.

Hamilton, Wool Capital of the World. The boast stood in bold letters under a statue of a group of curly-horned merino rams, there on the main street, to emphasise to the passer-by that this indeed was the centre of a new, immensely rich corner of the British Empire, where a new landed gentry had taken root and prospered.

High up on a hill above the town is the Anglican Christ Church. Every Sunday in 1914 the carriages and phaetons and the new noisy motorcars clattered and rattled their way up Gray Street, on their way to the morning services here. Past the Hamilton Club, a solid and cream-coloured building, its doors closed to all but the most worthy. Past the primary school, established in 1852, with its Latin motto in wrought iron on the front gates: *Semper sursum* ('Ever upwards').

Up the hill the street continues, along the avenue of poplars, past the old two-storeyed rectory with the bishop's room looking out from the front landing, and on to Christ Church itself. Back in 1914, the bluestone church was as solid as its Church of England traditions and stood opposite another steepled church on the hillside dominating the town, St Andrew's Presbyterian. This united Protestant enclave overlooks a town that was designed to remind the townsfolk of the old country, with its botanical gardens full of English trees and splashing fountains.

Hamilton was synonymous with patriotism. Hundreds of countrymen came forward from the Western District, all eager to enlist for this, the Great Adventure, rushing in, just in case it ended before they had a chance to be in it.

But the war wasn't over quickly. Set against Australia's current population compared with that of 1914-18, it has been suggested that the impact of the First World War casualties would now be the horrifying equivalent of losing nearly 300,000 men in just four years – almost five times the number that actually died, in other words. But there's been no such population growth in Hamilton in the last 90 years. It is around 10,000 today, as it was back then, and the deaths of Hamilton's young men had as devastating an impact then as it would have now.

One of this town's own, Edward (Ted) Ellis Henty grew up and worked in Hamilton. He was baptised and married in the church on the hill. Ted Henty came from a famous pioneering family. In November 1834, the original Edward Henty (Ted's great-uncle) landed in Portland Bay – today about a 40-minute drive from Hamilton – on board the schooner *Thistle*. He was credited as being Victoria's first permanent settler, the man whose horse-drawn plough turned the first sod of arable land. Edward and his brother Stephen pushed inland, opening up enormous stations, where merino flocks started producing the fabulous golden fleeces, and helping found centres like Casterton and Coleraine. These small towns, like so many others in the west of Victoria, would become a major enlistment source for the 8th Light Horse.

Ted's mother, Annie Campbell, had been working as a governess on a property a few kilometres from Hamilton when she married his father, Walter, a town merchant. They settled at 'The Caves', about 8 kilometres from Hamilton, on the banks of the spring-fed, ever-running stream that the Scottish settlers called the Grange Burn.

Walter and Annie had three children: Wilf, Archie and Ted (born in 1888). They grew up happily on the small farm. The cottage is still there today, now enlarged with later additions. A huge monkey-puzzle tree still stands outside the front, ideal for climbing by small boys. The house sits on a sloping hill overlooking a series of waterholes for swimming, with a limestone arch and a cave that invites exploring. There were apple trees and rich plums in the orchard to eat. The small gorge with its steep banks is famous for its fossils, exposed in a wide band at the creek's high-water mark. A perfect location for the trio of growing Hentys then, and the boys certainly got up to mischief. Wilf lost the sight in his left eye when he was hit with a rock fired from a slingshot by his brother, Archie. This had far-reaching repercussions after war broke out.

In May 1915, Wilf got a letter from a Lieutenant Colonel Geo Cuscaden at 3rd Military District Headquarters in Melbourne. 'Dear Sir,' it read, 'I beg to inform you that as it is necessary to read a certain Test with both eyes, it is impossible for you to be taken.' So Wilf was spared going to war. And Archie, who had joined the militia and was also keen to fight, could not go. Father Walter was now sick with a terminal illness and Archie was needed to run the farm.

That left Ted, who was already a good shot. There was no doubt that from the time he could fire a rifle and bring a hare home for dinner, Ted Henty wanted to become a soldier and go to war. And so he did.

Like other Australians of his generation, he grew up in an intensely patriotic, British world. Geoffrey Blainey described it best in *A Shorter History of Australia*:

> On the eve of World War I, Britain was close to the peak of its power. Australians bathed in the warmth of the British sun. In many ways the two nations were one. Between them the flow of migrants, commodities and ideas was usually smooth. In 1914 most of the high posts in Australia were still occupied by people born and educated in the British Isles. Australia's Governor-General and six State governors came from the British Isles. The Prime Minister, Joseph Cook, an Englishman, was succeeded at the start of the war by Andrew Fisher, a Scot.
>
> The accents of the British Isles could be heard in pulpits and newspaper offices … in private grammar schools the British link was strong. British scholars held at least half the university chairs in Australia and sent their brightest students who wished to do further study on to Oxford and Cambridge. Most of the popular songs and gramophone cylinders sold in the music shops came by ship from England. News from the British Isles studded the daily newspapers …
>
> In schools the geography of Britain as well as Australia was learned. Clever schoolgirls knew by heart the names of all the rivers and mountains of Britain. On Sunday they sang hymns that had converted the dry Australian-like landscape of the Holy Land into the green and fast streams of England. In the bookshops – and Australians were probably more avid readers of books than the British – most best sellers came from London.

Young Ted Henty would undoubtedly have read a local bestseller entitled *Deeds that Won the Empire*, by the Reverend W.H. Fitchett, published in 1897 from stories that had first appeared in the Melbourne

Argus. By the end of 1898 the book had gone into its ninth edition, and by October 1914, in the first rush of recruiting, it was in its twenty-ninth impression.

Written by the headmaster of Melbourne's Methodist Ladies College, the preface stated that the tales were not meant to glorify war but to 'nourish patriotism'. They represented, said Fitchett, 'an effort to renew in popular memory the great traditions of the Imperial race', and the examples were not only of heroic daring but of even finer qualities: 'heroic fortitude, of loyalty to duty stronger than life, of the temper which dreads dishonour more than it fears death, and of the patriotism which makes love of the Fatherland a passion'.

The foundations for such patriotic fervour had been helped by Australia's participation in the South African (Boer) War. Between 1899 and 1902, some 16,175 mounted men and 16,314 horses had served in colonial and Commonwealth contingents, and 606 had died in the cause of the British Empire. Monuments were soon erected in Australian country towns and the heroes were remembered in schools like the Hamilton and Western District Boys College – motto: *Humanitas facit hominem* ('Humanity makes the man') – which had been founded in 1870.

This is where Ted Henty was both educated and inculcated with a firm belief in the need to be able to bear arms. Among the school's amenities was a rifle range. 'Cricket, football and golf are all very well in their way, but they will not go far in assisting us to repel a foreign foe, if one should ever attack us,' insisted the school magazine, *The Hamiltonian*. Or, more directly: 'brilliant cricketers, great footballers and fine golfers have not been as conspicuous on battlefields as men who could shoot straight and ride well.'

At the turn of the century there was a great fear in Australia of aggression from abroad. One of the first federal laws passed in 1901 restricted Asian immigration and would soon be called, unofficially, the White Australia Policy. The European settlers had already been alarmed by the energy and success of the Chinese who had poured into Australia during the gold rushes of the 1850s. Those from China who were already in Australia were allowed to remain, but from now on, this was definitely to be a country for the white man.

In 1914 there was an additional worry emanating from the Land of the Rising Sun. There was the belief that Japanese militarism might be directed south; while, in the Pacific, the German Navy was flexing its muscles.

Australian politicians were united in a belief that Australia should learn to defend itself, as well as rely on the might of the British Empire – while, of course, still being in a position to help out the empire overseas if the call came. 'The nation peered at the rest of the world like a frightened unarmed man looking through very thin bushes at marauding tigers,' L.L. Robson observed in his 1982 study of recruitment for the First AIF.

In *The Anzacs*, Patsy Adam Smith wrote that the movement to set up an army cadet corps in Victoria had begun in 1884, and by the next year, 38 state schools alone had established corps. A high standard was expected of these schoolboy cadets: 'The members of the corps will have opportunities before leaving school of becoming versed in the use of the rifle and infantry field exercises and such of them as may hereafter join the militia or volunteer forces will have comparatively little to learn in order to attain efficiency.'

The Hamilton College cadet corps had been formed in 1890 and built up until in 1902 it totalled 60 in all ranks. In 1903 the official roll listed one Cadet Henty. The corps drilled regularly, with special drills on Saturday mornings for new recruits. By 1903 it was strutting out to its own fife and drum band. There was regular shooting practice at the school rifle range, using heavy Martini-Henry rifles. Cadet Henty scored well – in September 1903 he was firing off a handicap of 3 and scoring 31 out of a possible 35. By 1907 the cadets were assumed to be part of the Australian Military Forces, and by the Defence Act of 1903-11, all Australian boys were required to serve. All medically fit boys between the ages of twelve and fourteen were junior cadets; the senior cadets were older boys still at school or those who had left between fourteen and eighteen.

This compulsory part-time military training was extended after the 1909 visit by Lord Kitchener of Khartoum, when the British Commander-in-Chief in India was invited to visit Australia and report on its defences. (Ironically, of course, it would be the same Lord Kitchener who initiated an attack on Turkey in the Dardanelles in 1915, and a few months later, was forced to order the evacuation after the Gallipoli disaster.)

In his report the following year, Kitchener recommended a trained Australian military force of not less than 80,000 men. The school cadets would pass into a citizen military force until the age of 25, with an additional year in the reserves. Training would be done at annual camps. The whole of Australia was to be divided into military districts, with officers appointed to supervise the camps in each area. In addition, a military college was to be established to train career officers, resulting in the opening of the Royal Military College, Duntroon, in 1911.

After he left school Ted Henty threw himself into soldiering with the citizen military force and got a job as a clerk in a Hamilton bank. Aside from his passion for things military, in 1914 the countryside was in recession and the extra money gained from his part-time soldiering was much needed by the family living at 'The Caves'.

'He evinced a disposition for the Light Horse in which he was one of the enthusiastic spirits and which might be described as his only hobby,' *The Hamilton Spectator* said of Ted in its tribute on 23 August 1915. In May 1914, well before war was declared, he managed to get ten days' leave from the bank to go to Melbourne and attend a training camp at Flemington, where he graduated with a 'certificate of instruction'. And when war broke out, it was Ted who organised the guard of honour that saw off the first volunteer soldiers from the town.

Ted would have to cool his heels for a while in Hamilton, however. It was not until 21 September that he was appointed a lieutenant with the 8th Light Horse, which would not really form up as a regiment until October, although some of its members turned up at Broadmeadows much earlier. So the dashing young officer, slim and straight-backed as befits a natural horseman, dark-haired and dark-browed, turned his attention instead to marriage. His bride-to-be was Florence Grace Pearson, the beautiful young governess teaching English literature and poetry to two little girls on a property called 'Koornong', a short ride away from 'The Caves'. They settled on a date for the wedding: 18 November.

Meanwhile, other old boys from Hamilton College were coming forward to join the 8th Light Horse. One was Sergeant John Leslie (Les) Connor. Born in Coleraine, he had been captain of school before going up to Melbourne to stay at Ormond College and study mechanical engineering at Melbourne University. After graduation, Les went off to pursue a career first in the tin mines of Mt Lyell in Tasmania, then searching for gold at Mt Morgan in Queensland. In November 1910 he went to Western Australia as a surveyor in the Golden Horse Shoe mine at Boulder City. 'When resident in Boulder he joined the Citizen Forces, and as whatever he did he tried to do well, he studied the science of warfare, passed examinations and received a commission in the Goldfields Battalion,' his school magazine reported.

But Les Connor's fate was sealed in August 1914, shortly after war was declared. Back in Victoria on holiday, he arrived in Melbourne and tried to have his Goldfields commission transferred to the first expeditionary force, but there were no vacancies. Rather than wait to be offered a position as an officer, he joined the 8th Light Horse at Broadmeadows Camp as a trooper (private) instead. Aside from an eagerness to fight for his country, whatever the rank, there was an important reason for this decision. Les knew people like Ted Henty in the 8th Light Horse from their schooldays together; he knew others because they came from his hometown of Coleraine. The 8th would turn out to be a network of old school chums and university students, fellow townsfolk, old friends and close relatives, who all joined up to share in the Great Adventure.

They were mates – or, to use the preferred word of the time, they were *cobbers*. Like so many recruits from around Australia, each man would come to regard his regiment as something very special; a crack outfit, but also a special, close family.

Dudley Murton was another twenty-year-old Old Hamiltonian who joined the 8th, and would become a member of Ted Henty's 'B' Squadron. He was one of the few men in that squadron to survive the war, receiving a shattered elbow in what was then known to the school, late in 1915, as 'the famous Walker's Ridge charge'. Murton would spend two years in hospital before returning to Australia in 1917.

Another old boy, Keith Learmonth, a nineteen-year-old station hand, also enlisted at Hamilton and became a corporal in the 8th, but was evacuated ill from Gallipoli just a day before the Charge at The Nek. He survived the war and was invalided home after he had been transferred to the Postal Corps. Altogether, Hamilton and Western District Boys College, just one of a number of small country schools in Victoria, would send 124 of its old boys to the Great War and nineteen would be killed.

Ted Henty's wedding to Florence at Christ Church was Hamilton's society wedding of the year. *The Hamilton Spectator* brought details to its readers under the headline 'Soldier's Bride Honoured':

> A marked token of the high esteem in which Lieutenant Edward E. Henty is held by his fellow officers and men at Broadmeadows encampment was shown by the valuable and handsome gifts received by Miss Pearson on the occasion of her recent marriage with their popular young troop leader.
>
> From the C.O. and officers of the 8th Regiment, Miss Pearson was the recipient of a handsome oak case of cutlery, while from the non-commissioned officers and men comprising Lieutenant Henty's troop, a silver entree dish and salver were received.
>
> The latter was suitably inscribed as follows: Presented to Miss F. Pearson by the NCOs and men of A Troop B Squadron 8th Light Horse on the occasion of her marriage to their troop leader, Lieutenant E.E. Henty, 18th November, 1914.

The silver salver stands today on a sideboard in the home of Lieutenant Henty's great-grandchildren for, in October 1915, two months after her husband was killed on Gallipoli, Florence gave birth to a son. She called him Edward Ellis Henty, after his father, and two generations on they still remember him.

All 36 names of those in Ted Henty's light horse troop are engraved on the salver; only two would still be alive a year after the wedding. A random look at these names gives some idea of the diversity of the men who came forward to join the 8th Light Horse towards the end of 1914, as well as providing a roll call of the tragedy to come at The Nek.

The first name on the salver is that of Sergeant Henry James 'Bunny' Nugent who was one of the two survivors and a particularly interesting character. He was a Boer War veteran (so keen to fight that he had paid his own way to South Africa to enlist in the Midland Mounted Rifles), after which he returned home and became a VFL umpire. Then, just five weeks after being taken on at Broadmeadows as a trooper in September 1914, Bunny's fitness and experience saw him promoted to sergeant. His heroism during the war earned him a Military Medal and, later, a unique honour in football history: on opening day 1918, Richmond and Essendon lined up before the match and applauded the umpire – Bunny Nugent – onto the ground. He survived wounds, sickness and service in three wars to eventually die in 1955, aged 75.

Others in the troop were not so fortunate. Corporal Victor Nassau Raymond, for instance, was a 19-year-old warehouseman from Prahran, 5 feet 10¼ inches high, weighing in at 11 stone 7 pounds, with brown hair and brown eyes. Killed in action at The Nek. No known grave.

Lance Corporal George Thomas Hughes was 38 and a Presbyterian minister from Balranald in New South Wales; 5 feet 11 inches tall, with blue eyes and grey hair. His sister wrote after his death on Gallipoli: 'He was the Presbyterian Minister for two years before he resigned his charge to enlist. He sold some valuable horses, buggy, furniture and a motor previous to going away.' Killed in action at The Nek. No known grave.

Trooper Joseph Patrick McKay was a 24-year-old labourer from Yarrawonga, Victoria. He was 5 feet 8 inches tall and weighed 12 stone. By a twist of fate, he was saved from certain death when he was taken from the firing line suffering from piles, two days before the charge at The Nek. He would die at the very end of the war, by drowning.

Trooper William Arthur Hind was a 21-year-old apprentice printer from Hamilton, eldest of a family of eight whose father was the foreman at *The Hamilton Spectator*. The newspaper said in its tribute: 'He was of a quiet but obliging disposition and was well liked by his confreres. He also possessed the soldier's inclination and was not content until he threw in his lot with the colours as soon after the outbreak of war as possible.' One eyewitness later said he 'fell whilst waving his country's flag above the parapet of the Turkish trench'. Killed in action at The Nek. No known grave.

Lance Corporal John Boswell was a 21-year-old farm labourer from the tiny Western District town of Woorndoo, and also signed up at Hamilton. Killed in action at The Nek. No known grave.

Trooper Samuel James was aged 22, with blue eyes and light brown hair, and hailed from another minor Victorian town, Wychitella, in the wheat fields of the dusty mallee country. Killed in action at The Nek. No known grave.

Trooper Robert Kerr was a 31-year-old draper from the northern Melbourne suburb of Essendon. After he died, his personal effects were sent home – a pack of cards and his watch. Killed in action at The Nek. No known grave.

Trooper James Alexander Bell was a ruddy-faced 34-year-old labourer from Sale in the dairy country of eastern Victoria. Killed in action at The Nek. No known grave.

Trooper Donald Mathieson McGregor Johnson was a tall 18-year-old, a brass finisher from the city of Warrnambool, in the state's west. He had a marksman's badge from the school cadets. Killed in action at The Nek. No known grave.

Trooper Laurence Gerald Finn was a 23-year-old grazier who had attended the private Catholic school Xavier College, where he was known as 'Finny'. His proud parents said that he was the first man to volunteer from the Port Fairy district. Killed in action at The Nek. No known grave.

Just one year after Bunny Nugent had organised the engraving of this silver salver, he found himself in a hospital bed in Heliopolis, Egypt, where he lay wounded after being evacuated from Gallipoli. The respect and affection he felt for his late troop leader are obvious from the following letter he wrote to Ted's mother Annie:

Dear Mrs Henty

I received your kind letter and was very pleased to hear from you. I would have written to you only I did not like to intrude in your bereavement. I was going to wait till I got back if I was spared to tell you how your son died.

He was made second in command of the Squadron the night before the Charge, but he got permission to come out with his old Troop.

He said to me: I have been with you ever since I joined the Force and I am going out with you now.

He was killed in the first rush – a machine gun got him and he died without a sign. I got to him just as he fell but he never spoke nor moved. I think he died happy because he had the old smile on his face.

I was going to bring him in only I got hit just after him.

I would like to let you know the honour and respect we all had for him. We would have followed him anywhere and all the other Troops envied our Troop Leader.

They all used to say little Ted was the best man in the regiment. That expression shewed the feelings of every man in the Regiment. He always had a cheery word for his men. He was always doing something for their comfort in the trenches. He would help us build up the sandbag parapets for our protection with never a thought of danger for himself. He died like a Hero leading his men when he need not have gone into danger.

There are only another man and myself left out of the old A Troop that was in the Charge.

I always had a soft spot in my heart for him, we got on so well together. He was an Ideal Officer and I will always remember him if I am spared to get through all right. You can rest your mind easy that he died without any pain.

The report of his death that you sent me and any effort of mine can never tell what a fine soldier and gentleman he was, and I am in a position to know being closely connected to him both in Australia and on Service at the Front. I think his photo is fine – it is just him.

You ask about the black horses. I have got his black mare and will not let anyone ride her. I will send you a photo of her.

I would like you to tender my sympathy to his poor Wife. I hope that both the Baby and herself are keeping well. And if I get through I will call and see you myself when I hope to be able to give you better details than I can write.

I hope the Baby has been named after his Father because I would like to think there is still one with the same name and a Son of the Whitest Man I ever knew.

I also wish to express my sympathy with you in your sad loss of a son but I am sure it is the way he would have liked to go out.

Thanking you for your kind thoughts on my welfare.

I will now close.

Yours sincerely,

J.J. Nugent

Sergeant A Troop

B Squadron

8th L.H.

Many Gallipoli survivors honoured their fallen comrades in this way by writing to their loved ones and visiting them when they eventually returned to Australia. But Bunny Nugent's letter also shows how close the officers and men of the regiment were to each other. They were, indeed, a band of brothers.

Chapter 3

The Boys from Berry Bank

Charles Bean, the indefatigable official war correspondent who filled 283 notebooks with observations and detailed notes on his way to writing the multi-volume *Official History*, set out to define what made Australians different.

They retained many qualities common to all the British peoples, he said. They spoke the same language, read the same books, loved the same sports, and held the same ideas of honesty, cleanliness, and individual liberty.

But, said Bean, they were different. They looked different. They had bigger bodies because of an open-air life and more food. The active life and the climate 'rendered the body wiry and the face lean, easily lined and thin lipped'. They spoke differently. They were more resourceful because they often lived in lonely places where they had to solve difficult problems without help. Men were judged on what they were worth, not on class distinction. They didn't worship money and they tended to protect the weak and any discipline was self-imposed.

Then Bean began his paean to mateship: 'So far as he held a prevailing creed, it was a romantic creed inherited from the gold miner and the bushman, of which the chief article was that a man should at all times and at any cost stand by his mate.'

That was the creed of the 8th Australian Light Horse Regiment. And it was the creed of three mates, three brothers called Mack, who answered the call of the Empire, the call from Home. Jack, Ernie and Stan – they were the boys who rode away from their home at Berry Bank to join up in Melbourne.

They were tough men of the land. They stuck by each other and they survived Gallipoli.

Jack and Stan came home eventually. Ernie was killed later in the war and lies today in the sand of a war cemetery on an old caravan route between Egypt and Syria, shot at a spot near El Magdhaba in 1916.

The brothers wrote home frequently about what was happening on their big adventure. The letters were kept by their youngest sister, Mary – stored away carefully, tenderly, in a cardboard box inside a cedar chest of drawers – and were only discovered a few years ago, after her death.

Today, there's just a railway siding at the spot on the map called Berrybank. What was once a small country station building now leans, about to collapse on the rutted platform, across the line from metal grain silos. The interstate express from Melbourne to Adelaide whooshes through once a day, past the overgrown paddock that was once a football ground, the closed and shuttered Presbyterian church, and the thistle patch where a blacksmith's forge once stood. The semitrailers and other motor vehicles now roar past the site on the straight piece of highway that runs from Geelong to Hamilton. Berrybank is about halfway between the two, close to another small town called Lismore, with its war memorial and another bluestone Presbyterian church.

A sign on the highway points the way off to 'Berry Bank', the sheep station that gave its name to the settlement Berrybank. Today it still has 3,000 acres of some of the finest grazing land in the country. A white painted mailbox and a thick stand of sugar gums trailing shrivelled bark mark the way to a long, winding, dusty road that leads to today's modest homestead. Near the first bend of this road are three squat, bushy pine trees. The three pines were cultivated from seed gathered originally from the Lone Pine that stands on the heights of Gallipoli. Weather-beaten plaques at the base of their trunks record that the trees were planted 40 years ago in memory of Stan, Ernie and Jack Mack. That was the order in which the three brothers rode away from here, separately, down the dusty track to join the 8th Light Horse forming up Broadmeadows, north of Melbourne.

Beyond the pine trees, the rolling brown paddocks stretch to the horizon and to Mt Elephant, the broad-backed hill that dominates this landscape. This is the area where they still grow the finest wool in the world. The sheep are still shorn here at 'Berry Bank' in the bluestone shearing shed with the hand-hewn wooden beams and floors, rich with the smell of ingrained lanoline and sheep dung, and built over 140 years ago. The best long-stapled fleeces are still carried carefully in wicker baskets by the junior hands, to be sorted on a wooden table and pressed into hessian bales, all stamped with the brand: Berry Bank.

It was Joseph Gardner Mack, a lowland Scots farmer and grandfather of the three Mack brothers, who first came to this windswept landscape of native tussock grasses, in 1851, and founded a sheep station of what was then around 36,000 acres. With him were his wife and their seven children. They travelled in horse-drawn gigs and on horseback, with their stores and furniture following behind in slower bullock wagons. Joseph built a substantial two-storey house next to one of the Gnarkeet chain of ponds that dot the property and are spring-fed. The one nearest to the homestead is 10 metres deep and icy cold. Here, the family would later build a bathing box for the ladies and a proper diving board, from which Jack, Ernie and Stan could dive-bomb each other.

Their father, also called Joseph, had arrived at Berry Bank as a little boy of six. He grew up to carry on the family tradition of large families when he married Helen Dodds, youngest daughter of a family of five born to another Scots pioneer. Helen bore Joseph Mack five girls and six boys, including the trio of brothers who rode off to fight in the First World War.

Joseph Mack kept a large scrapbook. It mostly contained records of big hare-coursing meetings held at the station, and sales from his substantial merino stud; the notes and clippings were stuck down hard with homemade glue so they wouldn't lift. He also kept a small, succinct diary, in which the entry for 10 September 1914, written boldly in black ink, reads: 'Stanley went to Melbourne to be sworn in to fight against Germany.'

Stanley (Stan) Mack was the youngest of the trio, born in 1889. He was 25 years and four months old when he signed up on 11 September. He was taller and heavier than his older brothers, and was described on his enlistment papers as having brown hair and yellowish eyes.

Ernest Harold (Ernie) signed up next. He was born in 1886 and was aged 28 years and six months when he put his signature down on 18 September 1914. He was 5 feet 8 inches inch tall, weighed 11 stone, and had black hair and brown eyes.

John Dodds (Jack) would wait a while before joining his younger brothers in the army, possibly because he had more responsibilities on the station and so had a hard job persuading his parents that he should go too. He was born in 1880 and had grown up to be 5 feet 7½ inches high, a wiry man with brown eyes and black hair who weighed in at 10 stone 5 pounds when he enlisted aged 34 and three months on 6 January 1915.

The boys' favourite sister, Mary, had a lovely voice and was studying at the Conservatorium of Music in Melbourne. They would write to her about their adventures in Europe and, in her own way, she would join up, too. With other young ladies of the district she formed the Berrybank Concert Party, touring Victoria to give patriotic concerts and raise money for the Belgian Fund (and the war effort).

All three brothers had already spent time away from Berrybank, albeit briefly, to attend Geelong College, another well-known school that 'collected' students from the Western District properties. Altogether, nineteen Geelong College boys would join the Light Horse. But the Mack brothers' real schoolyard was 'Berry Bank'.

Jack, Ernie and Stan Mack had grown up happily on a large and thriving pastoral property, where good and bad seasons dictated fortune. They rode, they mustered, they dipped, they drenched, they crutched and they sheared sheep. In their spare time they shot, played cricket and football, or rode to neighbouring stations for tea and a game of tennis. It was an easy, interacting society. People rode for great distances, dropping in on properties for food and lodging. At 'Berry Bank' there could be up to three dozen sitting down for breakfast, more when there was a special event.

Everybody knew somebody else in the Western District. If not, they were related by blood, marriage or the old school. Brothers, friends and schoolmates – they would all join the Light Horse together.

On 11 September, the same day that Stan Mack signed his enlistment papers in the city, the grand vice-regal review of the first Victorian contingent of the AIF took place at Broad-meadows Army Camp.

The first unit of mounted men to be raised, the 4th Light Horse Regiment, paraded before dignitaries such as Governor-General Sir Ronald Munro-Ferguson, as did the infantry, the artillery and the 2nd Field Ambulance, with stretcher-bearers Harold Brentnall and George Fish. George said he was sharing a tent with nine other 'grand fellows' at Broadmeadows, while Harold reported that the training so far had consisted of 'squad drill, stretcher drill, routine marches and lectures'.

The troopers for what would be the 8th Regiment had begun arriving even before it had been announced on 3 September that Australia's contribution to the war would be expanded from the original first commitment. A second contingent was being formed at the same time and now overlapped in the crowded Broadmeadows Camp, as the first contingent had its departure date delayed because of fears that German warships were lurking near the probable sailing route from Australia to Europe.

On 17 September *The Argus* reported on the difficulties:

> The new men comprising the second contingent are coming in so fast that some difficulty is being experienced in housing them. Another batch of 250 men arrived yesterday, some for the Light Horse and others for the infantry. The volunteers for the Light Horse are called

out and the officer in charge explains to them that only really good horsemen are wanted, adding that they will be put through severe jumping and riding tests.

Like Stan Mack, some of the men turning up had brought their own horses. His was called Bob. Horses were in short supply, though, and new arrivals were put into one corner of the camp for some basic drill on foot. In Sydney, Lieutenant Colonel J.B. Meredith, in charge of raising a Light Horse brigade, reported that he only had around 400 of a total requirement of 563 horses; 200 new horses had been presented for inspection on one day but only twenty were passed as suitable. The price for good horses was going up – £20 for suitable hacks.

In Melbourne the horses were sorted out at a large army remount depot in the inner suburb of Maribyrnong, beside a river. Many of the owner horses that had been ridden to Broadmeadows by the country boys were found not to be suitable. Stan Mack would write to his mother at Berry Bank some weeks after he arrived that he had got 'a beautiful hack this evening from Maribyrnong as Bob stumbled and got rejected'.

The remounts were army horses bought by government purchasing officers from graziers and breeders. If a man's own horse met army standards it was bought by the government for about £30 ($60). The light horse mounts were generally called 'Walers' because they were from a strain bred to be stockhorses in New South Wales. They were characterised as being strong, great-hearted and a cross between thoroughbred and semi-draught, so they had speed, strength and stamina. The horses were branded with the government broad arrow and the initials of the purchasing officer, with a number also marked on one hoof.

When they were in camp the horses were tethered by head and heel ropes between other long ropes, which were called picket lines. Each trooper placed his saddle and equipment in front of him and slept close by, in a bell-shaped tent. There were eight men to each tent, feet pointing inwards to the centre. With big men selected, it was often a tight fit, and when one man turned in his sleep, the others often had to follow the leader.

When the trumpeter sounded reveille each morning the first job of the day for the trooper was to feed, groom and clean his horse before breakfast. A very strong bond was established between horse and rider, so much so that at least one trooper kept a picture of his horse with his diary, and faithfully recorded its food rations.

The outside world had a keen interest in the welfare of the horses also. A Miss Maude Harvie of Elizabeth Street, Melbourne, formed a devoted band of helpers to make bandages for the horses of the expeditionary force. The Defence Department paid for Miss Harvie to travel to Sydney, Brisbane, Adelaide and Hobart so that she could set up similar working bees.

The needs of the men were also keeping the community very busy. They were working to supply the Belgian Fund with a huge list of supplies needed for what would be the Victorian Hospital Unit, to back up the army. The list included 7,000 blankets, 15,000 flannel shirts, 10,000 pairs of socks, 12,000 single sheets, 5,000 cotton shirts, 4,000 pillows or cushions, 1,000 pieces of old linen, 5,000 pairs of mittens, 3,000 quilts, 12,000 towels, 5,000 knitted caps, 2,000 sweaters, 5,000 mufflers, 2,000 pairs of slippers, 20,000 white handkerchiefs, 5,000 'cholera belts', 2,500 pyjama trousers, 200 hot water bottles, 20,000 face washers and 2,000 pairs of bed socks.

Government House was a central collection point, with the Governor's wife heading a committee of volunteer women 'packing with deftness and despatch'. Each municipality was given a target, while its mayoress co-ordinated the local effort. Thus the mayoress and citizens of Hawthorn had gathered and provided 10,000 pillow slips; the mayoress of Caulfield was beating the bounds for the 12,000 sheets; and Malvern was to supply the pillows. Meanwhile most of Canterbury was hard at work making flannel shirts: 'in that suburb,' reported *The Argus*, 'the workers must be generous with their time and skilful with their needles, for the task they are working on is not a light one'.

As the men of the Light Horse drilled at Broadmeadows, a huge volunteer effort was at work outside to support them. Donations in cash and kind were flooding in. The Kodak Company sent 15 pairs of prismatic binoculars; Cawsey, Menck and Co. gave up large supplies of coffee essence; while Benset and Woodcock donated 1,000 tins of sheep tongues; and E.W. Cole, £100 worth of books. The citizens of Warrnambool promised to make and send a fully equipped field kitchen.

But there was no beer for a wet canteen at the camp – indeed, no wet canteen for the troops at all. As the weather at Broadmeadows grew warmer and the troops drilled harder, the executive council of the Sons of Temperance National Division of Victoria and South Australia had met and passed the following resolution:

> That we most heartily congratulate Senator Pearce, Minister for Defence, in abolishing the 'wet canteens' from the camps of the Expeditionary Forces of Australia. We feel assured that his action will meet with the thankful approval of thousands of parents and hope that he will not

falter in his desires to protect our forces, on land or sea, by the entire elimination of the most insidious foe to be found in intoxicating liquor.

There were also stern warnings about other temptations. Mr William Shackle of Port Melbourne published a poem, which read, in part:

> You're going to a country where the singing bullets fly:
> Where you're wakened up at midnight by a sudden sullen roar,
> And overhead the shrieking shells come dropping from the sky.
> That's war, my boys, that's war!
>
> You're an automatic rifle; you're a bayonet's motor nerve:
> You're a hammer, when the iron is hot, to smite;
> But Australia expects you to remember and observe
> What's right, my boys, what's right!
>
> If women welcome you in ways you don't experience here,
> You're to look upon the children at their side;
> And say a prayer, and face the South, where mothers hold you dear –
> Their pride, my boys, their pride!

There would be no temptations on Gallipoli, save for some small solace from the rum jars. The reality of this war would unfold a long way from this noble poet of Port Melbourne.

With one Victorian light horse regiment already raised (the 4th), the army had initially planned for the state's new recruits and their squadrons to be drafted together to form a body to be called the 6th Light Horse Regiment, which would be part of the 2nd Light Horse Brigade, drawn from elsewhere in Australia. But as yet more and more men came forward and the Imperial Government in England welcomed more reinforcements, the plans changed again. An official notice proclaiming the formation of the 3rd Light Horse Brigade would appear in District Order No.54, issued on 23 October:

> His Excellency the Governor General, acting with the advice of the Federal Executive Council has been pleased to approve of one Light Horse Brigade being formed of persons who voluntarily agree to serve beyond the limits of the Commonwealth in the Australian Imperial Force, in addition to the units referred to in the Commonwealth of Australia Gazette No.56 of the 13th August 1914 and Commonwealth Gazette No. 74 of the 19th September 1914.

So the proposed 6th was now to be renamed the 8th Light Horse Regiment, and as it was beginning to come together at Broadmeadows, the two other regiments that would join it to form the 3rd Brigade were also under construction. The 9th would have three squadrons of over 100 men each, two squadrons from South Australia and one from Victoria. The 10th's three squadrons would all be made up of Western Australians.

The overall commander of this widely separated 3rd Light Horse Brigade, the man given the task of welding the three regiments together into an effective fighting force, was also named. The brigadier was to be the promoted Colonel Frederick Godfrey Hughes, from Melbourne, described by Charles Bean in just one withering line in his *Official History* as: 'An elderly citizen officer belonging to leading social circles in Victoria.'

Hughes was nearly 57 at the time. He had already spent a lifetime in and out of various kinds of uniform, even if he had never been to war. He was keen enough all right, only excused from going to the Boer War because by 1899 he was already a married man with children. Come the outbreak of the First World War, he was ten years older than most other brigade commanders in the AIF.

Here was a man to whom the Charge of the Light Brigade in the Crimean War was almost recent history, an amateur cavalryman who regarded being presented to Her Majesty Queen Victoria on no less than four separate occasions as the highlight of his military career. Tall, straight-backed, his hair grey with white at the sides, and sporting a large trimmed bushy moustache, Frederick Hughes would ultimately command the men who charged and died at The Nek, and would contribute to their deaths by being … too old.

As Hughes' second-in-command, the defence authorities decided on a seasoned Boer War veteran, a very different person. 'A well known Australian permanent officer of South African fame,' Bean would write of the brigade major, 'who, although very senior for this position, had been straining every nerve to get away in some capacity'.

Lieutenant Colonel 'Jack' Antill was from New South Wales. He was a square-jawed toughnut. After he had joined the brigade in Melbourne, the magazine *Melbourne Punch* carried this biting description of the man who would later become known to the 3rd Brigade as 'Bull' Antill, or simply 'the Bullant':

> When he instructs, he flails the instruction into his pupils with his tongue. Some officers to whom he tells the raw, uncloaked truth about themselves are apt to become offended. It is unfortunate, but to

divorce Antill from his own particular manner would be to rob him of his effectiveness.

Few men of his age could live long with him in a set-to. He is of the hard-hitting, finish-early school – a dangerous man to face. He can ride to a standstill the worst of buckjumpers, and loves to do it. He has the clear-cut face; the close shut mouth and the hard eye of the determined man. When he speaks there is a decisive ring about his words, which are as few as possible. He is a soldier all through.

This uncompromising officer's martinet manner and sheer pig-headedness would play a critical role in later events.

Chapter 4

Sound 'Boots and Saddles'

Auburn Douglas Callow was among the very first to 'be there' – to join the 8th Australian Light Horse Regiment. In fact, like many of its troopers, he was so keen that he got there before it had actually come into being. Aub Callow was aged just 18 and a half when he rode up on the cool, showery morning of Tuesday, 8 September at Broadmeadows, astride his horse, Friday.

He had ridden Friday all the way from Ballarat, 130 kilometres away, where he was training to be a veterinary surgeon like his father Andrew, who practised there. Andrew was one of 14 children born to Thomas, a bookmaker, and his wife, Jane, both of whom had migrated to Melbourne from the Isle of Man in 1870. Andrew, the vet, called his son Auburn after the suburb where he was practising at the time, and Douglas after the main town on the Isle of Man.

Young Aub had already spent 20 months in junior cadets and three years in the senior cadets (including two years as a lieutenant) before he set out. The army wanted men with military experience aged between 19 and 38, so he squeaked in with his father's permission, as he was underage.

He was entering an army which still thought in terms of cavalry and bayonet charges but where battle would be decided by high-explosive artillery shells, shrapnel busts and machine guns. Aub Callow was enrolled as Trooper No.10 and directed to report to the Signalling School, where he was issued with a makeshift uniform, a floppy white hat and two semaphore flags to practise with.

Within a few weeks, however, one of his fellow troopers went down with measles, so the whole school – signallers, tents and equipment – was placed in quarantine and taken by horse and cart to a far corner of Broadmeadows. There, they spent their time skylarking and taking pictures of one another being tossed in a blanket.

Stan Mack had gone to Melbourne from Berry Bank on 10 September, enlisted at Victoria Barracks the next day, and was despatched to Broadmeadows the day after. He would be Trooper 67. On 14 September father Joseph noted in his diary: 'Ernie and Mary went to town. Former going to war.' He was given the number 66; perhaps, following his brother's enlistment number, it had been reserved for him. Jack Mack did not enlist until January 1915. Many more men had come forward by then and Jack's trooper number would be a distant 524.

The Macks were not the only set of brothers to join the 8th. Lionel and Dyson Cole were young farmers from the hamlet of Cobrico; Alex and Bert Evans came from Lindenow. None of these four would return home from Gallipoli. There were also the Borthwick brothers and the Carthews, from other parts of Victoria.

Within a few weeks of Aub Callow's arrival at Broadmeadows, enough men wanting to be light horsemen had been formed into five training squadrons, each about 150 men strong, after having been tested for riding, general smartness and being drilled on foot by regular sergeant majors.

The 8th Light Horse could afford to take the very best for its three squadrons. 'From these the Regiment picked its personnel and, as by this time the staff had got a fair idea of the best men, a splendid type of manhood was selected,' wrote Tom Austin, the 8th's unofficial historian. A station hand from Lake Bolac, Tom had also been boxing champion at the elite Melbourne Grammar School and was among a group of five of that school's old boys ('OMs', they called themselves) to join the regiment.

On enlistment in a country town, city centre or at Broadmeadows itself, each trooper would have completed three pages of Attestation Papers.

On the first page he answered 14 questions, ranging from simple identification – what is your name? In or near what Parish or Town were you born? Are you a natural born British Subject or a Naturalized British Subject? Are you married? – to the more direct – 'Have you ever been discharged from any part of His Majesty's Forces, with Ignominy, or as Incorrigible and Worthless, or on account of Conviction of Felony, or of a Sentence of Penal Servitude, or have you been Dismissed with Disgrace from the Navy?'

The enlistee signed the first page, solemnly declaring that 'the above answers made by me to the above questions are true and that I am willing and voluntarily agree to serve in the Military Forces of the Commonwealth of Australia within and beyond the limits of the

Commonwealth'. If he was married he also agreed to allot not less than two-fifths of his pay to support his wife and children.

The person being enlisted then swore the following oath:

> I will well and truly serve our Sovereign Lord the King in the Australian Imperial Force … until the end of the War, and a further period of four months thereafter unless sooner lawfully discharged, dismissed or removed there from; and that I will resist His Majesty's enemies and cause His Majesty's peace to be kept and maintained; and that I will in all matters appertaining to my service, faithfully discharge my duty according to law. So Help Me God.

A medical examination followed and personal characteristics were noted – height, weight, chest measurements, complexion, colour of eyes and hair, and any distinctive marks such as vaccinations. Unsurprisingly, many of the country boys had scars on hands and legs from their work on farms and stations.

The medical officer then signed an embracing certificate, a document that read:

> I have examined the above-named person and find he does not present any of the following conditions, viz: Scrofula; phthisis; syphilis; impaired constitution; defective intelligence; defects of vision, voice or hearing; hernia; haemorrhoids; varicose veins beyond a limited extent; marked varicocele with unusually pendant testicle; inveterate cutaneous disease; chronic ulcers; traces of corporal punishment, or evidence of having been marked with the letters D. or B.C. [signifying the letter D (for Deserter) and B.C. (for Bad Character) were branded on soldiers dishonourably discharged from the British Army for these reasons in the nineteenth century. This was consistent with the harsh discipline meted out to many, including men of the 1st AIF.]; contracted or deformed chest; abnormal curvature of spine; or any other disease or physical defect calculated to unfit him for the duties of a soldier.
>
> He can see the required distance with either eye; his heart and lungs are healthy; he has the free use of his joints and limbs; and he declares he is not subject to fits of any description.
>
> I consider him fit for active service.

The commanding officer also signed a certificate – 'I certify that this Attestation of the above-named person is correct, and that the required forms have been complied with. I accordingly appoint him to ...' – before going on to enter in ink, either A, B or C squadrons of the 8th Light Horse Regiment. The bold, flowing signature under the certificate read: 'A.H. White, Major.'

The army's military order No.575 had appointed officers to the 8th Light Horse and named its CO, Major Alexander Henry White. He would become a key figure at The Nek.

Like Lieutenant Ted Henty, Alexander White, aged 32, had been a keen peacetime member of the militia and was one of the first citizen force officers to volunteer for active service. Born in Ballarat, one of a family of ten, he was an enthusiastic amateur sailor with the local yacht club. Alexander joined the family malting firm, Joe White Maltster Co. Ltd, which provided malted barley to the Foster's Brewery in Collingwood. After first working at the malting itself, at Wendouree, he moved on to Melbourne and became a company director and right-hand man to his brother, Joe.

Business was good. The Foster brothers from America had imported a steam-driven ice-making machine and pioneered the first cold beer in Victoria. White was a popular man, particularly through his connection with the Commercial Travellers Association, which he joined in 1907. He would carry his membership fob on his watch chain to Gallipoli.

He married Myrtle Louise Glasson, daughter of the manager of the Ballarat Trustees Company, at 'a very pretty and smart wedding' in St Peter's, Ballarat. Alexander and Myrtle adored each other.

On 21 September 1914 she presented him with a son, Alexander John Middleton White, who was born in their Melbourne home at 11 Cole Street, Elsternwick. Their pet name for the baby was 'Bill', and the proud father wore a locket around his neck containing a photo of his 'dear little wife' and 'dear little button mouth'. As historian Peter Burness observed in his book, *The Nek*, 'White's long letters to his wife and baby written on his way to Gallipoli and from the Peninsula reveal him to have been a kind, gentle and decent man'.

His wife said later that his whole heart and soul was in his military work from the time he joined the old Mounted Rifles in Ballarat after leaving school. White had been a private in the Victorian Mounted Rifles before gaining a commission in the light horse in 1904. He had risen quickly in rank until in 1914 he was made brigade major of the 5th Light Horse Brigade of the old militia before transferring to the Australian Imperial Force on 21 September and given a new command.

Although he had volunteered his services for the AIF soon after war was declared, he forsook a possible place in the first contingent because little Bill had just been born. He was held back at Victoria Barracks to organise his family affairs. Then came promotion to lieutenant colonel and command of a brand new regiment, the 8th. He was aged just 32 years and six months.

At 5 feet 11 inches tall and weighing 12 stone 12 pounds, the colonel was stockily built and enjoyed his food. Sandy-haired, slightly ruddy-cheeked, he was popular with his men, who called him a true officer and gentleman. 'Gallant' was the word most used to describe him. The commander of the Anzacs, Lieutenant General Sir William Birdwood, himself wrote of Alexander White: 'I always felt such complete confidence in him and knew that while he was here all was going right in his regiment, for there was no detail escaped his attention, and he was the life and soul of his regiment, being idolised by both officers and men.'

White had a certain sense of style, too. Watching his troopers exercise in Australia before leaving, he would have a wicker picnic hamper packed, and stand sipping tea from a fine china cup as the men rode past.

There was idealism in Alexander White, mixed with a sentimental streak, yet at the same time a strong sense of discipline and Victorian morality. Within a day of sailing from Australia, for instance, he would record: 'I caught six men gambling in the crew's quarters. I intend to stop this, will allow no one in the Regiment to gamble!'

Two days later: 'Today I tried a man for swearing. I intend putting down this filthy language.' And the next day: 'Found some of my men drunk and find that some of the ship's people are selling beer at 1/3 and whisky at 8/6, so will soon stop this business ... the inspection today went off better but there still remains a lot to be done – the men would live like pigs if they were allowed, some are dirty devils and no mistake.'

When White went off to war, he stuck a newspaper cutting in the pocket-size red leather New Testament he carried with him. The cutting was headed 'A Creed', and went:

> Let me be a little kinder
> Let me be a little blinder
> To the faults of those about me
> Let me praise a little more;
> Let me be when I am weary
> Just a little bit more cheery
> Let me serve a little better
> Those that I am striving for.
>
> Let me be a little braver
> When temptation makes me waver,

Let me strive a little harder
To be all that I should be.
Let me be a little meeker
With the brother that is weaker
Let me think more of my neighbour
And a little less of me.

But the man who would lead his men to certain death at The Nek also stuck this enigmatic poem into the front of his carbon-copy diary:

The fellow who sits in the game of life
With only a deuce and a tray
May feel that with trials his hand is rife,
And it's scarce worth the trouble to play;
But still let him play it the best that he knows,
Nor e'er his depression reveal,
But when the hand's played it is fair to suppose
That the Dealer will give a new deal.

The appointment of White's other officers dated from 21 September. A captain commanded each of the three squadrons, 'A', 'B' and 'C', with four lieutenants (including Ted Henty) in each squadron as troop leaders.

As in the case of the overall 3rd Brigade command structure – with Brigadier Hughes, the civilian soldier, and Brigade Major Antill, the professional, in charge – the army decided that White's second-in-command should be another Boer War veteran. Major James Charles O'Brien was the man, a 52-year-old who had also served with the British Army in India.

The 8th under White set out to be a crack regiment. They decided on a motto: *More majorum* – loosely, 'After the manner of our ancestors'. They chose as their badge a horse rampant, rearing on its hind legs under a crown and between two sprigs of wattle. The officers went further, wearing blue-and-gold enamelled regimental badges with the distinctive rearing horse on their smart, fitted and tailored uniforms, and bright cherry-red forage caps. They took to writing on crested notepaper with the horse also engraved at the top.

The 8th Light Horse also decided on a distinctive look for each of the three squadrons: chestnut horses would be ridden by the men of 'A' Squadron, bays and light brown horses went to 'B' Squadron, and the dark browns and blacks to 'C' Squadron.

The regiment soon had its own trumpeters to sound calls, like 'Boots and Saddles', and a mounted band was formed to play the regimental march, 'Keel Row'. Lance Sergeant Francis Oliver Boyle, a 25-year-old draper and bandmaster from the town of Sale in eastern Victoria, was a natural to lead these men. Their silver instruments flashing and blaring, kettledrums rattling and harnesses jingling, before long they were a brave sight.

The keen young troopers were now shedding their civilian clothes and their initial camp dress of floppy white hats and blue jackets and trousers for their new, utilitarian but smart light horse uniforms.

They were issued with a 'wool serge', a comfortable khaki, upper garment with rising-sun badges on each collar peak and Australia badges on each epaulette. Later on, rectangular blue-and-gold patches were worn on the sleeves. The blue colour at the top designated the 8th Light Horse Regiment; the gold the 3rd Light Horse Brigade.

A polished brown-leather bandolier, with nine pockets, each capable of holding ten rounds, was slung across the body from the left shoulder, meeting a broad polished tan-leather belt with a brass buckle. From the belt on the left side hung a scabbard containing a 1907 Pattern bayonet, with a 43-centimetre-long blade, the attachment ring to the rear.

The light horseman's riding breeches were made of Bedford cord, laced up beneath the knee and held up by fireman-pattern khaki braces with a small stretch strap at the back.

The trooper wore well-polished brown leather lace-up boots and spiral-strap polished leggings that reached to just below the knee. The boots were worn with regulation spurs, with a tan leather butterfly on the spur strap. To top it all off came the slouch hat, with its rising-sun badge, puggaree and chin strap – adorned with what became the light horseman's most distinctive and jaunty trademark: the emu-feather plume.

This plume became the symbol of the light horse and soon part of its legend. The men of the First AIF used to say they were their 'kangaroo feathers', and the troopers were soon portrayed as being 'very sure of themselves, at times almost cocky or verging on the larrikin, their hats at a jaunty angle and appearing nothing less than the epitome of their hardened colonial background'. Even a drill manual suggested that the hat should be worn with 'a rakish tilt'.

Extraordinary men were still coming forward to join this extraordinary regiment. 'I was young and I was single. I could ride and I could shoot. I thought I was just the man they wanted,' Trooper David McGarvie said in 1976. That was when he sat in the parlour of his farmhouse with his grand-daughter Christine Gascoyne and friend Alison McKenzie, and tape-recorded interviews that lift the veil on this survivor's life and times before, during and after Gallipoli.

David was a crack shot and would be put to good use as a sniper on Gallipoli. A God-fearing Presbyterian, he went into battle with a Bible in his breast pocket and said his prayers every night. He never swore; 'blast' was the strongest word he ever uttered in his life. David was in Ted Henty's troop in the 8th and was one of only two survivors. Born with a harelip and a cleft palate, incredibly, the resulting speech impediment would end up saving his life.

On Gallipoli, he said matter-of-factly, shooting Turks on the open ground above the trenches was just like shooting rabbits. David McGarvie kept shooting rabbits on his farm he called 'Huntly' almost to the day he died in 1979, aged 87. He was known to his large and loving family simply as 'Pa'. Grandson Jamie Collyer remembers that Pa's arsenal had consisted of two weapons: 'One was an old single-barrel shotgun with broken extractors. In order to get the spent cartridge out you had to drop an old bolt down the barrel. The other weapon was a lightweight .22 rifle that also had broken extractors. To get its cartridge out you carried a piece of fencing wire with you to poke down the barrel ...'

In 1914 the arsenal was different. David McGarvie was a careful man who kept a neat pocket diary in pencil, and on the flyleaf of his 1915 diary, he made a list of the weaponry-related items he had been issued with:

Rifle
Bayonet
Scabbard
Oil Bottle
Pull Through.
No. 26378.

Like the other troopers, his rifle – serial number 26378 – was the short magazine Lee Enfield (SMLE), probably one made in Britain, as full production of an Australian version was only just getting under way at Lithgow in New South Wales. The rifle had evolved from weapons tried and tested in the Boer War. It was easily maintained with an oiled pull-through, and was accurate, sighted to 2,000 yards on the leaf and 2,800 yards on the long-range side plate. It was tough and sturdy, a bolt-action rifle that fired .303 bullets, which were fed into a magazine, five rounds at a time, using disposable clips. These clips can still be found on the Gallipoli battlefields, sometimes in little rusty piles where the action was fiercest.

David had a miserable beginning. William and Jean McGarvie were shocked when their son was born with the harelip and cleft palate, and although they had his harelip repaired before he was three, the cleft palate remained, giving him his distinct speech impediment, which he had until the day he died.

When he went to the Pomborneit School in January 1897 aged only 4½, his teacher, Mr Joseph Mumby, tried to get David to sing. But although he could hum along in tune, singing was an impossibility for the little boy. So Mr Mumby thrashed him, almost daily. David's cousin, Richard, who was at the same school, would attempt to hide the teacher's strap when it was obvious that Mumby was working up into one of his foul moods. The situation became impossible and eventually David's father had him transferred to another bush school, at Weerite.

But there was more to come. In 1900 Jean McGarvie, who had been renowned as a fine mezzosoprano and pianist, contracted tuberculosis and went off to take the sea air at Princetown near Port Campbell. She died there in 1901 and within 12 months William had married again, this time to Mary Edmonston, an old friend of his first wife. But Mary could not abide her stepson's handicap. As many did at that time, she took his strange way of speaking as a sign of mental deficiency. While she accepted his two brothers, Keith and Hector, she spurned David and gave him a very hard time.

Then came the war. David's elder brother Keith was the first to enlist. He became an original Anzac, joining the 8th Battalion, and went ashore at the landing on 25 April 1915. He too was an excellent rifle shot and survived the war to become a leading dairy farmer, agriculturist and politician, representing the electorate of Warrnambool. In 1965 he was among the veterans who returned to Anzac Cove for the fiftieth anniversary.

Keith had also been to visit the grave of their younger brother, Hector. In June 1916, word had apparently come from Britain, via his old school Geelong College, that ex-public school boys were being sought for training as officers in the British Expeditionary Forces. So Hector paid his own fare to the UK, trained as a second lieutenant with the Royal Field Artillery – only to be killed instantly on 8 July 1917, by a bomb blast near Ypres in Belgium. He was just 21 years old.

William McGarvie was furious when David enlisted. Perhaps he thought his middle son would never be accepted with his cleft palate. And he nearly wasn't.

'I volunteered at Camperdown,' David told his granddaughter in 1976, 'and of course they were volunteering all over the place. But they were only taking *fit* men. Well, the doctor wouldn't have anything to do with me at all. He said: "Go and put your clothes on. You're only wasting my time." Then the sergeant major, he tried to soften the blow by saying … "You couldn't do sentry duty".'

But David McGarvie was determined to do his bit for King and Country. 'There was a fellow at the factory who wanted to learn how to shoot. Well, I took him up to the rifle range to show him how to shoot on the Saturday. On the next Saturday, instead of going to shoot, I drove right on to Colac and I enlisted at Colac. That was on the third of October 1914.'

'Why did he want to enlist?' asked his grand-daughter. 'Did he think it was going to be fun?'

'Oh no, it wasn't fun,' David replied. He searched for a valid reason before adding: 'I suppose you'd say, my sense of patriotism. And I thought, well, there was no one depending on me and there was no reason why I shouldn't …'

Other volunteers came from much more cosmopolitan backgrounds. Trooper No.41 had enlisted simply as 'Roger Palmer' when he turned up at the recruiting office in Geelong on 11 September. But his full name was Roger Ebden Harcourt Palmer and he was already a citizen of the world.

He gave his father's address as 11 Broadway, New York, and although he had been born in Kew in Melbourne, he had gone to school at King Alfred's College at Taunton, in the English county of Somerset, between 1906 and 1911. He had been head prefect, captain of the cricket team and had won the school's 'Fortis and Fidelis' prize for being a good all-rounder. He was a natural leader and, after being a sergeant in the cadet corps and a member of the school's shooting team, had served in the Officer Training Corps with the 2nd Somerset Regiment. Yet he enlisted as a humble trooper in the 8th Light Horse, having refused a commission in the infantry. Within a month he had been promoted to sergeant.

Roger was 21, nearly 6 feet tall, dark and handsome, and a good friend of the Mack boys from Berry Bank. He was a direct descendant of John Palmer, who held the position of commissary general, in charge of stores, on the First Fleet when it sailed to Australia. Roger's father was a mining engineer who travelled the world with his wife and three children. At various stages they lived in Britain, Canada and the USA. But the parents separated and then his father died while testing a new explosive.

Instead of entering Magdalene College, Cambridge, after school as planned, Roger and the two other children were sent home to Australia.

His elder sister, Maude, got a job as governess on 'Yanko' station near Jerilderie in the New South Wales Riverina district, where she also looked after their younger sister. Roger got a job as a tutor on a station called 'Caramut' near Hamilton, close to Ted Henty.

Maude married the 'Yanko' station overseer, John Cameron, and in time they moved to Coleraine in the Western District. After the war, John Cameron would take his wife to meet an old friend – Trooper 480, Preston Maitland Younger, a stock dealer and the first man to enlist from Coleraine. He'd been invalided home after that dreadful day on 7 August 1915; a Turkish bullet had ripped into his armpit, exploded out of his shoulder, and left a livid scar on his neck. The bullet fragments had torn jagged holes in his sun helmet, which he'd brought home as a souvenir.

Maude asked him about her brother, Roger, officially reported as missing. The army had sent her his belongings: a safety razor, a history of Egypt and one silk handkerchief. Preston Younger told her the story about that day, how he had been beside Roger in the forward trench, saw him go up and over ... saw him get into the Turkish trenches just as he himself was knocked over by the bullet.

Others would say that it was Roger Palmer who waved the vital marker flag, a scrap of red and yellow, at the place they called The Nek.

Back at Broadmeadows, the 8th Light Horse began training together in their sections and squadrons. With their horses now chosen, they could call themselves full-blown troopers.

Space was becoming available in the camp as the first contingent of mostly infantry soldiers began to move out, down through the city to the docks, and set sail. The first contingent's flagship, *Orvieto*, sailed from Melbourne on 26 September 1914. The troops crowded the rigging and sang while the band played *Tipperary*. A farewelling crowd broke through barriers and rushed the pier, throwing streamers and fluttering their handkerchiefs.

Stretcher-bearers Harold Brentnall and George Fish were soon on their way too, alongside the men of the 4th Light Horse aboard the transport *Wiltshire*. George was now going out with Harold's sister, Jessie, after their meeting in Broadmeadows. Another friend, Sergeant Frank Carr of the 2nd Field Ambulance, sketched a picture of the pretty girl in a rakish hat waving goodbye, and named it 'Our Last Sight of Port Melbourne'.

Phillip Schuler, now a war correspondent, described the occasion:

> Never shall I for one (and there were hundreds on board in whose throat a lump arose) forget the sudden quiet on ship and shore as the

band played the National Anthem when the liner slowly moved from the pier out into the channel; and then the majestic notes of other anthems weaved into one brave throbbing melody that sent the blood pulsing through the brain:

Britons Never Will Be Slaves

Blared the bugles and the drums rattled and thumped the bars with odd emphasis until the ribbons snapped and the watchers on the pier became a blurred impressionist picture, and even the yachts and steamboats could no longer keep pace with the steamer as she swung her nose to the harbour heads.

The lighthouse at Point Otway flashed 'Good Luck' as the stretcher-bearers with the first Anzacs left Australia.

Chapter 5

The Father of the Regiment, Uncle Fred and the Bullant

While the men of the 8th Australian Light Horse Regiment were assembling at Broadmeadows, the other two regiments that would make up the 3rd Light Horse Brigade were forming up in Perth and Adelaide.

In Perth, the 10th Light Horse Regiment was almost entirely the creation of one man – its commanding officer, Lieutenant Colonel Noel Murray Brazier. Christened 'the father of the regiment', Brazier was the driving force and chief recruiter for the 10th. The regiment was a very personal thing to him; it was his preoccupation, his other family.

Noel Brazier was a peppery, stout man with strong views and a convivial character, who enjoyed the companionship of fellow members of his Perth club, where they could all relax over a whisky and a good cigar. He was known as 'Colonel' even to his grandchildren until the day he died, aged 80, in 1947.

Born in Victoria, the fifth child of eight in the family of the Reverend Amos Brazier and his wife, Jessie, he moved to Perth in the 1890s and got a job as a surveyor with the Public Works Department. In 1893 he married well after becoming engaged to Edith Maude Hardwick, daughter of the Swan Brewery's general manager, an influential figure in tiny, colonial Perth.

Brazier travelled widely, getting to know the state well, and was attracted to the fertile south-west. Here he bought a property in the Upper Capel area, just west of the present town of Kirrup. He called it 'Capeldene' and set out to make it a showplace farm and a place to raise thoroughbred horses.

Together with this tough personality and the passion he had for the new regiment, Noel Brazier also came equipped with an extremely short fuse. And being one to brood long and hard over insults and slights, real or imagined, his personal relationships with the commanding officers in the 3rd Light Horse Brigade would be a major factor in the drama that lay ahead at Gallipoli.

Western Australia in 1914 was vastly underpopulated. Despite the gold rushes of the 1890s there were only about 300,000 people living in a state that occupied a third of Australia. Most men were on the land, working on the great sheep and cattle stations in the north, the flat wheat belt that spread beyond the Darling Range near Perth, or in the fertile pocket of arable land in the south-west. Here was the natural habitat of the light horseman. Others worked in shallow shafts or deep underground in the goldfields of the flat red desert country that extended out from Southern Cross, Coolgardie, Kalgoorlie and Boulder. These mining skills would soon be used to help construct the maze of burrows, tunnels and saps that would house the light horse on Gallipoli.

When war broke out in August 1914, Western Australia had one mounted regiment, known as the 25th Light Horse. It had troops scattered throughout the state and had trained for a couple of years under Brazier, who had been promoted to lieutenant colonel after sitting for an examination in 1913. Sometimes the local light horsemen paraded on his property, 'Capeldene'.

The state already had a long tradition of mounted units; the Pinjarra Mounted Volunteer Rifles had been raised in 1862, followed by the Guildford Mounted Rifles and the Bunbury Rifles as well as several troops in Perth. During the Boer War, Western Australia had sent nine mounted units. There was enormous disappointment, then, when at the first call for enlistment for service overseas in 1914, it became known that no mounted troops were being asked for from the West.

The ranks of the 25th rapidly became depleted as troopers left, deciding to sign up for the infantry. The rest persevered in the belief that sooner or later mounted troops would be needed from Western Australia. At last, almost grudgingly, the authorities announced that a squadron of light horse would be accepted from Western Australia – as long as each member supplied his horse for free.

On 22 September 1914, Brazier noted in his diary: 'Went to Perth and reported for duty.' Four days later he saw a parade of the first contingent of Western Australians to leave the state. 'Fine looking men,' he wrote. 'March discipline only fair. Lump in my throat all the same.'

By the first week in October a squadron of light horse was in training at the old remount depot once used by the Guildford Mounted Rifles. The original plan was that they would become part of the 7th Light Horse, joining up with other squadrons being raised in Queensland and New South Wales.

Brazier was hard at work lobbying. Continual applications were being made from men eager to serve in the light horse, but were shelved or turned down because only a squadron was authorised for the state. Soon enough, the breakthrough came.

'Repeated efforts were at last crowned with success, authority to form a Regiment was granted, and the 10th Light Horse Regiment was accordingly formed. In this respect great credit is due to the personal effort put forth by Lieut-Col. N.M. Brazier, who may rightly be called the "Father of The Regiment",' wrote Lieutenant Colonel A.C.N. Olden, the regimental historian. The original squadron raised became 'A' Squadron of the 10th, and now two further squadrons could be raised to make up the full regiment of over 300 men, which would become part of the 3rd Australian Light Horse Brigade.

Brazier was already busy recruiting men and selecting donated horses (or buying them) for this, *his* regiment. He was riding out to the countryside and contacting old friends, recruiting their sons and the men he had met as a surveyor on their farmlands.

'Left for Beverley at 7 am,' he wrote in his diary on 30 September as he set out for the wheat belt. 'Crops look rotten and feed scarce. Outlook very gloomy. Very hot. One horse only at Beverley. Got 16 men at Narrogin. Seven horses given.' At another wheat town, Wagin, the next day, he signed up fourteen men, four with horses; at Katanning the day after, '15 men with horses, another 16 without'.

The new regiment's headquarters were set up at Claremont Showgrounds, where a party of officers under Captain Tom Todd was putting prospective light horsemen through their riding tests aboard a tall chestnut called Doctor Mac.

One such test was recorded. Todd asked one youngster, after he had fallen off Doctor Mac three times, 'My boy, what made you think you could ride?'

'I don't, sir.'

'Have you ever been on a horse in your life?'

'No, sir.'

'Well, what the hell did you come here for?'

'I didn't say I could ride, but I don't mind having a try, and I want to join the regiment.'

'That's the way to talk. Well, go away for a week and practise riding and I'll give you another chance.'

'Thank you, sir.'

The next week the boy came back. This time he stayed aboard Doctor Mac and was accepted.

The determination to join the 10th was extraordinary. One man rode nearly 300 miles overland from Kimberley to Wyndham, and then caught a ship down the coast to Fremantle to join up. Another was medically rejected because he had a malformed big toe. A week later he reappeared again at the showgrounds with a grin, asking, 'Will you take me now?' He had been to hospital and had the offending toe amputated.

Training in the West proceeded at a furious rate. By November 1914, Brazier would note: 'Men jumping over hurdles and tent pegging. Two men seriously hurt. Pace too hot, must be slowed.' But it continued just the same.

As Perth hotted up for a long, dry summer, the regiment moved down the Swan River aboard the ferry *Zephyr*, out through the harbour mouth at Fremantle and south to a dusty, dirty camping ground at the coastal settlement of Rockingham. Here the men would train until February, with the merciless heat and the persistent bushflies. Only a daily swim in the ocean and visits by friends laden with picnic hampers made life bearable.

A Mrs P. Law-Smith presented a regimental standard here. It was emblazoned with a black swan on a yellow background and the motto *Percute et percute velociter* – 'strike and strike swiftly'. His Grace Archbishop Riley, chaplain-general of the forces, blessed the standard as the men of the 10th stood with the sea breeze ruffling the emu feathers in their slouch hats, and the flag was solemnly handed over to the regimental sergeant major by Mrs Law-Smith herself.

In Adelaide, the nucleus of the 9th Australian Light Horse Regiment had also come together. Two squadrons of light horsemen would be recruited from South Australia, another vast state, which then had a population of only about 420,000. They would come to Melbourne after initial training and join up with a Victorian squadron to form another full regiment, the third arm of the 3rd Brigade.

The South Australian command went to Lieutenant Colonel Albert Miell, commanding officer of the 24th Light Horse Regiment, Citizen Forces, described in the regimental history as 'an energetic and capable officer of long standing'. Miell was 44 years old and a veteran of the Boer War, while Major Carew Reynell, his second-in-command, was described as having 'untiring energy … day or night he was forever at his post and ready for any task, however arduous'.

As in Western Australia, troopers rushed to enlist. Early days at the camp in Morphettville were also described in the regimental history:

> Strict training was carried out by officers and men, who soon began
> to show signs of perfect physical fitness for the hard tasks they would
> be called upon to face at an early date.

The horses supplied to the regiment were a splendid lot and reflected the greatest credit to the officers on whom the responsibility for their selection and purchase rested. As soon as the horses had been allotted to the various troops, each member was put through a thorough riding test, much amusement being caused by some, who, though anxious to serve with a mounted unit, had evidently never ridden a horse in their lives. As a result of this test a number of men had to be transferred to dismounted units, much to their disappointment. The remaining members immediately commenced troop and squadron training.

A Mrs Richard Bennett then presented the 9th with its own standard – 'a magnificent piece of work bearing the regimental crest, a lion rampant on a white Australia, the whole being on a scarlet field with a diagonal gold cross'. On this scarlet field, in white, sat the motto of the 9th Light Horse: *Pro gloria et honore* ('For glory and honour').

The two squadrons paraded through Adelaide's streets before leaving from Mile End station at the end of November on the train journey to Melbourne. They arrived at Broadmeadows with their horses at 11 pm, but 'rain was falling heavily and as the night had to be spent in the open, the impression formed that night of Victoria was far from complimentary to the sister State'.

The next day, the Victorian squadron, under Major T.J. Daly, rode up to join the two squadrons from South Australia. The 9th was now complete.

Within days the 9th would join with the 8th for training. The brigade commander himself – that 'elderly citizen officer belonging to leading social circles in Victoria' – would bring his personal supervision and special attention to 'musketry and bayonet fighting'. Colonels Miell and White could now have a closer look at the 3rd Light Horse Brigade's commanding officer, Frederick Godfrey Hughes.

The brigadier had been born in Windsor, Melbourne, on 26 January 1858, one of three boys born to Charles and Ellen Hughes, who had met in England but married in Victoria after migrating separately. Charles' early death led Ellen to take in sixteen young lads attending Melbourne Grammar School and offer lodgings with 'good food and a Christian environment'. Young Frederick would also go to Melbourne Grammar, where he was a keen sportsman. He left school to work as a clerk for a land valuer, and set up his own business around 1884.

Hughes began his military career at the age of 17, when he joined the St Kilda Artillery Battery as a horse driver. He became a sergeant in

1883 and was commissioned as an officer a year after that. The battery was one of the many pre-Federation military units notable for their dashing young men in self-designed uniforms. This one was under the command of Major Frederick Sargood, a wealthy businessman who would later be knighted and become an influential minister for defence in the Victorian Government. The uniforms had 'S.K.' (for St Kilda) on the shoulders, but the locals claimed the initials stood for 'Sargood's Kids'.

Frederick Hughes had a long connection with the seaside suburb of St Kilda. He would serve on the St Kilda City Council for 24 years, during which time he served two terms as mayor (in 1900-01 and 1911-12). He loved uniforms and being the centre of attention, and the garb of mayorship was another excuse to don fur-trimmed robes and gold chains.

His move into Victoria's high society was confirmed when he married Agnes Eva Snodgrass. She was a formidable lady, founder of a patriotic and conservative organisation called the Australian Women's Nation League, which at the outbreak of war boasted 50,000 members. Judging by a piece from *Bulletin* magazine's 'Melbourne Chatter Page', this entitled Hughes to some sympathy: 'Larry Rantoul was not trying to be either funny or insulting, but he convulsed an Empire Day gathering at the Town Hall when eulogising Brigadier General Hughes by declaring: "Nobody was surprised when General Hughes went to the war, for is he not the husband of Mrs Eva Hughes?"'

Eva's father, Peter Snodgrass, was a member of the Victorian Legislative Council, long regarded as the bastion of squatters' rights, and both families could boast that they were original settlers in the Port Phillip District of New South Wales.

Eva's sister Janet had also married well. She was now Lady Clarke, wife of Sir William Clarke, one of the richest landholders in Victoria. Janet had been governess to the four children born to Sir William's first wife, Mary, who had been killed in a carriage accident. Janet went on to bear him another seven children.

Sir William was the squire of 'Rupertswood', the mansion he had built 40 kilometres from Melbourne at Sunbury, and named after his son and heir. He also had a keen interest in military matters and used his money to help raise an outfit called the Victorian Nordenfeldt Battery. The Nordenfeldt was a primitive ten-barrel machine-gun mounted on a light carriage, and while the colonial government supplied the guns, Sir William provided the horses to draw them. He also supplied the new commanding officer – Frederick Hughes, who became its captain through the Snodgrass family connections.

The social cachet of being the commander of the battery was enhanced even further when another squire, Andrew Chirnside of 'Werribee Park', offered to support a unit of horse artillery. Chirnside inhabited a 60-room mansion outside Melbourne, said to be the largest private residence ever erected in Victoria. His property spread over 93,000 acres. Here were two squatters trying to outdo one another with their private armies.

The government decided to harness the military contributions of the two squatters by amalgamation. The Victorian Horse Artillery Regiment was born, with Hughes again as commanding officer, now promoted to major.

The Horse Artillery was a very flash unit indeed. The white helmets, highly polished riding boots, the blue uniforms with the gold braid and lace were all copied from the Royal Horse Artillery in the UK. And it was there, in 1893, that Hughes took a team of the Victorian Horse Artillery, to take part in an annual military tournament at Islington and shooting competitions at Bisley. Sir William Clarke (Baronet) footed the bill. But four years later, government support for the unit faded, a recession followed a land boom and bust in Victoria, and after Sir William's death, the regiment was formally disbanded.

Hughes was transferred and became a staff officer at headquarters in Melbourne, where in 1900 he was promoted to lieutenant colonel. After Federation, the old colonial mounted units became regiments of light horse, and in 1903 he was given command of the 11th Light Horse Regiment. Four years later Hughes was promoted to colonel.

Historian Peter Burness describes Hughes as 'an active and gregarious fellow' and goes on to comment: 'He was a man's man who mixed easily and enjoyed a range of masculine interests. In middle age he remained physically impressive. Although not considered intellectual he was "an alert, articulate, observant and sometimes irascible man (who) mixed urbanity and geniality with toughness and shrewdness".'

In 1907 Hughes could put on more gold braid when he became aide-de-camp to the Governor-General. And nepotism still ruled. It was time to return some favours as he became more senior in the army.

Sir William Clarke's youngest son, Reginald, was appointed adjutant of a regiment over the heads of other officers and then made brigade major when he followed Hughes, who was appointed to command a peacetime brigade. Later, Hughes made some suitable arrangements for his bright young nephew Wilfred Kent Hughes, known to everyone as 'Billy'.

Billy Kent Hughes (later in life to be knighted and become a prominent federal politician) had also gone to Melbourne Grammar, and enlisted in the army on 17 August 1914, as a private in the infantry. He got his sergeant's stripes ten days later because he had been in the school cadets, and sailed for Egypt with the 7th Battalion in the first contingent of the AIF. Soon after his arrival he received a cable from Melbourne telling him he had been awarded a Rhodes scholarship.

Sergeant Kent Hughes would call on his uncle soon after the brigadier arrived in command of the 3rd Light Horse Brigade and tentatively enquire about transferring from the infantry to one of the light horse regiments. The result was far more than he could ever have hoped for. He wrote excitedly to his father:

> I am now Uncle Fred's orderly officer (or practically A.D.C.). I made a suggestion to Uncle Fred about transferring, and he went to an awful lot of trouble to get things fixed up, although when I first asked him I had no idea of any promotion.
>
> The step from platoon sergeant in the foot-sloggers to A.D.C. to the brigadier of a mounted force seems a tremendous change from one point of view, though on the other hand I had been doing an officer's work for the past four or five weeks as my platoon commander has had charge of the reinforcements.

Now Lieutenant Billy had a batman, three horses and a groom. He was thrilled with his new job because in action 'it will probably mean dispatch-riding and that will be ripping'. On Gallipoli it would mean following Uncle Fred on the wearying climbs up and down Walker's Ridge and conveying his confused orders. Later on, the brigadier's own son, Arthur, would be commissioned and transferred across to Gallipoli.

After taking command of the 3rd Light Horse Brigade in October, the old brigadier seems to have let his brigade major, Lieutenant Colonel Jack Antill, have his head in the training of the men.

John Macquarie Antill – widely known as 'Bull' Antill, or simply 'the Bullant' – was a tough professional soldier, vastly experienced, but also both a martinet and a bully. Aged 48, he had been appointed second-in-command of the 3rd Light Horse Brigade on 17 October 1914. A photograph taken of him later on Gallipoli shows him standing, legs apart, arms akimbo, glaring square-jawed at the camera. His tie is done tightly up, shirt sleeves rolled up to the elbows; long shorts cover his knees almost touching the tightly furled regimental puttees and he is grasping a fly whisk in his right hand, as though he is ready to swat any nuisance that gets in his way.

The picture was taken in September 1915. By then Jack Antill would have taken command of the brigade from Hughes (who was invalided home from illness).

Antill was born on the family property at Picton, the historic little town south of Sydney, on 26 January 1866. As Peter Burness sums him up: 'Jack Antill was descended from a distinguished line of British Army officers from whom he inherited an interest in history and a sense of his own destiny.'

His grandfather, Major Henry Golden Antill, had served in America and India before coming to New South Wales, where he served as aide-de-camp to Governor Lachlan Macquarie. Granted land at Picton, he called the property 'Jarvisfield' in honour of the governor's own estate in Scotland.

Young Jack grew up and learnt to ride at 'Jarvisfield' before going off to school at Sydney Grammar, where he boxed and fenced, and got his first taste of military life in the school cadet unit. Like Noel Brazier, he first became a surveyor after leaving school, and also joined the local militia when he was 21. Two years later, he raised a squadron of mounted infantry at Picton that would become part the New South Wales Mounted Infantry Regiment (later the New South Wales Mounted Rifles) under the command of a Captain Henry Beauchamp Lasseter. The latter, from a prominent Sydney retail merchant family, married Antill's sister, and this may have helped Jack come to the attention of Major General Edward Hutton, the commander of the New South Wales military forces.

Hutton arranged for Antill to be sent to India in 1893 to get experience with the British Army. He served with the Devonshire Regiment and the 2nd Dragoon Guards. When he returned in 1894 he was commissioned into the new Commonwealth Army. Five years later, with the outbreak of the Boer War, Jack Antill was promoted to major and given command of 'A' Squadron of the New South Wales Mounted Rifles.

Bull Antill made his mark in South Africa. His squadron took part in a number of major actions, including the capture of a major Boer force led by General Piet Cronje. Antill was among the first into the Boers' camp after they surrendered, and he sent the white surrender flag home to Sydney, where it became a major attraction in the window of Lasseter's store.

His commanding officer reported: 'On two occasions he led his Regiment at the gallop against positions held by the enemy. Proving him to be a fearless and valuable leader in the field. He has shown great capacity in command of his regiment.'

Antill returned to Australia on 8 January 1901, but was back in South Africa in March, as second-in-command of the 2nd New South Wales Mounted Rifles (commanded by his brother-in-law). In action again, he took part in a series of night marches that resulted in the capture of over 1,000 prisoners.

He came home to be married, something of a minor war hero, with seven clasps on his service medals, having twice been Mentioned in Despatches. He was appointed a Commander of the Order of the Bath (CB) and promoted to the rank of brevet lieutenant colonel. After being appointed chief instructor for the Australian Light Horse in New South Wales, Jack emulated his grandfather by becoming aide-de-camp to the Governor-General, Lord Northcote, from 1904 to 1906.

After turning 40, Antill retired from the army for a short while, but in 1911 he got the call to join up again as commandant of the Instructional Staff Schools. His blunt, uncompromising manner landed him in hot water, however, when he was appointed to the army's inspection staff and required to attend militia training camps and submit reports to the inspector-general.

'The assessment he made of a one-week camp held by the 5th Brigade at Liverpool in November-December 1913 plunged him into trouble and became the lowest point in his peacetime career,' wrote Burness. 'In his report he condemned the lack of discipline, the control and proficiency of the officers, the supervision, filthy lines, poor rifle exercises, bad marching, dirty band instruments and the appearance of the men.'

He even criticised one of his brother officers whom he had served with in South Africa – cruel comments that were described as 'grossly unfair' by a court of inquiry called to look into the report. The court heard claims that Antill was harsh and tactless, and found that parts of his report were 'unjust, unfair, misleading and not supported by evidence'.

Although no action was taken against the Bullant, there was a suggestion that he should be transferred to another state and the controversy hung over his career, which had now stalled somewhat. He had held the same rank for over a decade and had seen officers he knew well, and some junior, promoted over him. 'The truth was that, while he was an intelligent man,' Burness continued, 'he was rigid in his thinking and did not possess the quickness of mind or the fertile brain of those whose promotions he coveted'.

When war was declared, Jack Antill couldn't wait to get away. After a period as enrolment officer for the AIF in Sydney, responsible for selecting the men for the first contingent, a selection board decided on his appointment interstate as brigade major for the 3rd Light Horse Brigade.

It must have been something of a shock to be number two and not in command. Even more so when Antill discovered that his new CO was 'an elderly citizen officer belonging to leading social circles in Victoria' and that the commanders of the 8th, and 10th regiments were militia men who had never heard a shot fired in anger.

Antill threw himself into the task of making his presence felt. The Bullant began doing the thing he was best at – throwing his weight around. First he went to Adelaide to have a look at the South Australians before they moved east to Broadmeadows to join the 3rd Light Horse Brigade.

'Major J.M. Antill, C.B. who had been appointed Brigade Major to the Brigade, arrived from Melbourne about the middle of November to inspect the Regiment on behalf of the Brigadier,' wrote Major T.H. Daley, stiffly, in his regimental history *With the Ninth Light Horse in the Great War*. 'After spending two days, during which he subjected the Regiment to a thorough overhaul, he returned to Headquarters.'

In reality, Antill had simply dressed them down. A local newspaper reported that his remarks were 'resented by every man in camp and the officers had the greatest difficulty in keeping the men in hand'. The tongue-lashing had been so bad that the NCOs asked to be discharged, and the officers made their protests directly to their colonel. Somehow, things were defused, so that before returning to Melbourne, Antill would describe the troops as 'a fine type of men'.

Brigadier Hughes, meanwhile, went off separately to visit Colonel Brazier and his men in Western Australia, telling *The Argus* on his return that he had found the 10th Light Horse Regiment to be 'very hardy and tough'. Antill would wait until January before going to Perth and he would sail with the men of the 10th early in February for Egypt.

But this visit, and the long voyage that followed, would produce a deep and bitter enmity between Brazier and Antill.

Chapter 6

The Best-Loved Man
in the Regiment

In September 1914, a charming young doctor and OGG (as the old boys of Geelong Grammar were called) wrote a note to *The Corian*, the magazine of his old school on the outskirts of the Victorian port city. 'I have volunteered, and though I have not heard definitely, am hoping to be taken in one of the Field Ambulance Corps with the 2nd Expeditionary Force,' he told the magazine. 'I have seen some other OGGs who are going with the First Force. My work if I go will not be as arduous or dangerous as theirs, but a man must do what he is most fitted for.'

Sid Campbell was writing from his study inside the austere quadrangular Gothic splendour of Ormond College, at the University of Melbourne. The college bears the name of its principal benefactor, Francis Ormond, son of a Scottish sea captain, and an early self-made Victorian grazier and philanthropist. Founded to serve the needs of the Presbyterian elite in Victoria, Ormond College is a severe-looking nineteenth-century institution, with its 165-foot tower and baronial dining room with open fires in the winter and a high table for the academic staff. Campbell, previously an undergraduate here, had now returned as resident medical tutor for the first two terms of 1914.

A month later he was in very different surroundings, and wrote, 'First attempt at keeping a diary – how long will it last!' The first entry read modestly enough: 'Entered Broadmeadows Camp 14th October 1914 as M.O. to 8th Light Horse knowing nothing of military work.' Within a few weeks, however, Sid Campbell would be known to officers and troopers alike as the most popular man in the regiment.

Sydney James Campbell was just 27 years and four months old, an all-round sportsman, a complete product of the wealth and privilege of the time. He was born in 1887, fifth child in a family of eight, in Portland, home port for the pioneering Western District families, especially the Hentys and the Campbells. Indeed, Sid was related to Ted Henty, the keen young lieutenant from Hamilton, and it may well have been Ted who helped persuade him to join the 8th.

Sid Campbell's father had become very wealthy and in 1895 bought a magnificent mansion called 'Maretimo', where the family spent many happy times. His schooling took place at Hamilton College, where he was probably a weekly boarder, and then Geelong Grammar, from 1900, as a day boy. He quickly excelled in both studies and sport. In 1905, Sid won a scholarship to Ormond to study medicine, and five years later he graduated with final honours in medicine, surgery and pathology, plus winning a scholarship in pathology with first-class honours. He moved on, just down the elm tree avenue of Royal Parade in Parkville, to become a senior resident at Melbourne Hospital. After a year he was back at the university as Stewart lecturer on pathology and acted as assistant in that department to Professor Sir Harry Allen, 'taking the lectures to the dental students'. During the first two terms of 1914 he was resident medical tutor at Ormond before he joined up.

In one way, Sid Campbell is still there at Ormond – in the form of a photograph staring down from a wall as today's students hurry along the corridor in their jeans and T-shirts. The picture is of a rowing crew and includes one of his friends, Mervyn Bourne Higgins. Merv, or 'Buggins' as he was known, would also become a brother officer, both serving together in the 8th.

Merv Higgins was the only son of the first president of the Arbitration Court, Mr Justice Henry Bourne Higgins. After a year at Ormond, Merv went on to Britain to study classics and history at Oxford University and was a member of the victorious Oxford rowing crew in 1910. He returned home to practise as a barrister and then joined the army.

Ormond College followed the rest of Australia in its enthusiastic response to the outbreak of war. It was a continuum: you owed it to your family, school, college – and yourself – to answer the call. On hearing the news, eight Ormond students immediately cut short their studies and 'volunteered to flap a towel in Great Britain's corner during the encounter at present "on" in Belgium's stadium', quoted Stuart Macintyre in his 'Ormond College Centenary Essays'.

At least one other Ormond man joined the 8th. Eric Whitehead, a grazier's son from Minhamite, had been a medical student. He came to Ormond from Geelong College, where he had been a prefect, a member of the cricket XI and a rower in the senior fours. Eric enlisted as Trooper 545 and would die in the dust at The Nek, with no known grave, as a temporary second lieutenant.

Altogether, 437 Ormond students, past and present, would serve in the First World War. Of the 356 medical men, graduates or undergraduates who joined up, 142 would be killed. More names on yet another one of those long wooden honour boards that survive today, with carved laurel leaves and surnames and initials written in faded gold, asterisks marking the fallen, the Glorious Dead.

Among the new recruits that Sid examined at Broadmeadows was John Dodd Mack, the third of the Boys from Berrybank, who signed up early in January 1915. Jack was now 34 and a station manager. Sid noted that he had small moles on his back and a scar on his left hand between the thumb and first finger. He pronounced him fit for service. The commanding officer of the 8th, Colonel Alexander White, scrawled his signature again boldly and appointed the eldest Mack brother to 'A' Squadron.

Jack was to find that the pace of training was quickening. The 8th and 9th were being licked into shape, now that two-thirds of the 3rd Light Horse Brigade were stationed at Broadmeadows. The Bullant, as usual, was making his presence felt. Regardless of Antill's approach, Trooper Tom Austin of the 8th reported that 'the instructors had a congenial task because every man was so keen ... everybody getting most impatient to get away to the scene of operations, serious doubts began to arise in many of our minds if we would get away at all. Every imaginable rumour was spread about, regarding German defeats and the Kaiser's death that we almost began to despair.'

Dave McGarvie, the sniper from Pomborneit, just kept going to church regularly on Sundays, sometimes holding prayer meetings in his tent with his new friend Lance Corporal George Hughes, the Presbyterian minister from Balranald who had ridden down to Broadmeadows and joined Ted Henty's troop. 'Lecture on attacking positions and practical demonstration,' noted Trooper McGarvie one day during this time. As usual, he was writing in pencil in his pocket diary. 'In afternoon, lecture on defending position. Demonstration.' Then, 'Parade at 8 pm till 9.30 pm for night work'.

But after the long days and nights during the week, with the surprise turnouts, the weekends at Broadmeadows were often lonely for a young man from the country. 'Wrote letter to father. Had some pistol practice – 50 shots. I am the only one in the tent tonight. Very few men in camp,' Dave recorded one Saturday.

Nothing too exciting on the Sunday either, it seems: 'Had a shower bath. Church parade near YMCA tent. Warm day. Had a quiet time all on my own. Went to service in Church of England tent. Text: "Lord Teach Us to Pray".' And after he prayed, Dave McGarvie would make sure he'd entered his scores from that day's shooting at the Williamstown rifle range, neatly, in pencil: 'Grouping 20 out of 20, 100 yards; 200 yards 19 out of 20; 300 yards 18 out of 20.'

At the same time, Aub Callow and the signallers were practising semaphore with flags and transmitting messages in Morse by means of heliographs and electric lamps. Field telephones were still primitive and unreliable, as shown in an account of signal training at the time: 'Particular attention is devoted to buzzer work. The buzzer is fitted to a field telephone and instead of the voice the receiving signaller hears a succession of long and short buzzes that would be distinct above the sound of battle.'

Wireless was in its infancy and there were no portable walkie-talkies. For signallers training in Australia, these were still the stuff of dreams. In 1913 the government had bought the first six wireless sets ever in use in the Australian Army, known as 500 Watt Marconi Wireless PACK sets. They had more than 250 kilograms of gear, and in the field were carried on four horses and needed six men to set up. Each set had two 10-metre-high antenna masts, which had to be erected 100 metres apart using guy ropes and earth mats, and a petrol engine to generate power. The sets had a range of almost 50 kilometres, sometimes a bit more in clear conditions. Four of the sets, accompanied by 30 men and 40 horses, would be sent to Gallipoli, where they were mainly attached to British Army units and used to help artillery observers aboard Royal Navy ships pinpoint attacks.

In Australia, flags, flashing lights and buzzers on field telephones all sounded fine – and looked fine when rehearsed on the flat fields of Broadmeadows. In practice, on Gallipoli, communications were a nightmare. How could a signaller wave his semaphore flags above the parapet in trench warfare without getting his head shot off? Or erect a heliograph on a tripod? If there were no effective radios in existence, how could orders be transmitted between the different units dug in on the ridges, and how could they be received from senior commanding officers who chose to float offshore in ships far removed from the front lines? Field telephone lines on Gallipoli were often destroyed in the shelling, so messages would have to be delivered by runners dodging snipers' bullets as they dashed between the trenches.

And as for the field telephones, Antill himself would write in his war diary in November 1915: 'Phone connections rotten – same all through – no wire, bad, obsolete phones and commutators – and we are using phones condemned in Australia before the war we cannot get any others. This means disaster in an attack, but no one appears to bother – requisitions have been in and renewed for nine months …'

This was a reality of a frightening, new type of warfare. It would be just one of the many revelations for these troopers who were still being trained in the ways of cavalry from the era of the 1854 Charge of the Light Brigade.

But now it was the beginning of 1915 and the men at Broadmeadows were ready for action. On 20 January 1915, the 8th and 9th regiments of the 3rd Light Horse Brigade paraded through Melbourne. It was a day that stopped the city.

Joseph Mack travelled up from 'Berry Bank' and stayed at Scott's Hotel the night before. He noted succinctly in his diary afterwards: 'Good horses and men looked well. Jack, Ernie and Stanley amongst them.' *The Age* had plenty more to say on the subject, having despatched a team of reporters to cover the momentous event. It was a huge day for everyone, and, for many, it was the last opportunity to see the pride of Australia's young men before they rode to war.

The following day, the four decks of headlines read:

AUSTRALIA'S LIGHT HORSE
MARCH THROUGH CITY
WELCOME TO THIRD BRIGADE
ENTHUSIASTIC CROWDS LINE STREETS

Below which the reporters wrote:

By 8 o'clock the long column of 2,000 men was formed in fours and the head of the column was already moving out of camp. Through Essendon, Moonee Ponds and Flemington the brigade reached Melbourne shortly after 10 o'clock and, at Campbell and Sons horse bazaar on the outskirts of the city, halted for a few minutes to water the troop and transport horses – just time to smoke a cigarette, then tighten girths and straighten slouch hats, ready for the two mile parade before the eyes of Melbourne.

Meanwhile Melbourne was ready and waiting their arrival. Every suburban train that reached Flinders Street or Spencer Street station before 11 o'clock, and every tram car that ran on city routes helped to swell a crowd that lined the whole marching route three deep and gathered in mass round the saluting base.

Collins Street and Bourke Street were avenues of flags and bunting, shop and office windows from ground floor to roof were crowded points of vantage. Prompt, at 11.40 am the head of the brigade turned from King Street into Collins Street and met the first cheers of the crowd.

'Where's your hankies?' called a mother to her girls. 'You'll have to give a shout for Cyril.'

Shout they did – and not for Cyril only.

As the head of the column wheeled into Collins Street, the mounted band struck up a swinging march, the men stiffened on their horses, and it took the most persuasive calls from sweethearts at the barricades to get the least flicker of recognition from the trooper on parade.

An old gentleman watching eagerly leaned out of the crowd with a handkerchief tied to the end of his umbrella ready to raise it frantically as his son rode by. He received a grave, dignified nod of the head, and waved so frantically that the line of horses shied and nearly broke the column.

All along the route of march it only required one voice to raise a 'hip' and a hundred voices finished the cheer.

Another reporter took up the story at Parliament House:

Punctually at noon three khaki horsemen swung into the road from Collins Street. A rattle of applause, the shrill notes of a distant band and the thudding of a drum announced the approach of the troops; in another minute the leading squadrons came into view and the march past had begun.

Three military police head the column, acting as outriders, and, sitting like statues in their saddles, with rifle butts resting upon their right thighs. Then came the staff officers, Lieutenant-Colonel Antill and Captain McFarlane and they in turn were followed by the brigadier, Colonel Hughes, riding at the head of a group of buglers and headquarters details.

The Governor-General's hand rose to the salute, a sword blade glistened in the sun. The head of the column passed by, and then followed the brigade, squadron after squadron, passing at a walk and led by the mounted band of the 8th Regiment with burnished instruments and drums swathed in the Union Jack.

In many respects the march past of cavalry differs from that of infantry. Infantry march by solemnly with a mechanical effect of swinging legs and arms and swaying rifle barrels. Cavalry pass with a merry dash. They typify the joy of life in a military spectacle, passing with a music all their own and a lilting air of irresponsible jauntiness.

So it was with the Light Horse yesterday. The six squadrons of the 8th and 9th Regiments rode by to the shrill bell-like treble of jingling chains; the staccato rattle of hoofs on the hard road and the soft creaking of burnished leather. They rode with sheen and sparkle of burnished chains, a glitter of spurs; and in the sun the officers' swords gleamed and flickered as they were brought up to the salute.

And so the light horse clattered away from the city towards the outer-Melbourne suburb of Heidelberg, to camp beside the River Yarra. Their transport wagons had been loaded with rations and baggage. With absolutely no idea of where they were going, and almost completely untrained for the realities of the close-quarter, brutal trench warfare that lay ahead, the innocent Australian mounted infantry prepared to sail on their adventure.

Chapter 7

Sailing into the Unknown

After months of training and frustration, the 3rd Light Horse Brigade was finally off to war. On 2 February 1915, Major James O'Brien, second-in-command of the 8th Light Horse, left Melbourne with an advance party, aboard the troop transport A43, HMAT *Barunga*. The troop transports had been requisitioned by the Commonwealth Government to transport the AIF and its supplies overseas. Most of the transports were British steamers, but a few were captured enemy ships, as in the case of *Barunga*, which was previously a German merchant vessel called *Sumatra*. All the ships were better known simply by their transport ship initials.

A few days later, Captain Archibald McLaurin sailed out in charge of transport A25, HMAT *Anglo-Egyptian*. He was another Melbourne Grammar old boy and had been running a vineyard with his brothers Bob and Reg near Rutherglen when war broke out. With him on *Anglo-Egyptian* went 55 troopers, 130 horses (mostly draught horses) and three lieutenants – the eager young Ted Henty from Hamilton, together with Frederick Thorne and Wilf Robinson. These last two were both country Victorians, used to working the land. Thorne was a horticulturist from Mildura and a Boer War veteran, while the large-framed Robinson was a wheat farmer on 'Murra Warra', the property near Horsham settled by his pioneer father in 1874.

At the same time, there was movement over in Western Australia. By 8 February the men of the 10th Light Horse had arrived in Fremantle from their base further south at Rockingham, and were gathered on the wharf as their horses were put aboard the British-India steamer *Mashobra*, known as transport A47. The horses, according to regimental historian Lieutenant Colonel A.C.N. Olden, 'for the most part behaved wonderfully well, considering it was their maiden embarkation, the sling being brought into requisition in one or two cases only'. Due to lack of room on the vessel, however, one squadron was forced to leave a few days later in another ship.

There was much speculation as to the destination, which because of security reasons was kept under wraps, but the betting in Perth was on Egypt because word had come through that the AIF's infantry and artillery were there along with some light horse. But nobody was quite sure where the 8th, 9th and 10th would meet up exactly.

Meanwhile, the crowds poured into Fremantle to say goodbye. The German cruiser *Emden*, which had been operating in the Indian Ocean, had been put out of action after the first contingent of the AIF had sailed in secret from Albany, Western Australia, on 1 November 1914. As a result, there were no restrictions now on a public send-off, as Olden noted:

> It is doubtful if ever such a huge and representative assemblage of Western Australian people had previously been seen at Fremantle to compare with that which gathered together on the wharf that day to bid adieu to their one mounted unit. A spirit of boisterous enthusiasm prevailed, both amongst the troops and their friends on shore. Doubtless much of it was assumed in order to conceal the deeper heart felt feelings of wife and sister or husband and brother.
>
> But it was a spirit proper to the occasion. Western Australia was giving of its best for King and Country and she was giving, as she always has done, cheerfully and with confidence.
>
> At five o'clock in the afternoon the *Mashobra* drew slowly away from the wharf to the accompaniment of cheer upon cheer, the National Anthem, and the many battle cries, now so familiar to everyone. A final waving of hats and handkerchiefs, a last long 'good-bye' as the steamer passed the Mole and the 10th regiment had gone!

There was an overnight anchorage in Gage Roads before transport A47 joined three other ships, carrying infantry reinforcements, and formed up in convoy off Rottnest Island. Sure enough, and typical of what would grow to be the Anzac legend, someone on board *Mashobra* had soon written a poem, which was circulated in a newspaper they called *The Mashobra Bully Tin*:

> Well! At last we have fairly got going
> And a few hundred miles out to sea,
> And we're heading Nor' West, without knowing
> What our mission in future may be.
> But whatever the job is, they'll find us
> No less eager to start – nor sincere;

Still, we cannot forget that behind us
Is the Girl on the Fremantle Pier!
We've got a good many things in our favour,
Our troopship is comfy and new,
And the tucker possesses a flavour
Unlike the old Rockingham stew,
We are done with the dust for a season
We've a chance to envelop a beer
Still we miss – and not without reason
That Girl on the Fremantle Pier.

'It was a happy family aboard the *Mashobra*,' the regimental historian would write. 'Lieut-Colonel J.M. Antill, the first Brigade-Major of the 3rd Light Horse Brigade, was in command of the troops, and, whilst enforcing a rigid discipline throughout the voyage, did everything possible to ensure the comfort and well-being of the men.'

In truth, it was far from being a happy family, certainly at the top. The Bullant had arrived in Perth and gone to the 10th's base before sailing with the regiment. He soon set out to demonstrate who was really boss. A clash with Lieutenant Colonel Noel Brazier, commanding officer of the Western Australians, who had almost single-handedly raised the regiment through all his friends and contacts throughout the state, was inevitable. Added to this, perhaps, were the fierce independence of most Western Australians and their inbred suspicion of outsiders, especially those they called 'wise men from the East'.

At the back of a notebook, Brazier began to write furiously in pencil a litany of what he called 'Episodes' of the 'Treatment' he received from Antill. Brazier's first two 'Episodes' entries read as follows:

1. During the BM's visit to Rockingham he was the essence of oiliness and wired to Brigadier [Hughes] that 10 Regt was easily the best. The other COs eventually told us that owing to the continual buttering up of the 10th they got to hate us.

2. The *Mashobra* left Fremantle at 5 pm on Wednesday February 8 and 15 minutes from casting off, while all hands were waving, the BM came round near me and yelled out 'This is the worst disciplined regiment I have ever seen'. He was CO troops although I am his senior.

I said nothing but felt a lot.

Later on he came near me and made nasty remarks and I told him there were two adjutants on the ship capable of doing their duties and if he expected me to chase them around continually and worry them he was mistaken. He shut up and two days later got very oily again …

The list of Episodes continues, page after page, detailing a relationship that was doomed from the start and would worsen, with disastrous consequences on Gallipoli. Scrawled across the last page of the Episodes is a note, written in ink, and signed by Brazier on 12 December 1926. It reads: 'THIS IS WAR!!! And words fail after 14 years to express one's thoughts.'

On the other side of the continent, the South Australians and the Victorians in the 9th sailed from Melbourne on 11 February aboard the transports *Karoo* and *Armidale*.

By 20 February, the majority of the 8th Light Horse knew that they would be sailing four days later. There was just enough time for packing suitcases and kitbags, and some home leave to say goodbye.

The officers took with them a brown leather trunk, a leather kitbag and a brown canvas valise. They packed for every eventuality. After all, they still had no exact idea where they were going – to the front in France or Belgium was the general belief, but, via where? Egypt?

Sid Campbell thoughtfully packed some evening gloves and white ties; Ted Henty took along a rabbit-skin coat and three pairs of mittens. They packed their polished dress boots and shiny Sam Browne belts for ceremonial parades, and Sid also stashed away his own revolver and pair of binoculars, just in case.

There were farewell presents, too. Peter Burness writes of the gifts given to Colonel Hughes as being perhaps 'appropriate for a senior officer at Waterloo' but 'of little comfort on Gallipoli'. St Kilda City Council gave its esteemed former mayor a silver 'campaigning bottle', while the members of the St Kilda Tradesmen's Club gave a silver cigar case and matchbox.

Ernie Mack wrote jocularly to his sister, Mary (he called her 'Jones'), at 'Berry Bank' to tell the family to come up to town to see them before they struck camp at Broadmeadows. The regiment, he said, was going to 'ride through Melbourne as a phantom host and not get disturbed by a crowd'; he added cheekily, ' – you know a lot of people would collect just to see Stan and myself clear out'.

The family did indeed come up to Melbourne. Joseph Mack made three entries in his diary:

> 22 Feb. Mother and I went to town to see boys go to the War.

> 23 Feb. About camps.

> 24 Feb. Said good-bye to John, Ernie and Stanley as they start early tomorrow morning.

On the evening before the regiment left Broadmeadows, Stan bought a letter card, wrote it in pencil, affixed a 1-penny stamp, and addressed it to his mother at her hotel.

> My dear Mother
> Well here we are close to leaving now so I thought I would slip over and write a final letter from B'meadows,
>
> We are all as happy as ever we were in our lives so for goodness sake don't worry and think we might be getting cold feet now that we are so close to sailing.
>
> If you notice a small tick on our p'cards then you will understand we have heard from home. Ted Wilson got me a beautiful hack this evening from Maribyrnong as Bob [Stan's own horse] stumbles and got rejected.
>
> Good night Mum and don't do any more work than you should
> Your ever-loving son
> Stanley.

The next day, Helen Mack would reach for a piece of notepaper, headed in blue 'Scott's Hotel, Melbourne', and write this poignant letter to her three boys in the 8th:

> My dear Sons
> We got up this morning as soon as we were told you would be passing through but we were too late.
>
> We saw the B & C [squadrons] through & followed the latter in a Taxi with Mr Edgar to the Wharf but could not see any of you. We may get some one to take us down this afternoon.
>
> I am glad you got a good horse.
> With all good wishes for your safe return and with much love from
> Your ever loving
> Mother.

Helen Mack would never see her boys again. She died suddenly from illness on 29 September in a private hospital – just one week before Stan returned from the war.

Like the Macks, most of the 8th were given leave on the two nights before sailing. With the temptations of the big city on offer, however, some men returned late to camp and had to face the consequences. Trooper Ernest Butcher was one such unfortunate. Not everyone was from the country – about a third of the regiment had some kind of urban background – and before enlisting, 22-year-old Ernest had driven a milkman's cart around the streets of Port Melbourne, past the pier where the regiment would soon embark. Butcher was charged with being absent without leave from 2.15 to 6.30 am, and fined 15 shillings.

In the main, though, the troopers' behaviour was exemplary. Young Aub Callow, for instance, the trainee vet from Ballarat, went into Melbourne to visit family before he left, while Dave McGarvie was seen off by his friends, Mr and Mrs Holt. The previous Saturday he had gone to the Protestant Hall and listened to a lecture (entitled 'The Second Coming of the Lord') before returning to Broadmeadows. In that last week he also engaged dutifully in some useful bayonet drill before packing his kitbag and being issued with his identification tags.

Sid Campbell, the universally popular Ormond College medic, had strolled along St Kilda pier that last evening of leave with a friend called Mary. The pier is just down from Luna Park, where an avenue of tall palm trees rustles in the sea breeze. Perhaps they had paused to buy an ice-cream cone from the grand old kiosk at the end of the pier. He wrote later about remembering the stillness of the night and the moonlight on the water.

The final night at Broadmeadows was a cold one, made worse by the fact that, with the camp all packed up, there were no blankets available. Aub Callow described the early morning start:

> Thursday 25th: We moved out of camp mounted this morning between 3 and 4 am. The morning was very dark and cold with cold showers at intervals. The regiment moved onto the Sydney Rd. and made for Port Melbourne. We arrived in the city at about 7 am and Port Melbourne at 7.30 am. We marched on to the pier, off saddled and commenced loading horses on the troopship A16, SS *Star of Victoria*. Then saddlery was packed away in the harness rooms and we were told off into our different messes. Everything was ready at 3.30 pm. We were towed out and anchored about a mile out. This was our first night on the boat.

Sid Campbell noted proudly: 'The Regiment embarked in a manner which evoked praise from the very critical embarkation board who described it as the best embarkation from Victoria of any unit to date.' Despite these high standards, there was little the light horsemen could do about the transport they'd been saddled with.

The *Star of Victoria* was a Commonwealth & Dominion Line steamer of 9,152 tons that chugged along, spewing smoke from its coal-fired boilers, at up to 14.6 knots, although normally it could make about 11. Transport

A16 was under the command of Captain Beck, with Chief Engineer Hunter in charge of a sometimes temperamental engine room. Normally it would carry 17 first-class passengers and 95 crew; now the ship was fitted out with seven lifeboats, enough for 364 passengers, together with eighteen large lifebuoys and another 114 life jackets and belts for the troops.

Its previous role as a luxury liner aside, *Star of Victoria* was not built for comfort. This would soon become apparent when, out in the open seas, it would pitch, roll and corkscrew like the worst Luna Park roller-coaster. Before long, the troopers were complaining that they were 'packed like sheep in a truck'. The horses took up two decks and the men slept in hammocks slung above the tables in a large communal mess room. When the weather got warmer they would sleep on the open decks. The men griped that the officers had comfier quarters and much more deck space than the hatchways they could use.

The first night aboard was relatively peaceful, although Tom Austin, the Melbourne Grammar boxing champ and the 8th's unofficial historian, observed that not being allowed to say goodbye to relatives on the pier had 'hurt many of us very hard'. He went on to describe the mood as those on board contemplated what lay ahead and what they were leaving behind:

> A few hours were spent leaning over the rails looking at the lights of Melbourne and speculations of our future doings were many and varied.
>
> Bunks tried at a late hour but as this was the first big sea trip for many the excitement and noises did not conduce to a sound sleep.
>
> However, on awakening next morning, the boat was well under way and we were soon passing through The Heads at a slow pace.
>
> The world was now before us and though full of eagerness and glad to be on our way to the front, many of us looked back on our Broadmeadows days with a sigh. The life there had taught us much. The Country man had got to know a good deal of the city, and the city man had grown to love the open air points of a soldier's life, such as fatigue dodging, orderly rooms, etc.
>
> We knew that the YMCA was the place to find a man when he was required for fatigue or guard, that the dirtiest man in the camp was the cook, and that night time was the time to make up all shortages in kit and saddlery, and that the Quartermaster Sergeant was the best man to buy beer for.

As the ship steamed down Port Phillip Bay, Lieutenant Colonel Alexander White turned his new field glasses on the shoreline, searching the foreshore at Elsternwick for a last glimpse of home. This he would describe in his first letter to his wife, Myrtle: 'I looked at Cole Street and saw Armstrong [a neighbour] and dog, but could not see you at all, could easily pick out the old shed – glasses quite good – missed you somehow.'

Star of Victoria was sailing in company with transport A54, *Runic*, which carried another 1,500 men or more, mostly infantry reinforcements for the first contingent of the AIF and with some light horsemen to fill gaps in units already in Egypt. As the two ships cleared the broad protected waters of the bay on the morning of 26 February 1915, and steamed through the narrow and treacherous Rip at the entrance, they soon met the heavy rollers marching in from the Southern Ocean.

With these ocean swirls came the inevitable seasickness. 'Sick as soon as out of port,' wrote Major Arthur Vivian Deeble; the next day: 'Sick all day.' Major Deeble would be another key figure in what was to happen to the regiment on Gallipoli. Born in Ballarat, on the goldfields, in 1879, one of a family of 14, Arthur Deeble graduated from the University of Melbourne with a Bachelor of Arts degree and became a schoolteacher. He also served as a captain in the 29th Light Horse of the militia.

When he enlisted in the 8th he was the principal of Essendon High School, a slight, precise man with a moustache, used to giving short directions to his teenage pupils and, therefore, not always popular with the troops when he acted like a headmaster. Deeble would marry late in life. His only son, Professor John Deeble (architect of today's Australian Medicare system), describes his father as having been a 'kindly, gentle man who would not eat veal because he did not believe in killing calves'.

Captain William Archibald Moore, the chaplain, who valiantly tried to hold the first Sunday service for the regiment as it lurched away on active service, was originally from South Australia. He was never popular with the men, for two reasons. Firstly, because he was the chief censor for the 8th and therefore read all the regiment's letters, with the help of six officers. The chaplain checked the officers' letters himself, and appears to have tackled the overall task with a heavy hand, crossing things out unnecessarily. On the other hand, as Sid Campbell, the doctor, admitted, the task of regimental censor was no easy one:

> [Captain Moore] has been through 1,000 odd letters eliminating dates, names of ships and places tho' most writers conform to the regulations & a glance through their letters is sufficient.
>
> One man started: 'My dear Mary. I've been having a hell of a time. It's a bugger being sick.' One can imagine the kind of lady Mary must be …

The other reason for William Moore's unpopularity, and the thing that the light horsemen could not forgive, was that he was hardly an inspirational figure to men about to go into battle. 'The only time we saw him throughout the voyage was at Sunday Service,' Tom Austin would write of the chaplain, 'and then his dismal dirges made us angry. He never visited the Troop Decks and was a very poor example of cheer and help. His last service prior to disembarking will live forever with those who heard it. As a masterpiece of gloom.' Mercifully, no doubt, Captain Moore did not go on to Gallipoli. Colonel White dismissed him shortly as 'a waster and an old woman'.

Major Deeble was sick, the chaplain was sick, Jack and Stan Mack were sick, even the doctor was sick. In fact the only man aboard who was well appears to have been the commanding officer, Colonel White. He wrote cheerfully after his first night at sea: 'Slept like a top woke this morning at 6 am feeling grand – Jones [his orderly] was very ill, also a lot of the men – had a huge breakfast, porridge, fish, bacon, rolls, toast and coffee.' The day after the first Sunday service he recorded: 'The band played the hymns, had a huge breakfast and lunch, it is wonderful what one can eat, I am ashamed of my hunger.'

The others could only groan. Dave McGarvie wrote in a shaky hand in his pocket diary: 'On stable picket from 5 am to 8, cleaning out stables. After breakfast felt a bit sick. Lost breakfast overboard ...'

Sid Campbell confirmed that the conditions were taking their toll on the men:

> They have been sleeping in any odd corner about the main deck although the majority have stuck it out on the troop deck where I have only been fit to venture when it was compulsory i.e. at ship's inspection, 10.30 am. About a doz were bad enough to put in hospital where I had one bad case of diarrhoea which gave me some anxiety ... [One] horse has gone overboard (pneumonia) and several others are going the same way.
>
> In some mysterious way, whisky, brandy and beer are being sold and one man was found drunk yesterday. We are maintaining a strict dry canteen in the mess – officers may take it to their cabins.

As *Star of Victoria* ploughed through the Great Australian Bight, another factor emerged to worsen the lot for the many seasick troopers. In the troubled engine room the main steam pipe burst, forcing *Star* to limp through the swell at some 8 to 9 knots.

'I mustered every man on the top deck – some are still very sick, last night was very rough,' wrote Colonel White again, before going on cheerily: 'Had a huge dinner then yarned to the Captain. Went down to the saloon and some of the officers sang songs, the most popular song is "I'll Never Love Another Girl Like I Love You" – my word we do sing it feelingly. At 9.30 went to bed, though I was thrown out of my bunk several times it was so rough.'

The CO could always be relied on to see the upside in every challenging situation, it seems. But the only real positive in this latest engine-room drama was that *Runic*, which had been struggling to match the pace of *Star*, was now able to keep up with the lead transport.

Six days after leaving Melbourne, the two ships reached the sheltered deep waters of King George Sound, on the southern coast of Western Australia. The sight of the tranquil bay was a source of huge relief to everybody on board, not least of all Captain Campbell:

> We are full of praise for the beauties of King George's Sound. It's a very magnificent harbour. The coastline outside with the projecting granite peaks scantily covered reminds me of the pictures of the Antarctic coast brought back by the Shackleton and Scott expeditions. Its coast is so bleak and barren one can readily imagine that one is in McMurdo Sound or Ross Sea (the names stick in my mind – whether I use them correctly or not I am not sure) and that at any moment one may see the base of a huge glacier projecting into the sea or a bit of the ice barrier round the next point.

As if to underline this turnaround in the 8th's nautical fortune, the doctor's next sentence was given maximum emphasis:

> EVERYONE IS HAPPY AND SMILING AT BEING SAFE AND SNUG in this pleasant place with a calm sea, a gentle breeze and a warm sun.
>
> Many of the men are fishing with improvised lines. The officers are reading and writing letters and the padre is gradually filling his mailbags. No one is in a hurry to depart …

The medical officer had mastered his seasickness enough during the first leg of the voyage to detect one case of diphtheria among the men and two cases of venereal disease. Speaking of this second dreaded affliction, on the very day that *Star of Victoria* sailed from Melbourne, the Reverend Dr J.L. Rintoul had caused a furore in the newspapers by claiming that a 'camp of evil' existed close to Broadmeadows. 'It was a camp of what had been called "harpies",' he said, 'the kind of womanhood which having been degraded and ruined by man's lust, sought now to degrade young men down to that level ...'

'Not far away,' he went on, 'and all through our city were the camps of the liquor traffic and other camps of evil. These demoralising forces were tending to the destruction of the glory and esprit de corps of our young army and the undoing of the glory of Australia.'

The diphtheria and venereal cases aboard *Star of Victoria* were quickly unloaded at the quarantine station at Albany. A New Zealand transport ship was also in the harbour, homeward bound from Suez with 25 sick soldiers aboard. Dr Campbell thought that some of them might be 'unsuitables' – that is, soldiers who had dallied at the houses of sin. Venereal disease was to be a constant problem in the expeditionary forces.

Picking up on the latest information from the New Zealanders, after the Albany visit Colonel White would call his NCOs in and tell them to pass on to the men that 500 Australians had contracted 'a certain disease' in Alexandria and Cairo, which meant they would be returned home as unfit for service. What's more, said the commanding officer, these men were doomed as the disease they had contracted was incurable.

The New Zealand transport brought other items of news and gossip, which soon circulated among the men. The ship had left Suez just as Turkish troops had been reported appearing at the canal, and apparently conditions were rough at a place called the Mena Camp. It now looked as though Egypt could be much more than a mere port-of-call for the light horse – but aboard *Star of Victoria* nobody was absolutely certain of the destination or what was developing elsewhere.

Even the commanding officer was left in the dark. Colonel White visited the ship's wireless room later on in the voyage, but was not allowed to send a message home and thought it 'pretty rotten of the navy to block press coming through, we of course, don't know what is happening'. Some on board wished the ship would sail directly to Marseilles where they could disembark and then travel north to join the Western Front.

Destination plans for the Australian Army had actually changed late in November, just after the very first AIF troop convoy had left Aden on the southern tip of Yemen, still bound for Britain. The Canadian Expeditionary Force had arrived in the UK ahead of the AIF and had been sent to train on Salisbury Plain. Wooden huts were supposed to house the men, but couldn't be erected in time before the winter, so the Canadians were forced to pitch tents. Under canvas, the 'training' became a fight for health and existence, with the camps becoming, in Charles Bean's words, 'archipelagos of tents in a knee-deep sea of mud'.

Urgent representations were made to prevent the Australians being sent to the same quagmire, after which a telegram was sent from Sir George Reid, Australian High Commissioner in London, to the first Australian contingent at sea: 'Unforeseen circumstances decide that the force shall train in Egypt and go to the front from there. The Australians and New Zealanders are to form a corps under General Birdwood. The locality of the camp is near Cairo.' Instead of landing in Europe as originally planned, the first Australian troops disembarked in North Africa on 3 December and began moving by train to Cairo.

There was no prospect of anything foreign or exotic in the four days spent at Albany, however, let alone catching anything unsuitable. For a start, the men were not even allowed shore leave. 'I do not intend to allow anyone ashore – fancy some of the beggars might desert owing to sea-sickness,' observed their colonel.

'New Zealanders in here a fortnight ago "painted the town red", officers as bad as men,' Sid Campbell explained, 'hence only men allowed ashore here were two large parties from *Runic* for route marching, which proved too much for a good number'.

Boat races were organised between the officers and men of *Runic* and *Star of Victoria*, while many fished for mackerel over the sides of the steamers.

However, Colonel White and one of his officers managed to go ashore. After a day of being entertained by the locals, the brass returned 'rather full … judging from their full, sweaty faces and the fact that they brought back a grey kangaroo on I board with them as a mascot,' wrote the doctor.

Star of Victoria left Albany on 6 March and, as Ernie Mack reported to Mary, the men were soon having 'the time of our lives'. The seasickness had all but disappeared and the conditions had improved markedly: 'The most beautiful weather all the time – not enough to make the ship roll, but apart from that it is rather muggy and you can't do very much without perspiring. Reminds me of a hot day at home after very heavy rain …' To his father he wrote:

> We may have looked a smart lot of soldiers when we were in camp but no one could say that about us on board nowadays. The most popular dress is a singlet and a pair of pants and bare feet though shoes have to be worn if one does much walking on the decks not protected from the sun as the boards get very hot. Most of the decks are covered in awnings. My work being in charge of 60 horses with six permanent stablemen and six fatigue men to help lead horses generally finishes at dinner time and the rest of the day we have to

ourselves to have some sleep as we only have about nine hours each
night ...

There were some preparations for war. A parade was held and all the
bright fittings on saddlery and stirrup irons, mess tins and brass
buckets, even buttons, were painted a dull colour. 'My sword belt looks
awful with the buckles painted,' Colonel White confided to Myrtle,
'and my sword is the limit. Am going to rub it off my belt, can't stand
it'.

Travelling almost a fortnight ahead of *Star of Victoria*, Ted Henty with
the 8th's advance party aboard *Anglo-Egyptian* had written his first letter
home, to his brother Wilf on the farm at 'The Caves', near Hamilton.
Nothing remains of the love letters Ted would have sent home to his
new wife, Florence. At the time of his sailing she would have just
become pregnant with the little boy who would be christened Edward
Ellis, after his father, when he was born in October 1915.

The letter to Wilf Henty was dated the day Ted left port, 2 February,
although it obviously wasn't written until later in the voyage:

> Dear Wilf: I'm just sending you a few lines to give an account of some
> of our wanderings since we left the country, though can't give you
> any names of places, ships, etc.
>
> My job is a good one, not a great deal to do and plenty of time to
> do it in. Only missed one meal through seasickness, but a darn week
> through vaccination.
>
> Had a hell of a time, fever, mild blood poisoning, neuralgia inside
> and general absolute knocked-outness. Couldn't rest for two days and
> nights and then the doctor gave me a sleeping draught, which gave
> me a little broken sleep, and I improved.
>
> I'm better now but not much use yet, though daresay I'll pick up
> from now. Didn't say much about this at home, but don't get vacci-
> nated unless you have to.
>
> We have lost four horses so far which is good considering the class
> of some of the NSW remounts, which are in pretty poor condition.
> The boat is pretty big, built to carry 11,000 tons cargo and has some
> first class cabins for emergencies. We are really fixed up though there
> is not much accommodation for men. The horses are ranged in three
> decks, the lower one of course being the worst because of the heat.
> It's the very devil down there in the tropical weather we are getting
> now. Crossed the line [the Equator] a couple of days ago weather
> beautiful with a nice breeze blowing. This breeze had been with us for
> about a week but previous to that we had some hellish weather for the

horses and men though only a couple of days when we got a tropical downpour.

The Indian Ocean is like a big sheet of slowly heaving glass and the old boat just ploughs away, day after day, night after night. We have seen swarms of flying fish they rise from the water like a mob of sparrows and fly gracefully away for 50 to 100 yards.

They look white in the sunlight and are something like the shape of a trout or perhaps a garfish without the beak, being about four or six inches in length. Don't know how the war is going as we haven't heard anything for 16 days. It's a fine irresponsible sort of life. Here we are in our little show, plugging along not knowing where we are going to or how things in the world are doing.

Land loomed up this afternoon, high and mountainous and tonight we will be in port and hear some news again.

Must now shut up.

Love from Ted.

Back on board *Star of Victoria*, Corporal George Leslie Rayment had been appointed a clerk on the staff of the 3rd Light Horse Brigade headquarters, which was also sailing with the ship. One of three brothers who would serve with the AIF, George described the new routine on this second leg of the journey:

After the first week on board the novelty of the trip began to wear off. However life on board was not one of laziness as there were 500 odd horses to be looked after, saddlery and equipment to be cleaned and branded as well as lectures to attend. Then for our benefit there were concerts, sports and competitions, the officers providing prize money to the extent of about fifty pounds ... personally to keep out of mischief I had 500 copies of a lecture delivered by General Birdwood to the troops in Egypt to type together with as many covering letters from our Colonel, and this occupied my spare time for a good deal of the trip.

As the corporal observed, singsongs and concerts were often held in the evenings. By the end of the voyage a 30-voice choir would be performing regularly, and Trooper Charlie Gribble, a salesman from Ballarat, had won the solo performance competition. In 1915 poetry readings were popular too, and tongue twisters like *Sister Suzie* would be recited as fast as possible:

Sister Susie's sewing shirts for soldiers
Such skill at sewing shirts

Our shy young sister Suzie shows!
Some soldiers send epistles
That they'd sooner sleep in thistles
Than the saucy, soft, short shirts for soldiers sister Susie sews.

New friends were being made aboard *Star*. Sid Campbell had met Trooper Alex (Lex) Borthwick and his brother Lieutenant Keith Borthwick, both of whom were friends of the Mack brothers. And there was Lieutenant Charles Carthew, born in Happy Valley, from up Myrtleford way, where they grew tobacco. He had a brother called Fred who had moved to Western Australia before the war and had enlisted as a signalman in the 10th. They would meet again on Gallipoli.

Keith Borthwick hailed from the Sale area, in the east of Victoria, and was quite a character, according to Sid:

> A most interesting and entertaining man – young, probably 32, but with a good deal of experience packed into his short life. His most interesting experiences connected with horse and cattle shipping, former chiefly to India but also along coast to NSW. Has been through India, in Tibet, Straits Settlements, Queensland, NSW, Vic. Last night he told us a yarn of an experience shipping horses to NSW from Melbourne on a small boat. A story which many a magazine writer would like to have.

The doctor was being kept busy inoculating the men against typhoid:

> We do about 140-150 an hour provided the men are supplied to us smoothly, left side then right side. One man paints with iodine then the patient comes to me and is inoculated. By my side is a table on which is a bowl of cool sterile water into which the needles are dropped from the steriliser bowl continually boiling on a primus stove. I have about 12 to 15 needles each is boiled after using for one inoculation. One syringeful does for roughly four inoculations but varying with the size of the dose … after inoculations, especially second dose, all experienced pain of varying degree and extent. Two fainted a few hours later, two or three had bad diarrhoea, two had severe pain in stomach, two had rash. I got an attack of migraine.

The ship was now moving along to a smooth routine. The wellbeing of the horses was the primary concern. Each day they were led out for exercise, for between two and three hours, and Tom Austin was in doubt as to the benefits of these promenades around the decks:

This to a great measure served to keep down swelled legs, besides giving the animals a breath of fresh air. A horse boat is not by any means a holiday home for horses. The poor beasts are clamped as close together as possible in skeleton kinds of stalls and can move neither sideways, forwards or backwards.

The decks are simply stifling especially in the tropics and a big draught has to be created by a huge fan rigged at one end of the ship to help keep the temperature somewhere near normal. A fair number of the horses caught colds and chills but the veterinary staff worked so well that on reaching Egypt a total of nine horses only had died on the way, chiefly from pneumonia, first caught during the rough weather experienced in the Bight.

This was a very small percentage of casualties as we had on board over 600 horses and it clearly shows that each man had his eye on his horse throughout.

As well as the various tasks assigned to the men, there were regular fire and collision drills, during which two guards would be posted to each lifeboat, bayonets fixed, to prevent rushing. The favourite job aboard ship was to be detailed for the kitchen or bakery, and failing that, mess orderly. The regiment's unofficial historian noted that the food was 'exceedingly coarse and rough' and that certain purchases from the canteen on board 'helped the meals along considerably'.

Although no liquor was available from the canteen officially, it always seemed to be about 'in fair quantity'. The head cook was the obvious suspect. As other diarists observed also, he was pretty popular in the evenings; but, Austin wondered, 'why he should be able to sell liquor to troops on a dry ship, thereby making treble profits that a canteen would, when the stuff could easily be regulated from the canteen, is puzzling'.

The ship's carpenter had built a stage on one of the hatches and this was lit up each night for the concerts and later, boxing tournaments. Tom Austin himself was in training for the boxing competition – 'we will have our money on Tom and are keeping him a dark horse,' Stan Mack confided to his sister.

Despite physical exercises and tug of wars between the squadrons – with a £4 prize donated by the officers – many of the men were conscious that they were putting on weight. 'Dinner – soup, whiting, roast turkey and ham, ice cream, fruit, cheese and coffee – is it any wonder we are getting fat?' wrote Colonel White, who had taken up skipping. 'The men are as fat and lazy as pigs and so are we.'

'I am sadly neglecting my own exercise,' the athletic Sid Campbell admitted. 'Turned out in shorts one day, punched the ball, skipped and had three rounds with the gloves with Wilson, receiving a nasty jolt to the jaw. Which has cooled my enthusiasm for boxing for a few days.'

'Wilson' was Lieutenant Eliot 'Ted' Wilson, from another prominent grazing family in the Western District, the eldest son of Dr J. Gratton Wilson, federal MP for Corangamite. It was Ted who had found a new horse for his mate Stan Mack just before the regiment sailed.

One night, a debate was held between 'A' and 'B' squadrons on the motion, 'A White Australia: Yes or No'. 'B' Squadron won the £3 prize awarded by Colonel White, after some 'fierce and varied arguments'. Tom Austin remarked that at the time no thought was given to a debate on conscription – 'I do not think anyone ever dreamt that Australia would be found wanting even to the last man'.

The band under the baton of bandmaster Sergeant Francis Boyle was busy, too. The men voted the band 'well worth the money', with *In Druids' Prayer* a favourite tune. The brass section led a singing contest, using *Lead Kindly Light* as the test piece for the competing twenty-men choirs. 'C' Squadron would win the £3 prize this time.

Dr Campbell delivered a talk on 'Venereal diseases of the East', at the request of Colonel White. ('I am keeping this subject before the men and warning them all the time,' said the colonel.) The lecture was apparently well received, the apprehensive Sid noting that he was 'not once hooted in spite of the fact that I had inoculated most of them that day'. He also noted that he was now treating five cases of gonorrhoea.

Even less entertaining, one would imagine, Chaplain Moore preached one of his stern moral sermons the next day. This time, it seems, with the colonel's approval: 'It was good.'

All in all, these were the happiest of days for the 8th Light Horse.

Star of Victoria was now steaming steadily towards Colombo, the capital of Sri Lanka (or Ceylon, as the country was then known), making between 280 to 310 miles a day, despite an erratic steering gear, which made it hard for *Runic* to anticipate changes of course. Shoals of flying fish were also skimming ahead of the ship, and on one day the troopers rushed to one side to catch a glimpse of a giant sunfish – 10 feet long with 'a yellow and brown striped hide'.

On 16 March, *Star* crossed the Equator. As with the 10th travelling aboard *Mashobra*, everybody from the commanding officer down took part in a traditional ceremony to honour the ancient sea god Poseidon, or King Neptune. A crew member, carrying a triton and suitably dressed in a barnacled robe, with a long flowing beard made from old rope, and a golden crown on his head and accompanied by his 'mermen', pretended to climb out of the sea to hold court as King Neptune. He examined those aboard to see if they were Shellbacks (people who had crossed the Equator before) or Pollywogs (newcomers). Pollywogs were cross-examined before being thoroughly dunked in seawater; they were then given a certificate to say that they'd crossed the Line and were entitled to become members of the Royal Society of Shellbacks.

A canvas swimming pool was erected on the deck of *Star of Victoria*, after which the king and his courtiers came aboard. The CO was the first to be arrested by Neptune's 'police' and subjected to treatment as a Pollywog. The victim later wrote of his ordeal, with good grace:

> I was the first man pounced on, led down, questioned, condemned to be shaved by the big razor and ducked. They lathered the whole of my face and neck with lime put on with a white wash brush, scraped with razor 3 feet long and suddenly tipped into the bath, grabbed by the merman, and ducked, and shooed out the other end. You should have heard the yells of delight from all hands.
>
> I enjoyed it, every Officer was done, and done well, then the NCOs and men.

Dinner, with plenty of ice cream, was followed by the start of the boxing competition. This Colonel White would also describe to his wife: 'I do so wish you could have seen it, the men were piled up in tiers – six rows high and every man yelling, and oh, the fights were funny and exciting. I yelled loudest of any, I think.'

Two days later they were off Colombo. 'Great mountains could be seen running up to sharp peaks thousands of feet high,' wrote Aub. 'It was a splendid sight. We sighted Colombo at about 7.30 and were inside the breakwater and anchored at 9.30. At about 11 am, the natives had their barges alongside us and started coaling [that is, throwing lumps of coal] about 12 noon.'

There had been trouble in Colombo when earlier Australian contingents had behaved badly. As a result, Colonel White had a 'dickens of an argument' with the port commander before being allowed to let the men ashore – half that day, the other half the next.

For those who stayed aboard that first day, like Stan Mack, used to living in a white Australia, the locals came as a shock:

Hundreds of Coolies are coaling us. They are very funny, nearly stark naked and a lot of them are about ten years old and swarming all over the ship. We have to have somebody on our little deck all the time to keep him or her off, as they are terrible thieves. They are as black as pitch; the young ones … squint down and look at you, blinking their eyes.

The heat here is terrible – at the present moment I have my pyjama pants on and the perspiration is pouring out of me, never felt like it in all my life. What we want is a good feed of fruit and we are going to get it tomorrow. By Jove, the coal is making a mess of this ship and I am very gritty so must have another shower.

As a diversion, some of the troopers still aboard enticed the locals to box one another, for the princely sum of 6 pence each, pugilism being very much on the mind of everyone in the regiment at this point. 'The Ship's 1st Mate nearly took an apoplectic fit when he discovered what was happening,' Tom Austin reported, 'and some of our shearers licked their lips in admiration of his withering vocabulary'.

When it came to the shore leave, everybody in the 8th behaved splendidly, and the CO would have no reason to regret his earlier efforts on behalf of his men. 'Every man turned up, not one drunk or missing,' he later wrote, with obvious pride. 'The police and military people tell me we established a record. I was delighted.'

There was no delight for those in command of *Runic*, however. Although there were some light horsemen among the 1,500-plus on the transport, the 8th regarded *Runic* men as 'a very rough lot'.

As a result of their bad form while route-marching in Albany, they were refused shore leave in Colombo. And, in retaliation, just before the two ships were due to sail off again, the men on *Runic* mutinied. Locking some of their officers in the dining room while they were having lunch, and threatening to throw overboard anyone who interfered, the mutineers took possession of the ship's boats. Five boatloads got clear of the ship, two of which reached shore.

Foghorns sounded aboard *Star of Victoria* and signals flew to alert the authorities on shore. Three armed guards of troopers were issued with twenty rounds of ball cartridges each, and told to fix bayonets and go in pursuit.

They managed to block three of the boats and send them back to *Runic* and then about 100 of the 8th went ashore to search for the rest. 'We had to take a hand and there was not a *Runic* sympathiser on the *Star of Victoria*,' wrote Stan Mack in a letter in which he warned he would 'tell the main facts but don't let it out of the family, as we have special orders not to mention it'.

But others wrote, too. Lex Borthwick described how most of the men from *Runic* had been rounded up without too much trouble: 'The party I was with got five privates and a Lieutenant – their Adjutant – out of a hotel. I had a struggle on the ground with one of the prisoners but he was half drunk and I came out of my first action a winner. These men on the *Runic* were a disgrace to Australia, and our men at Colombo were itching to have a go at them.'

'Our men were in stern mood,' Sid Campbell agreed, 'they themselves had behaved splendidly …' According to Stan Mack, the inter-ship antagonism was due to continue:

> We did not fire a shot but the *Runic* men say they will get even with us for going against them. They passed close to us once and the whole lot of them leant over and hooted at us – it's a wonder you did not hear them in Australia.
>
> We would be very pleased to give the swines a good hiding but expect they will be kept away from us. The leader of them must get at least four years and some of their Officers got a rough handling.

The ships set to sea again at 4 am on 20 March 1915, now heading for Aden. Of the *Runic* mutineers, 30 men were still unaccounted for.

Two days out, Sid Campbell was busy again, vaccinating the men against smallpox. 'I was the first to be vaccinated,' wrote Colonel White, always leading from the front. 'It sure did hurt a lot. Six of our chaps fainted.'

That night big Tom Austin won the heavyweight division in the boxing competition. Meanwhile, a second attack by Turkish forces had been repulsed on the Suez Canal.

Chapter 8

Sand and Pharaohs

A s *Star of Victoria*, accompanied by *Runic* and its surly complement of reinforcements, ploughed on through the tropics, the first letters from Harold Brentnall, dental mechanic turned stretcher-bearer, were arriving at the humble family home in Nicholson Street, Brunswick. Like hundreds of others in the First AIF, he was struggling to describe the amazing sights they were seeing in the Land of the Pharaohs to those sitting around the kitchens of inner-suburban cottages and homesteads in the bush.

The first convoy had begun assembling in King George Sound off Albany in September 1914. Sailing was delayed for over a month before the ships set out on 1 November, with orders to sail via the Cape of Good Hope to Britain. But the course for this first fleet changed due to developments elsewhere, including the suppression of a small Dutch revolt in South Africa which might have involved the aid of Australian troops. Then, with the removal of the German raider *Emden*, the route was clear via Colombo and Aden and on to Europe through the Suez Canal. But Turkey had decided to side with Germany. Suddenly, the canal itself would be threatened. Charles Bean speculated: 'News of war being declared by England and Russia on Turkey … shall we be stopped in Egypt?'

Bean's surmise was right. The official reason for the diversion was because of the need for a new training ground for the Empire's troops, as the Canadians struggled in the quagmire that was Salisbury Plain. Lord Kitchener, British Secretary of State for War, was still focused on the critical situation that existed in France. He wanted the new Anzac troops in Europe, but they could be held in Egypt.

Only a few days after the 31 October 1914 declaration against Turkey, Winston Churchill, First Lord of the Admiralty, had sent a naval force to bombard Turkish forts along the Dardanelles. This was regarded as a purely naval operation, a softening-up show of force before an even bigger naval exercise would occur in March. That, it was thought, should lead to the easy occupation of the Turkish capital, Constantinople.

It was, of course, to lead instead to the Allied armies launching an ill-planned and fatal invasion of the Gallipoli Peninsula.

Much to their disappointment, the men of the first convoys from Australia found themselves not in the UK then, but camped in a square mile of desert, a 10-mile march out of Cairo in the shadow of the pyramids and close to a smelly piece of marshland. Here they were, far from Europe and green fields of glory. Instead there was sand and more sand, glare, dust, dirt, heat, disease, and a population who seemed bent on ripping them off.

The first troops set up camp here from 4 December and soon got down to business, according to Bean:

> Almost from the morning of arrival, training was carried out for at least eight hours, and often more, every day but Sundays. The infantry marched out early in the morning, each battalion to whatever portion of the brigade area had been assigned to it. They then split into companies. All day long, in every valley of the Sahara for miles around the Pyramids, were groups or lines of men advancing, retiring, drilling, or squatted near their piled arms listening to their officer.
>
> For many battalions there were several miles to be marched through soft sand each morning before the training area was reached, and to be marched back again each evening. At first, in order to harden the troops, they wore as a rule full kit with heavy packs. Their backs became drenched with perspiration, the bitter desert wind blew on them as they camped for their midday meal, and many deaths from pneumonia were attributed to this cause.

On board *Star of Victoria*, Dr Campbell was hard at it again as the ship steamed on the next leg of the voyage: eight days across the Indian Ocean from Colombo to Aden. Having begun inoculating all on board against smallpox shortly after leaving Ceylon, he now found that many of the men were sick, a side-effect of the vaccination: 'Hospital very busy. Usually 12 to 15 in hospital ... a cold with temperature for several days ... bronchitis and possibly some pneumonia.'

Dave McGarvie experienced no immediate problems after he was inoculated – 'had a talk with Private Kipping on Theosophy', he wrote – but four days later: 'Paraded sick. Got bandage on arm where it was vaccinated.'

Among the sick was Stan Mack. It was the first bout of an illness that was to dog him all the way to Gallipoli. He made no mention of it until later on, when he wrote a second letter to his mother, from a hospital in Egypt: 'On thinking it over I may as well tell you I got yellow jaundice on board the boat. Someone who does not know what's wrong with me may write I've got something worse, like pneumonia, but jaundice is what I got and I became the colour of a new Sovereign.'

For the rest of the troopers, the third leg of the voyage was almost a pleasure cruise. Major Arthur Deeble wrote of a 'sentimental song' competition, humorous recitations, and concerts with Scottish and Irish songs. Ernie Mack's description confirms that end-of-day entertainment was still very much part of regular life on *Star*:

> The bugles blow the Retire at nine o'clock and Lights Out at a quarter past when everybody is supposed to be in bed. Up on our little deck we generally sit and talk till about half past nine before we turn in …
>
> We have tea at five and unlike our old camp we have meat for tea, in fact the meals supplied to us are very good except that the meat is generally on the tough side, except when made as a stew, but that is only to be expected as it comes straight up from the freezing chamber to the kitchen. Some of us have been greatly amused at times on the voyage, as we have seen the stewards plucking mountain duck for the officers' mess.
>
> Every evening for the last week or more there have been music and elocution contests but have been of a very third rate class as there does not seem to be a decent singer in the regiment. Our band is just the thing as every evening and afternoon it plays selections. The evening performance is always for the officers' benefit, as they play on a horsebox outside the dining room. Perhaps the music helps them masticate the mountain duck.

Although the two transports were now sailing alongside passing warships, no more information was forthcoming. 'Everyone is in total ignorance as to where our destination will be,' the second of the Mack boys continued, 'but it is pretty well certain we will land in Alexandria, but for how long remains to be seen, perhaps only to spell the horses.'

At around noon on 28 March, the ships reached the port of Aden, described by Ernie as 'the most forsaken place on the globe & it makes one weary just to think of having to live there. Built on an island, the cliffs of which facing the ocean, rise to a height of about 300 ft and are very rugged.' Shore leave was out of the question, the stopover here lasting only a matter of hours, a relief no doubt to this Berrybank man.

As at Colombo, the locals came out to greet the new arrivals, but instead of being on the receiving end of a hail of coal projectiles, 'We were soon surrounded by natives in small boats selling tobacco, fruit, lollies, etc.,' Aub Callow wrote. There were some bargains to be had here. Ernie Mack noted how, 'Everything seemed to be cheap ... Cigarettes that cost 15 shillings per 100 in Melbourne were bought for two shillings and sixpence', as well as commenting on the Yemenese themselves: 'Totally different from the coolies in Colombo, being bigger, and what we saw of them slightly more intelligent.'

It was a busy port, Aub continued: 'Shipping moving in and out of harbour all the time ... About 3 pm this afternoon an armed merchantman came into the harbour. We saluted her by every man standing at attention until she passed and the band played *Rule Britannia*.'

'Did not land,' Callow concluded, without a trace of disappointment, before adding the final instalment in the mutiny saga: 'Ringleaders taken ashore from *Runic*'.

Star of Victoria sailed at 6.30 pm that day, on the last leg of the voyage to Cairo. Sid Campbell was concerned about the increasing sickness aboard and noted he was running out of drugs. To add to his troubles, a number of the men had bought oysters from the boatmen who had come alongside at Aden, and they were now suffering from what they called 'toe jam poisoning'.

As they entered the Red Sea, the ships passed a number of desolate islands. 'One poor beggar on one of those islands signalled us by Morse lamp to give us some war news as he had none for weeks so our signallers gave him the little we knew,' Ernie Mack wrote. 'We heard today that two English warships were sunk by mines in the Dardanelles & as the names were given I expect it is true.'

Then, suddenly, the war seemed to have found the light horse. 'Unprecedented excitement today,' Ernie reported on 31 March. 'Ten o'clock this morning a wireless message informed us that the Turks had made another attack on the Canal yesterday; 3 killed 15 wounded British and between 150 and 200 killed and wounded Turks; also that we were to prepare our boat for an attack when going through the Canal; also that we might have to disembark to attack the enemy.'

Turkey had mounted an ill-fated expedition to attack Britain and the Suez Canal in Egypt in February 1915, believing that imperial rule there was weak and lines of communication stretched thin. The attack was repulsed, mainly by Indian troops, and although Australia and New Zealand forces garrisoned trenches afterwards, no Australian regiment was involved. The Turkish losses were regarded as those of a small 'native war' and, as Charles Bean observed: 'There was a heavy fall in the current estimate of the fighting value of the Turkish Army. This was not without its influence on future events.'

This lowering of the Turks' reputation translated into jubilation on board Ernie's ship:

> [Everybody] is going about as if they had won a 10 pound jackpot. By Jove won't it be funny if we at once get into the firing line.
>
> Troops of men are hard at work filling bags with coals & cinders & piling them along the starboard side of the ship so by the time we reach the Canal we ought to be a floating fort so it will be bad luck if we don't have a shot & of course it would be bad luck if a bullet cut my promising career short especially after writing such a long letter so in case of accidents I'll make arrangements to have it posted.

As the bags of ashes were piled high, a machine-gun position was erected above the horseboxes. Sid Campbell was told to prepare for possible casualties, although he thought there was 'very little likelihood of an engagement'.

The next morning, at 4.30 am, the officers were roused from their bunks and told to assemble in the saloon, where they would be addressed by the commanding officer, Colonel White. The date was 1 April. 'We all went like lambs, on arrival finding it was an April Fool's Day joke,' wrote Sid.

On Friday 2 April – Good Friday – both *Star of Victoria* and *Runic* anchored off Suez. At last the regiment had its orders: it would be disembarking here and heading west to Cairo by rail. Prudently, the transports would not be proceeding up the canal.

There was a general bustle to get ready. The men were paraded to see if any items of uniform were missing before they packed their kitbags.

Then two officers came aboard to see Sid Campbell and Colonel White on an urgent mission. Venereal disease was cutting a swathe through the ranks of the first contingent troops, they warned; the problem was Cairo itself, which the men would regularly visit from their camps near the pyramids. 'By all accounts this city is very awful for vice of the worst sort,' Colonel White reported afterwards. 'What I have heard is unbelievable. It seems that Port Said and France are quite respectable now – every one has come on here.'

Bean would later elaborate on this 'vice of the worst sort', reporting that 'proprietors of the lower cafes … pressed upon the newcomers drinks amounting to poison and natives along the roads sold them stuff of unheard-of vileness' while 'Touts led them to "amusements" descending to any degree of filth'.

Added to this local encouragement was the sheer number of men let loose at one time in the Egyptian capital. Early on, following the arrival of the first contingent, 20 per cent of the force was granted leave in Cairo. The result, as *Age* correspondent Phillip Schuler reported, was an often wild invasion of 10,000 troops from afternoon until 9.30 pm, when leave was supposed to end in the city. By April 1915, regulations had been tightened up considerably, with leave reduced to 10 per cent, and the visiting Australian High Commissioner to London had made an impassioned speech to the men, appealing to their better nature, their duty to King and Country, and urging them to 'cast out the wrong uns from their midst'.

Still, on the very day that the 8th Light Horse anchored off Suez, the famous 'Battle of the Wozzer' took place in Cairo. Brothels were ransacked by Australian and New Zealand troops, who believed they'd been ripped off by pimps and madams, and were catching VD from the girls. Beds, mattresses and clothing were piled into a bonfire in the street, an Egyptian fire brigade was harassed, and order was only restored after British troops were mobilised with rifles and fixed bayonets.

The ships moved into harbour at Suez on Easter Saturday as night fell, and orders were given for the men and horses to be loaded on board three trains, which left at 2.30 am on Sunday. Jack Mack described the trip to Cairo:

> [The] train stopped five or six times en route at villages where we all got out to stretch our legs and were instantly surrounded with swarms of men, women and children pushing, scrambling, knocking each other down regardless of size or sex, each with his hand outstretched to us, and everyone bawling 'baksheesh, baksheesh!' [a small sum of money given as alms].
>
> Arriving at Cairo, we at once lined up, handed over our rifles and overcoats to the baggage wagons, and took a horse each and walked about a mile through a corner of the town to a walled in enclosure to water the horses. Then we walked out here another 8 miles, arriving about 4 pm and had nearly four hours hard going before we were dismissed for the night.

The 8th was the last regiment of the 3rd Light Horse Brigade to arrive, joining the rest of the brigade at Mena campsite, just outside Cairo. The

10th Regiment, from Western Australia, and the 9th, mainly from South Australia, had begun arriving in Egypt from early in March.

Back in Albany, the men from the 8th Regiment had been warned about Mena – and the New Zealanders at Albany hadn't been exaggerating. The camp was condemned by all because of its bad water supply. George Rayment, one of the brigade staff clerks, outlined the problem:

> The water ran into a storage reservoir above the camp and it was necessary to keep a squad of men on duty daily to skim off the green slime which accumulated every hour. Orders were issued that no water was to be used for drinking purposes unless previously boiled, but little regard was paid to this order when men came in from a long route march over the desert.

'Most things are ready,' Sid Campbell wrote, before turning a more critical eye on the regiment's second-in-command, Major James O'Brien. The Boer War veteran, who had the led the first advance party from Melbourne, had 'shown himself to be absolutely incompetent', the medical officer confided. And there was that familiar scourge of the desert to contend with, much to Colonel White's irritation: 'Dust storms are the limit, sand everywhere, can't keep it out. We all wear goggles.'

On the plus side, Ted Henty and the others in the second of the two advance parties were judged to have done well in having the horse lines established for the regiment's arrival. The troopers also now had large wooden sheds for each squadron to have meals in, which Corporal Rayment thought 'much better than squatting on the sand like at Broadmeadows'.

Two things soon became apparent to many of the Victorians in the 8th: how close they were to the action (the Dardanelles being just two days and nights away by ship), and how easy it was to renew friendships from their home state. Dr Campbell, for instance, had met up with five friends from university days, 'all fit, well and eager for the front'; they left that afternoon, – 'Everything indicates Dardanelles as destination'. Jack Mack was another:

> This is an extraordinary place for meeting fellows; half my old school mates and most of the fellows under 40 years I ever knew in Australia seem to be here either in the artillery or one of the light horse regiments.
>
> It was a grand sight to see the artillery moving out of the camp just after dark last night, direct for the front. Grand horses, grand

looking men, and both men and horses drilled to a wonderful pitch of perfection.

We all wondered what all the wild cheering was for in their lines on Tuesday night, till we heard that the general had just addressed them, saying he wasn't just speaking to try and frighten anyone but thought it only fair to let them know they were going as fast as possible to the Dardanelles, where they would land under fire and go into action at once to take on a severer task than any artillery had attempted this war; he had seen enough of them to know that they'd be successful but that at least 30 per cent of them would be dead within a month!

It seems to be a fairly sure thing that we will follow on as soon as they've cleared the way for us to land, so we hope to see a little bit of fighting before we return.

His brother, Stan, told their mother that none of the other light horse regiments had left yet. 'They have been here since leaving Broadmeadows over four months ago and are longing to get over to the Dardanelles with the infantry,' he wrote, before adding optimistically, 'It will take us two months to finish off the Turks, you see.'

Among those who had moved on during the 8th's first week at Mena was the 2nd Field Ambulance, with Sergeant Frank Carr and stretcher-bearers Harold Brentnall and George Fish. They had big lumbering horse-drawn wagons, which flew large flags with red crosses. They might just as well have been setting out for the Battle of Gettysburg instead of modern trench warfare in the gullies and ravines of Gallipoli. 'Left Mena Camp at 5.30 pm for Cairo, arrived Cairo at 9 pm,' wrote George Fish, who had just celebrated his twenty-fourth birthday; 'entrained with wagons and left at midnight for Alexandria'. Horses, wagons and ambulancemen sailed for the Dardanelles on 10 April.

Jack Mack wrote to Nell, one of his sisters, describing how, one unit had left for the front the day before:

It was funny this morning at church ... the whole brigade formed up in hollow square, an imposing enough sight and our parson, in dolorous tones asked us to join in saying 'good bye' to the men of the machine guns (Lt Charles Arblaster and 27 other ranks of the Brigade's machine gun troop) who are leaving us for the front tonight – and we will never see them again etc. etc. (They were present, too!)

Immediately the sermon was over, Colonel Hughes addressed us and told us not to follow the padre's advice and say good-bye, as he was confident we would be with them again within a fortnight, but

[to] join with him in congratulating them on being the first men of the 3rd Brigade to have the honour of going into action, wish them luck and God speed – and now lads give them three cheers!!

The New Zealanders and First Brigade, Australian Light Horse got their orders to proceed to the front on foot, horses to follow as soon as they are secured. The first lot passed our camp at 7 pm last night and from then on at intervals through the night, regiment after regiment marched past to the railways station, cheering and singing, bands playing and all very happy to be getting away from Egypt to see a bit of action.

The men of the 3rd Brigade were now left to do their own intensive training. In another letter, this time to his mother, Jack set out a typical day for the light horsemen:

The discipline here is very different from Broadmeadows and as for work – well, in a month we ought to be fit enough to walk back home on our heads.

Get up at 6 am sharp, roll call at 10 mins past – and down you go if ten seconds late; then a third of each troop is told off to water horses, each man leading three horses to the trough a mile away through loose sand in which you sink to your boot tops; the rest of the men being told off into various parties to mix horse feed, dig drains etc.

Horses must be back groomed and fed by 7.30, when we are marched onto the parade ground where the day's orders are read and we are dismissed for breakfast.

At 9 am we lead our horses out for exercise, walking six or seven miles through the sand and coming home by the watering trough, feeding the horses and being dismissed for lunch about 12.30.

At 2 pm we either lead the horses again or do foot slogging and rifle drill till 4 pm, when the horses are again led to water, then fed about a quarter to five when two thirds of each troop is dismissed for the night and the other third told off as sentries and guards.

Another regular occurrence, leave permitting, was a visit to the Shepheard's Hotel in the city. The Mack brothers, Jack and Ernie – Stan having been hospitalised with jaundice – were now sharing a six-man tent, along with Tom Austin, twenty-year-old Trooper 'Jacky' Dale (a friend of Tom's and another Melbourne Grammar old boy) and Lex Borthwick, one of the two farming brothers from Sale. Naturally, a night out in infamous Cairo was not long coming for Ernie and his elder brother:

[We] only get paid two shillings a day over here as our highly paid services was having a bad effect on the English regiments stationed in Cairo … we were not much impressed with the place. Plenty of smell I think is the chief characteristic but we were able to get a good cup of tea at Shepheard's Hotel, which is the swell place of the town. The hotel was declared out of bounds for the soldiers as the officers wanted it for themselves but G.H. Reid [Australian High Commissioner to London, Sir George Reid] had the order cancelled … it was read out to us again on parade the other day but nobody takes any notice of it.

Colonel White was another to venture into the city, as he reported to Myrtle: 'The annual fete was held at Shepheard's Hotel last night, this is the swell hotel in Cairo. Well, we went in to have a look at it, hundreds of people throwing confetti over each other. Nearly all the ladies were French and they do enjoy this sort of thing.' He went on quickly to say: 'The Australian girl is the best in the world and can hold her own everywhere. Well, they had good string and brass bands, a huge garden with wonderful fireworks; hundreds of officers from everywhere, and inside the hotel dances were going. It was quite a swell affair …' But, he added reassuringly, 'needless to say we did not dance'.

It was such a strange new world for the boys from the bush, as this letter from Ernie to Mary shows:

Shepheard's Hotel is THE hotel of Cairo and on Saturday night at 10 o'clock there is always a concert or dance. You ought to see the place, as it is wonderful and would spoil anyone who was in the habit of living in the best Melbourne pubs. The Ballroom is wonderful and has a beautiful floor of some kind of polished wood whilst all round the room there are curious Eastern divans or couches.

Yesterday afternoon we took a guide and went over Hassan's Mosque and the Citadel. A person could stand under the dome which is 300 feet high and take hours looking at the sculptures and frescos all the way up the walls. What is most marvellous though is the acoustic properties of the big hall under the dome as a person talking in a natural tone at one end is easily heard at the other which is over 200 feet away. The Citadel is another wonderful place and from a certain parapet you can see all over Cairo and for miles all over the city. Cairo is a city of mosques and minarets, and what strikes you most are the flat roofs of the houses; a tremendous lot of the houses appear to be only half finished as they are without windows, or rather, the large openings are in the walls with no windows put in.

When coming back through the town we went through the native bazaars. These bazaars are in narrow streets and each street or section have their own peculiar wares, and each race of people have their own bazaars. The shops are only squares of about eight or ten feet in stone walls and all the goods are hung around the walls, on the floor and nearly always right out onto the street while the proprietor squats in the middle of the heap. The silver and copper smiths do all their work in the street and we watched them for some time putting fancy designs on the silver and copper walls. If only we had a camera and knew how to work it we could take most interesting photos, but it would cost a lot in buying films as there would be such a lot of things to snap ...

Meanwhile, putting an end to any fun and games, would be Colonel Jack Antill, the Bullant, busy with his surprise drills again.

'On Tuesday and Wednesday we were aroused out of our beds at 2 am and had to march out to the desert on foot, if you please,' Ernie wrote to Mary. 'We had practical instruction in field firing and bayonet charging.'

He continued, perhaps with some premonition of what was to come:

For the latter work one wants plenty of wind, which is an article we are sadly lacking, and I am of the opinion that if we were doing the real thing we were too much out of breath to do much damage by the time we reached the trenches.

It was most interesting though & I hope to be able to tell you one day what the real thing is like. You know, it must be great satisfaction to run a bayonet through the enemy.

One hopes that the last two sentences here were not too disturbing for Ernie's youngest sister. Perhaps the Bull's methods were starting to rub off on his men ...

The surprise turnouts, with Brigadier Hughes and his brigade major, Antill, riding into the regiments' lines, before dawn sometimes, and calling for an immediate muster of the troopers for inspection, were now developing into a continual annoyance for the three commanding officers. White, Miell and Brazier regarded the Bullant and Hughes as nuisances who were unnecessarily interfering with their authority and the smooth running of their regiments.

Colonel White was away from camp one day, attending a court of inquiry into the *Runic* mutiny, and was most displeased with what he discovered on his return:

My chaps very savage, they had been ordered out in marching order for a route march through the sand and had to double up a hill owing to being cussed by the Brigade. The leading regiment got up the hill slowly and once on top went off at a great pace, result 8th being behind, had to run up hill and deep sand. You can imagine how they felt. I was sorry I had not been in command, there would not have been any running. It's rot.

But the good-natured White seems to have had no personal antagonism towards Antill. He later described how Antill once offered him a lift into Cairo and insisted that he join him for an afternoon tea party – 'The Bullant is a good old bird and I like him a lot.' As for Hughes, White thought 'the old Brig' very decent but 'the old chap I think is ageing a lot'.

White also wrote to his wife about Hughes calling all of the brigade's commanding officers to his tent one night: 'The old man at the end of the table, me at the other, the rest all around. Everybody except myself got shut up, the Bullant snubbed and COs squashed. I said what I thought and got off scot free. Oh dear it is so funny at times.'

Noel Brazier's relationship with Antill, however, already poisonous before the voyage on *Mashobra* out to Egypt, declined further – especially as Antill kept himself very close to Hughes. Brazier noted in his furious list of 'Episodes' at the back of his notebook that while he had been holding a discussion with the brigadier on one occasion, the Bullant had been making faces at him behind the CO's back: 'Lt Col Antill, with his eyes covered by the peak of his cap, contorted his mouth in all shapes.'

Things really blew up when the prickly Brazier was carpeted by Hughes for having his second-in-command, Major Alan Love, drill the 10th Light Horse instead of drilling it himself. According to Brazier he was 'sent away like a whipped boy'. The matter worsened when Brazier asked to have the whole matter referred to Lieutenant General Sir John Maxwell, who commanded all the forces in Egypt.

Brazier now talked about his 'other war'. The bad relationship all but consumed him and would be a major factor in what would befall the light horse on Gallipoli. Later, he would write in a red message book: 'From the time the Brigade left Australia, Antill determined to get the Brigade for himself at all costs. I told Hughes that on Gallipoli.'

Unaware of the discord emerging at the top, the soldiers enjoyed the opportunities to go sightseeing. The Old Geelong Collegians of the 8th got together on horseback and had their photograph taken with the Sphinx in the background. Letters and photographs were now pouring back to Australia describing the wonders of Egypt. Sid Campbell and a party of 30 others from the 3rd Brigade spent a weekend at Luxor visiting the Tombs of the Kings.

Training, as always, came first – although it didn't always go according to plan. There was a 10-mile route march by the whole brigade in full marching order. Colonel White described what happened:

> A hot still day. The 8th to the right, then the 9th, then the 10th, then the signal troops, Brigade train and the L.H. Field Ambulance. A big show, the Brig complimented me on our turnout. Of course we had to wear everything, heavy tunics, sword, revolver, glasses, water bottle, haversack, whistle and field dressing, in fact we are just like a Xmas tree with all our stuff draped around us …
>
> After being inspected we started out in column of sections; had only gone a few yards when we came on a donkey in the road. That blessed donkey held up the whole of the Third L.H. Brigade. Our horses are very afraid of camels and donkeys. I saw the funny side of it and laughed though my horse was trying to climb a tree. Well, we got past the donk, then came on a camel. More fireworks … staff cussing, we laughing and the rear swearing like fun at the delay.

After three weeks at Mena, with increasing sickness among the men from the green slimy water supply, the brigade now got word that it was to shift camp to the Heliopolis racecourse, a 13-mile ride away.

Jack Mack explained the new base to his sister Nell:

> The town of Heliopolis was built at a cost of some millions by an American syndicate with the idea of out-rivalling Monte Carlo – only after it was built the local Government refused a gambling licence … so they got left. The smallest stable or hen roost is really gorgeous while the Sultan's grandstand overlooking the course and now occupied by Brigadier Hughes and staff is like a picture from the 'Arabian Nights'. The big base hospital with 3,000 beds is only five minutes walk from the entrance gate.

Next to the racecourse was a large Luna Park, much bigger than the one the 8th had left behind them in Melbourne at St Kilda. The men looked forward to the move at the end of the month. Horses and men were now very fit again and there were more diversions. Tom Austin had been in training for an unsuccessful heavyweight match against a man called Shouter, who had won an Australian championship and had a formidable reputation as a bruiser.

The Mack boys had organised a weekend expedition for a quail shoot as 'the guides can promise 200 birds for four guns'. They went off shooting on the Saturday.

That day Colonel White wrote to Myrtle: 'We are only 14 days from London. Don't fancy we shall see anything of France or London this year; fancy Austria will be our job, but then no one knows yet. Perhaps it will all be over in a week.'

The next day was Sunday, 25 April 1915. 'Terrible day. Hot and dusty,' wrote Major Arthur Deeble in his diary.

Far away from the Sultan's grandstand, on a remote peninsula that none of the light horse had ever heard of, Australians were going into action on Gallipoli.

Chapter 9

Blood and Trumpets

Shortly before 4.30 am on 25 April 1915, as a blue-black dawn rose on the jagged line of the ridge ahead, the first Australian troops stumbled ashore from open boats at Anzac Cove – their boots skidding on the flat grey stones at low water mark, scrunching through the gravel and coarse sand beyond, and then climbing, up, up, up the crumbly yellow brown of the ridge, with the chest-high scrub and the long-thorned gorse bushes tearing at their clothes. By evening, 16,000 men and stores would have landed. And by that night, the sand and the gravel and the stones would be covered with the blood of the wounded waiting for evacuation.

Over 2,000 men would be killed or wounded in the first 24 hours, and arrangements for their collection, treatment and evacuation were a disgraceful, ill-planned shambles. Like most things about Gallipoli, nothing very much, ever, went right.

Harold Brentnall, 'Brenty', the 19-year-old stretcher-bearer, had been among the first ashore. He wrote in pencil in his pocket diary, in jumpy handwriting: 'Collected wounded under heavy fire. First time under fire. Worked all day and all night. Two hours sleep.'

The next day: 'Collecting wounded all day and night under heavy fire. Beach crowded with wounded.'

And the next: 'Collected wounded all day very little sleep. Shells are bursting nearly all day and night around our hospital. All night and near morning we brought wounded for miles down a big gully which was swept with shrapnel shell and rifle fire. We are nearly all tired out. Snipers very bad.'

Sergeant Frank Carr, who was with Harold, described his experiences in a moving letter home:

Dearest Mother, Sister and Brothers:

Sunday April the 25th is a day I will never forget. The first boat to hit the shore was full of 3rd ambulance men, as they accidentally got ahead of the Infantry in the dark, there were eight of them killed and seventeen of them wounded out of the one boat.

After the 3rd Brigade landed and charged the cliffs, our Ambulance was embarked in the boats, only our stretcher-bearers, 108 of us.

I can tell you my heart beat rather erratically, for the deck of the Destroyer that took us in close to shore was strewn with wounded and dying, poor fellows who had been hit before they had reached the shore. At any rate Providence had a watchful eye over us and we landed without losing a man.

On reaching the shore our work began. The beach was strewn with wounded and dying Australians and Turks. Three of our fellows were hit before we went a dozen yards, but the sight of our wounded pals put a feeling of revenge into our heads, and into it we went after the Infantry. You should have seen the wounded; it is impossible to describe it. Anybody who went through those first three or four days will never forget it.

On the first Sunday I carried ammunition and water from the beach to a part of our firing line all day and on every return trip brought back a wounded man. On the Sunday night a small party had got into a difficult position and were cut off by Turkish reinforcements. We were there all day Monday.

I was looking after the wounded as they were hit – we had one officer with us, Major Fethers, he was killed, but his gallantry put heart in all of us.

On the Monday I was able to get back with the survivors. When I got back to our little crowd they were all overjoyed to see me as I had been reported missing. I immediately rushed in to stop it [the report] from going home.

Those first few days were like a huge nightmare to us, but the work our men did was glorious. Carrying men off the top of the hills under an awful hail of shrapnel, but the thanks and grips of the hands of the dying and wounded would only spur you on to do more. It was impossible to use a stretcher and four of us would have to do the job with a waterproof sheet.

Meanwhile, George Fish – Brenty's mate and future brother-in-law – had been put in charge of the 2nd Field Ambulance's hospital stores, and was lying offshore aboard a troopship, chafing at the bit to go ashore. He thus had time to write an extraordinary first-hand account of the landing and its aftermath, beginning at dawn on the Sunday:

I went straight on deck and in the dim distance I could see several battleships with the glare of the shells as they left the guns, and in the distant hills, the great clouds of smoke. We were then a safe distance from the shore and for about an hour we remained there watching the shells burst and listening to the roar of the guns. During this time we could see great numbers of small boats being towed to the shore by torpedo boats.

At about 7 am our stretcher-bearers went ashore. One unfortunate sailor came on board in a terrible state. His head seemed to be opened up. He was taken aboard another troopship and we have not heard how he got on and if he recovered or not.

All this happened before breakfast. The roar of the guns was terrible and goodness knows how many were firing. I had breakfast, and I may say it was a short one, and went on deck again. One hill seemed to be getting a terrible lot of shelling; they were landing in from all directions.

All this time we were not a great distance from the battleships and the sun was up strong and soon we could see the whole coastline for miles. A balloon ascended from one of our ships and whoever was in it watched operations from a good height. Later several seaplanes ascended and remained in the air for a long time. During all this the battleships never ceased firing, and then a terrific fire as if from Maxim guns opened up and they peppered away for a long time.

Of course we were watching all this from an apparent safe distance but we thought different when at about 9.30 am we saw several shells land not so far away. They caused a great fountain in the sea. We were all watching and waiting when to our surprise a shell went right over our heads and reached the water about 100 yards away. Another landed still closer but on the other side, so it was not long before our anchor was up and we were off to a safer place.

News came on board that our boys had reached the second ridge and were doing splendidly. There are sure to be a number killed and wounded, for according to reports the Turks were entrenched right down to the beach.

Monday April 26: News came through late last night that our boys had captured two field guns and two lines of trenches and are going well. I think we have recovered from the shock of those shells bursting on either side of us. The sailor who was at the anchor says he never got the anchor up so quickly before. All the Indians in the crew went for their lives and he was left alone to work the engine and had to get the assistance of some of the officers ... Altogether there were 12 shells landed in the water. The battleships are still peppering away at the hills.

Tuesday April 27: Well, it is another glorious day, the sea is lovely and calm and some of our boys are in bathing, while the others are on shore fighting and the firing is still going on from the battleships. It is a strange warfare I must say; here we are having a good time and just a little distance away men are killing each other.

We have been very busy today loading ammunition onto barges for our boys ashore. It has been very hard work and I am feeling pretty tired tonight.

Major Hearne went ashore today to see if we are needed. I hope we are because we are all anxious to do our bit.

Wednesday April 28: Received orders 1 pm that ambulancemen were wanted ashore. Great excitement prevailed as there are only 15 bearers including myself aboard, the rest being transport men (drivers for the useless horse-drawn wagons).

4 pm: At last we are off. I am one of the lucky ones to go ashore. The *Chelmer*, a torpedo destroyer, came alongside and took us off at 5 pm, and after visiting several other troopships we eventually landed at 8.30 pm amidst a shower of bullets and shrapnel from Turkish guns.

This was my first taste of battle and I cannot express my feelings as I stood in the rowing boat on my way to shore. As the bullets were zip-zipping in the water all round us, my thoughts flew back to my loved ones at home and I wondered whether I would see them again.

The night was anything but pleasant, heavy rain falling and bitterly cold. We dug ourselves into the side of the cliff and rested till morning.

As we drew away from the troopship, the crew of the *Chelmer* were besieged by us wanting to know all that had happened to the Infantry on the morning of the landing. Many a tale was told as we were rushing towards the shore by these brave men, of how the Australians had jumped from the boats in the water waist deep and holding their rifles in the air, waded ashore. They also told of towing boats loaded to the gunwales with men, reached the beach with only a third of their original number alive.

One incident related to us by a Jack Tar (of whom all Australians have the greatest respect) showed how cool our lads must have been under the most trying conditions.

One man had waited coolly in a boat smoking his pipe until she grounded, then he got up and jumped ashore, removed the pipe from his mouth, knocked the ashes against the keel of the boat, then, placing the pipe in his pocket, turned to his comrades with the remark: 'Come on lads, let the ——— have it!' All this had taken place under a hail of lead from the machine guns up on the nearest ridge fifty yards away and men falling all around him.

Anyone reading this would be convinced that the Australians were boasting but speaking for myself and others who landed with me, the feeling we experienced when we heard how well the lads had acquitted themselves, and remembering that we were a young nation and making our first effort before the eyes of the Navy, filled us with pride to think that the same blood ran in our veins as also ran in our forefathers who helped build up the British Nation.

We were thankful for being tried and more thankful still that we had not been found wanting but we had upheld the traditions of the nation for whom we would gladly lay down our lives.

Once ashore, George joined up with his mates, the stretcher-bearers, and then recorded an account of the first three days they had experienced ashore, as told to him by a staff sergeant – quite possibly Frank Carr. He began by telling George about the first morning:

The bullets were whistling around and the shrapnel bursting overhead but no one paid any heed to this. Our interest was taken up in staring about at the havoc that had been wrought amongst our troops who had landed first. Men were lying about just where they had fallen. We were quickly brought to our senses when one of our men cried out: 'I am hit.'

So we sought cover and marched round the beach under protection of the cliffs until we found a suitable place for ascending.

The order was give[n] by the officer-in-charge to collect wounded, so off we started to climb the first hill. As we advanced the bullets started to come from all directions. One of the boys moving along with his squad and hearing the continual zip-zip around remarked in all innocence that the place was as bad as Egypt for locusts, the noise being made by the bullets entering the bushes. But when he had mounted the first ridge and saw the ground being knocked up all around he was convinced it was more than locusts and dived for the nearest cover, which happened to be a Turkish trench not long vacated.

Most of us took cover in this trench for a breathing spell and while crawling along on hands and knees, the man leading in turning a corner came upon the dead body of a Turk propped up in the trench.

He retreated in all haste with his hair on end. We soon found on investigation that the Turk, who was stripped to the waist, had about four bayonet wounds through his body. Thus reassured we moved on to the next gully where we had to run the gauntlet of shrapnel as well as bullets.

All this time we had been dressing wounded and directing those who could walk back to the beach, where they were placed on barges and sent to the hospital ships.

Our work has none of the excitement that is attached to the man with a rifle. We try and relieve suffering, and a man placed on a stretcher is no light weight, and running from cover to cover is not practicable with a seriously injured man on the stretcher; and our feelings when crossing a clearing swept by machine gun fire can be imagined. It is a feeling like cold water running down the spine.

In attending to men who have fallen it is most heart-breaking – some of those brave men who have fallen badly wounded take little heed of their hurts in [t]he excitement; they feel it less than those attending them. Although it is no time for sentiment, the feeling comes over one to almost doubt the power of a Supreme Being in allowing it to go on. We pass from one to another attending to all as best we can and a lump rises in the throat as we look at some friend we have known and who is so badly hurt we know he is not long for this world, he whispers some message to be given to his loved ones at home, should we ever return. Then, again, we have the man who is cursing the wound that is keeping him from the thick of the fray.

At the time, snipers were doing a lot of damage to our men, picking off the stretcher-bearers as they wended their way down to the beach. The hills being thickly timbered, snipers had a chance to be hidden for days amongst the thick bracken and just pick off our men as they passed through.

One of them attacked a bearer with a fixed bayonet but by good luck the bearer was carrying a bill hook, a knife for cutting scrub, and, dodging the bayonet, sprang in and caught the Turk across the neck almost severing the head from his body.

Tuesday night was the worst time we experienced since the landing, the Turks evidently made up their minds to drive us into the sea – they came on in massed formations blowing all sorts of bugle calls. Whether they were trying to deceive our men I don't know but our cookhouse call was blown [Bugle call 'Come to the cookhouse door, boys'], also several others used by the British. But our lads sat tight and waited until they were pretty close before opening fire, then the carnage began.

Some confusions was caused by a German officer dressed in the uniform of our officers and giving orders to 'Cease Fire' but the ruse was soon found out before any great damage was done. A search was made for the man who gave the order and he can thank his lucky stars he was never found.

George Fish wrote that by Thursday, 29 April, the day after he had landed, a great change had taken place on the beach and up the gullies. A hospital had been erected on shore and 'amputations were being done before sending patients to the hospital ships'.

But the first four days after the landing were a period of complete chaos for the wounded. There was a failure in everything, from poor communications to a lack of hospital ships for the large number of casualties. There was a severe shortage of stretchers, and the bearers often carried men over their shoulders or they improvised with stretchers made from unwound puttees. The initial scenes of the wounded lying in rows on the pebbles of Anzac Cove were described in contemporary accounts as being a holocaust. The overcrowded beach was being raked by bullets and exploding shrapnel shells.

In the end a naval beach master ordered that every available floating craft, from barge to pinnace, be employed in getting them off. But this led to further chaos and suffering, as some of the wounded were taken from transport ship to transport ship only to be turned away – because either there were no hospital facilities on board or the doctors and orderlies had gone ashore.

In the first five days at Anzac, 965 Australians were killed, 161 died of wounds and 4,114 were wounded. The New Zealanders lost 275 killed, 78 who died of wounds and 698 who were wounded.

Four days after the landing at Anzac Cove the ships carrying the wounded began arriving in Egypt – just as the 3rd Light Horse Brigade was comfortably settled into its new quarters at the Heliopolis racecourse. The brigade was obviously delighted with the new camp, as evidenced by Corporal George Rayment's description:

Brigade headquarters occupied the Saddling Paddock and the Stewards' quarters, the Brigadier took possession of the Sultana's pavilion while the Officers mess was located in the pavilion of the sultan. The office which had previously been used by the stewards was constructed of stone and therefore cool while, to my great delight, a shower bath was fitted up in the corner. As I had been ordered to sleep in the office I made myself a bed out of three planks and had a most comfortable sleeping place.

Heliopolis is a wonderful city of the desert about five or six miles from Cairo and was built by a Belgian syndicate a few years ago on most modern lines at a cost of something like twelve million pounds. It is connected with the capital by an electric railroad the cars of which are replete with every convenience. The intention of the founders was to make the city a second Monte Carlo but the British Government put a stop to it. The Palace Hotel which alone cost nearly two million is the most luxurious hotel in Egypt.

Almost alongside the Racecourse is a great pleasure resort called Luna Park, very similar to Luna Park in St Kilda … here were scenic railways, magic caves, etc.

As hundreds of wounded began arriving from Gallipoli, the magic went out of Luna Park. It was turned into a hospital, along with the Palace Hotel, which accommodated 2,000 men. On the evening of 29 April, as the first wounded arrived at the Luna Park hospital, Captain Sid Campbell, medical officer of the 8th, was there and provided a fascinating report:

It was a sudden plunge into the realisation of the horror and absurdity of war. I certainly felt it as I went into the entrance hall and saw our brave fellows in their bandages and untidiness and dirt being put on the admission roll and sent off to their wards. Most walked in, some were stretcher cases. The motor service from the station at the back of the hospital seemed to be very quick and efficient. Three medicos with assistants took names, battalions, site and nature of injury and religion for wounded and detailed them to the various wards.

Rumours of disasters to the Australians were numerous. The story all told amounted to this:

Disembarkation about 4 am. First line formed by 9th, 10th and 11th Battalions. 9th and 11th suffered most and said to have been practically wiped out. Officers supposed to have suffered severely. Men got out of boats into chest-deep water and rushed for the beach under fire – rifle, machine gun and shrapnel. There was a small cliff close to water where men were able to form up and then a cheer and a bayonet charge cleared the Turks from their first line trench quite close. All day

104

our men used very little ammunition. The Turks never waited for them but evacuated trench after trench and position after position until our men by the end of the day were three to five miles inland.

Once or twice there were local setbacks. All the time our men were subjected to heavy gun and artillery fire and our casualties were heavy. Many were out of action as soon as they reached the beach; others were wounded or killed in the boats.

Found Lt. Col. Elliott, 7th Battalion, wounded in the foot. From him the following: Apparently some bungle – naval people could not find landing in dark and hence delayed landing of first line so that later parties were landing at almost the same time and suffered nearly as severely as first. Also tugs not released for towing so that e.g. the 7th Battalion had to row themselves ashore. Machine gun got onto one boatload at 150 yards range and killed nearly all including Heron, late university and M.G.S. footballer.

Last heard of, Stan DeKavin was doing fine work and going strong. Herb Hunter, Captain of Stan's company, sprained ankle getting out of boat but hobbled on. Eric Connelly and Major Blezzard wounded. Elliott found himself hit in leg but could see no wound in boot.

Showed me boot. I could not discover entrance until he showed it to me – small quarter inch slit below malleolus. Adjutant extracted bullet from sole of foot with wire cutters. Wound only slight … Our men had hardest job. They must have fought splendidly under very trying conditions …

Jack Mack was on the scene, too, and sent this description to his sister, Nell:

The big base hospital with 3,000 beds is only five minutes walk from the entrance gates and on Thursday we got our first information of our fellows being in action when a special train drew up with 200 wounded and then onwards all through the night the motor ambulances were racing in from Alexandria with the serious cases.

One chap who had been shot just above the kidney, the bullet going right through without touching bone or internals, escaped from the hospital while waiting to be dressed, wandered into our lines and had a great time telling our fellows all about it until an orderly grabbed him.

He was only shot last Sunday and was still in his shot-torn blood-stained uniform.

There's no doubt they had a hot time and did grand work, but there seems no doubt either that they went mad and disobeyed orders and did far more than they were required to do, with unnecessary loss of life.

In the first place the boats taking them ashore ran into barbed wire entanglements placed under water 50 yards off the shore, and while they were all mixed up, machine guns opened up at short range and killed scores. However, they got ashore, captured the guns, scrambled up the cliffs and took the fort on top, which was all they were required to do.

But the wounded tell us that in the fort they found a couple of scouts who had landed the day before, still alive, but with their eyes out and their kneecaps cut off. This sent them all raving mad, they killed every German and Turk in the place and rushed straight on for the next post two miles away; five machine guns ambushed them, but they never checked for a second, wiped the guns out, and on and into the fort. Bayoneted every man, on again and the same treatment to the third fort – when the survivors reckoned they'd done enough, so posted sentries and went to sleep!

It is reported today, and our officers believe it correct, that of one battalion only 22 privates and one officer answered the roll call the next day.

Jack then moved on to the subject of what the future held for the 8th Light Horse:

All the infantry reinforcements left last night – the 1st and 2nd Brigades of L.H. go next week and it's a sure thing we will go in three weeks if not sooner.

For those of us with enough sense to keep up with the Regiment, this trip will out-rival the best that Cook's ever organised. From Melbourne to the Pyramids via Ceylon, with free board and lodging and six shillings a day for exes – then on to Turkey, up through Bulgaria, Romania and Austria into Germany; later across France to England, and finally home again via Gibraltar.

'Wounded still arriving in great numbers,' Sid Campbell reported again, on 30 April. 'Reports of wiping out regiments and staffs continue but also we know that they succeeded in doing what was wanted. Our fellows seem to have rushed into the fight without a waver … they have fought magnificently.'

This same message was soon to resound around Australia. The carnage and confusion of the first desperate hours and days on Gallipoli, the shambles on the gritty sand of the Cove, the wounded piling up in the hospitals at Heliopolis, all of that went unreported while the unhesitating heroism of those who stormed ashore at dawn on 25 April would soon become a romantic national legend.

There was no instant satellite television coverage of war in 1915, no correspondents looking down the barrel of the camera reporting live from Anzac Cove. Charles Bean, the official war correspondent, had actually been there in the action – going ashore at 9.30 am with a later wave of Australians – but his first report would not appear for almost three weeks.

Through censorship and primitive communications, all reports from Gallipoli, then and in the future, would take a long time before they appeared in Australian newspapers. Although there had been a brief report from Athens, published on 26 April – stating that troops had been landed at three points in the Dardanelles – it was not until five days later that *Australian* troops in the Dardanelles were mentioned at all. Gradually, the coverage grew, as did the length of the casualty lists that began appearing in the papers.

On 8 May, a report from Ellis Ashmead-Bartlett, the dashing and flamboyant correspondent for the London *Daily Telegraph*, who covered the landing at Anzac Cove for all the Fleet Street papers, was splashed in all the leading Australian dailies. An experienced war correspondent, he had managed to get his story out well ahead of Bean.

Ashmead-Bartlett had sent off this first despatch on 29 April and marked it 'Urgent'. It went by ship to Alexandria, where postal clerks took 'Urgent' as a direction to telegraph it to London at vastly expensive cable rates. But it gave the *Daily Telegraph* the break, and the story was immediately telegraphed on to newspapers around the world.

Bean, meanwhile, had been stymied by red tape. His report went back from Gallipoli through the official channels, awaiting clearance. The staff at general headquarters had not recognised Bean as the official correspondent, so his account was not published in Australia until 15 May.

A week before this, *The Age* ran eight decks of headlines with Ashmead-Bartlett's story underneath:

GALLANT AUSTRALIANS
FULL STORY OF THEIR FIGHT
A Thrilling Narrative
TROOPS LANDED IN DARKNESS
ATTACKED ON SEASHORE
British Correspondent's Tribute
'NO FINER FEAT THIS WAR'
Heroes of Mons Equalled

They did not wait for orders, or for the boats to reach the beach but sprang into the sea, formed a sort of rough line and rushed at the enemy's trenches. Their magazines were not charged, so they just went in with the cold steel and it was over in a minute, for the Turks in the first trench had been either bayoneted or run away and the Maxim guns were captured.

Ashmead-Bartlett then described how 'this race of athletes' had stormed on up the cliffs, before turning his attention to the wounded:

I have never seen anything like these wounded Colonials in war before. Though many were shot to bits and without hope of recovery their cheers resounded throughout the night ... they were happy because they knew they had been tried for the first time and had not been found wanting ...

For 15 mortal hours the Australians and New Zealanders occupied the heights under an incessant shell fire, and without the moral and material support from a single gun from the shore. They were subjected the whole time to violent counter-attacks from a brave enemy, skilfully led and with snipers deliberately picking off every officer who endeavoured to give the command to lead his men.

No finer feat has happened in this war than this sudden landing in the dark, and the storming of the heights, and, above all, the holding on whilst the reinforcements were landing. These raw colonial troops, in these desperate hours, proved worthy to fight side by side with the heroes of the battles of Mons, the Aisne, Ypres and Neuve-Chapelle.

In Australia, the stories by Ashmead-Bartlett and Bean were published as a pamphlet in New South Wales and issued to all students in senior grades. They were cut out from the newspapers and kept with precious family records, along with the letters that started to come back from the men who had taken part in the landing.

At Heliopolis, the grim realities of war and Gallipoli continued to grow for the men of the light horse as the wounded still flooded in. Sid Campbell and four other Light Horse Field Ambulance doctors were now ordered into the hospital to help, and Sid was assigned to a ward, keeping concise notes as he went:

Wounds chiefly limbs and shoulders and back. The latter two types sustained while lying down or advancing in stooping position. Numerous shrapnel wounds, none very large ...

108

Many rumours of mutilation of wounded by Turks but I have not yet got any first hand information. I have yet to meet the man who saw a case. Similarly the reports of the wiping out of Regimental Staffs and regiments are probably greatly exaggerated.

Most of bullet wounds coming in now are septic. We are getting Monday 26th and Tuesday 27th wounded. The wound exit is usually large and explosive effects are common. Hence many of men think they have been hit by Dum-Dums and some are only convinced with difficulty this is not so.

Dr Campbell confirmed that the wounds he was now seeing conformed to descriptions given in an American (presumably Civil War era) textbook on gunshot injuries and 'the effects of the sharp pointed bullet'.

Unfortunately, the new medicos from the light horse discovered that the hospital staff were most unhappy with their existing commanding officers and how they were handling the crisis. Sid Campbell wrote that they had 'neither made preparations for a rush of wounded nor allowed others to make them, and apparently discouraged those who suggested such'. He went on, outlining the fundamental problems he faced:

Thus the hospital is unprepared for this rush. There is a shortage of dressings, instruments, saline bath and such like apparatus, sterilisers, splints. It is very bad. Nothing has been improvised to make good these deficiencies.

The method of admission and disposal of wounded is bad. Medicos are wasted on clerks' jobs. All wounded are admitted here instead of being classified on the train journey here. Cases admitted found to be mild are bundled off to Luna Park, where a hastily improvised hospital has been made in the skating rink. Just when the tired and dirty men have been cleaned, had their wounds dressed and are settling down to sleep, others are sent on to Mena.

Discontent amongst medical and nursing staff is very great and it is distressing and annoying and scandalous that in a Base Hospital wounded men are receiving in many cases the kind of treatment they could expect in a Field Hospital.

On his ward rounds, Sid found another old Melbourne friend, Lieutenant Jim Borrowman, among the wounded. He jotted down Jim's story in his diary:

His Battalion landed soon after the first line. They were waiting ready on board for some time, when the forts started they were ordered below. They were not altogether encouraged when the boats returned to the ship after taking ashore the earlier parties to see that some of the boats' crew were wounded and that also some of their own men were coming back wounded.

On landing they rushed for cover under the small beach cliff. Here they formed and advanced up the hill and a gully and into the firing line. They were subjected to heavy fire most of the time. At one spot, three shells in succession burst within 10 yards of where Jim and some of his mates were lying. Jim had his cap knocked off by shrapnel and showed me the cap with a hole torn through the back and front.

Later in the day he was shot through the shoulder but kept on until the increasing stiffness of his shoulder impelled him to stop and return to the shore. The going was heavy – the men became blown [out of breath] frequently – the climbing was steep. They threw off their packs climbing the gully and left a baggage guard.

Battalions and companies became mixed up with each other, men and officers became separated. Jim did not see a Turk, living or dead, and this made the experience all the more trying. Peppered with bullets from all directions and no chance of replying.

In about a quarter of an hour his blood was up and he feared nothing. This was when a small body of Australians with fixed bayonets were ready to charge – but nothing appeared on which to let loose their anger. Most of the time it was a game of dodging for cover and a gradual advance through country covered with thick scrub.

While the wounded were giving their first-hand combat reports, of the hills and gullies of Gallipoli, of snipers, machine-guns and bursting shrapnel overhead, the light horse continued to carry out mounted drills in the Egyptian desert as if preparing for the Charge of the Light Brigade or some other cavalry engagement from 60 years before. And, once again, the cracks began to show in the chain of command as Brigadier Hughes and Brigade Major Antill ('hard in the face as ever', noted Stan Mack) had pushed aside the three regimental COs to take over the training routines.

As before, Colonel White discovered that the two were riding into his troopers' lines at 6 am. 'These fellows shouldn't come into our lines at all,' he wrote, detailing how he was very unpopular with 'the old chap, the Bullant and Tintacks', the latter being his nickname for Captain Percy McFarlane, an officer on Hughes' staff. The reason for this fall from grace was that he had protested in writing with the support of the other commanders. When meeting with Brazier of the 10th and Miell of the 9th, White had noted how 'they also have their little growls and worries, my advice to them was to take their gruel, it is all in the job and one has to get growled at some time or another'.

But Antill got his way, as Ernie Mack explained:

> Instead of our Colonel (White) detailing the work, the week's work is detailed by the Brigadier, Colonel Hughes. We arise every morning at five, breakfast at half past six, saddle up at seven and are on the parade ground at a quarter past. Being camped in the middle of this small town, we take about three quarters of an hour to reach our parade ground which is the Sahara desert about three miles from here.
>
> On reaching the spot picked we have a spell of 15 to 20 minutes before we start work. Our work finishes about eleven, when we come back to camp, water our horses, feed them and put the saddles away. It is then about half past twelve and that finishes the work for the day except for 'Stables' at four, which takes about three quarters of an hour.

Hughes and Antill had instructed the men on a new drill they called 'Shell Attack Formation', a strategy that was never going to be possible on the rocky inclines of Gallipoli. As Ernie commented in a letter home, 'That is the way we attack artillery ...'

By now, frustrated by the continual interference by command and the lack of information about their role in the continuing war, tempers were running short. 'They do not want us in Turkey, no place for Light Horse,' wrote an exasperated Colonel White, 'in the mean time we get burned up by the sun, cussed by the Old Man and eaten by flies, our tempers are being destroyed. Egypt is a rotten place, only fit for natives.'

On 5 May, with Hughes away on a visit to Alexandria, Antill had decided to hold a 'Brigade Drill by Trumpet Call'. Sid Campbell suddenly exploded as he sat down to write after a day of total farce:

> Our officers seem to be getting heartily tired of the course of events in our Brigade and Regiment. Too much Brigade Hqrtrs interference with Regimental training, too much Reg. Hqrtrs interference with Squadron O.C.s.
>
> Oh! For some competent officers in the higher commands. What a disappointment a great deal of military life has been to me – the boasted military organization, keenness, and intelligence.
>
> What a large proportion of the officers are thickheads and fools, or smoodgers and crawlers or wasters and incompetents. And as I write

of them I think of the things I might ought to have done – well, it's not too late to make up lost ground now.

An intelligent man, this Ormond College graduate, Sid was careful to record these feelings in his diary rather than a letter home. White described what had happened that day:

> Of course I saw the ridiculous side of it and laughed till I cried. Two thousand men and horses tearing over the desert, the dust was awful. The Bullant in charge, the Old Man away for a couple of days.
>
> Suddenly a weak trumpet call in the distance. Goodness knows what it meant. The CO's tearing around in circles for orders, squadron leaders cussing, troop leaders passing rude remarks.
>
> The Bullant surrounded by trumpeters telling them off like fun for not sounding the right call. The men and horses wondering what on earth was happening … gee it was a circus.

The next morning the brigade and regimental staffs 'had a pow wow' during breakfast. 'Subject – the Dardanelles,' wrote Sid. 'Are we being asked to volunteer or are the Brigade Headquarters acting on their own initiative? Shall we go dismounted? Shall we wait in the hope that we will go later as mounted troops?'

It was now obvious that the forces that had landed on Gallipoli on 25 April had got a foothold on the peninsula but were well short of their objectives. At Anzac, despite the great heroism and bloodshed, the amount of ground held was little more than a second toe in the scale of things. Reinforcements were urgently needed. As Ernie Mack put it:

> This Turkish war is assuming big dimensions in regards to the number of men wanted there. Practically every Australian infantryman has been rushed over, that is of the reinforcements, and several English territorial Battalions that have been over here to garrison Egypt have been sent, till now Egypt is practically only guarded by the native troops and a few thousand Indian troops who are on guard down the Canal.

On 6 May, Ernie said, there was 'great excitement' in the camp:

> On Tuesday the 1st Brigade of L.H. and the N.Z. Brigade got orders to leave for the Dardanelles next Monday without their horses – these are to be sent on when they get into country suitable for horses.

Today word is going round that our Brig. Col. Hughes has got the same offer and he is to decide by tomorrow if he will take us and leave the horses. We, or rather most of us are most anxious that he will let us go immediately, as we do not mind whether we have horses or not, as long as we get there!

Colonel Noel Brazier, of course, pressed on ahead by himself, anyhow. He assembled the 10th, his beloved regiment of Western Australians, and addressed them: would they volunteer for dismounted service? 'The idea met with such a burst of enthusiasm,' the regimental historian recorded, 'he was in the proud position of being able to report to the Brigadier, General Hughes, that the Tenth had volunteered "to a man".'

The other two regiments were then paraded and all had volunteered to go to the front – as dismounted light horsemen. Then, on 11 May, orders came to prepare to move out to the Dardanelles.

But Hughes and the Bullant had another card up their sleeves. Here was the opportunity to offload Brazier, who they considered to be bluff and irritating. Somebody had to stay behind with the horses, in command of the camp at Heliopolis. Somebody had to stay in charge of the 25 per cent of troopers who would remain and act as grooms. Somebody had to stay and be in charge of the reinforcements still arriving in Egypt. Step forward, Colonel Noel Brazier.

'Naturally a lot of heart-burning was caused, but the position was reluctantly accepted by the officers and men detailed for this work when the great importance of keeping the horses fit was impressed upon them,' wrote the regimental history, tactfully. Major Alan Love was appointed to command the 10th as the three regiments spent their last few days in Egypt together, preparing for action.

With this latest development, Colonel White sent a playful but heartfelt letter to Myrtle:

> It is very hard to leave our horses. They are looking so well and fine, all clipped and in great heart. I know quite well they will never be landed. It will all be per foot.
>
> Now then old chap, stick your toes in and be game. If you hear that I am shot, do not worry, it will be only a wound, which I am sure to get sooner or later – bound to get two or three of them – but nothing serious, so you have nothing to worry about.
>
> Do not be anxious little girl; I am going to be all right. We are wanted very badly and I am glad to help our other brave chaps at the front.

To his brother, Joe, he wrote:

> Now old chap, do not be anxious about me or worry. I shall be right
> and shall come back to you all just as soon as possible. I know what
> a rotten time you will have waiting for my return but all will be well.
> I miss you all, especially now.
>
> All my love Joe old man – be game – you dear old chap.
> From Alex.

Chapter 10

A Sharpening of Bayonets

Now there was an enormous hustle and bustle as the light horsemen transformed themselves into infantrymen – or 'beetle crushers' as they had once referred loftily to the foot soldiers that had landed on Gallipoli. Brigadier Frederick Hughes had assembled his three regiments and told the men that 'the Australian Infantry had made a great name for themselves and we must live up to it'.

Many light horsemen could hardly bear the thought of giving up their horses, even for a little while. Trooper William Hodge McGregor, of the 4th for example, a farmer from Gisborne, carried a small snapshot of his horse (branded No.645) and a notation of his feed mix ('30 chaff, 15 bran, 5 oats') carefully tucked in the back of his little diary. They would find the diary in his tunic pocket after he was killed in action on 5 June 1915 – just under a month after the 8th had worked with their horses for the last time on the sands of Egypt.

But as they packed up their saddles and wrapped up their bridles on 12 May, most of the officers and men presumed that this was going to be a short, sharp expedition. The invasion of Gallipoli would be taken care of very quickly with the light horse now in action, surely. The Dardanelles would soon be won.

'Tomorrow we hand over our horses and saddle and get issued with puttees and infantry equipment and full supply of ammunition,' Jack Mack wrote the following day. 'Next day we entrain for Alexandria in full fighting kit, destination unknown, but as we do know we embark at once and are expected back in three weeks to recuperate, make up losses, collect our horses and get back to the scrap as mounted men, we are all tipping it's an unexpected attack in force on Smyrna [Turkey's third largest city on the Aegean coast].'

Others thought that although they were probably going to Gallipoli, once a proper port had been established there their horses would be brought to them. Many of the men still harboured dreams that they would ride in triumph beside the Bosphorus, past the ancient mosques and minarets of Constantinople, and then on to glory on the battlefields of Europe.

The excitement was palpable. Ernie Mack wrote to his sister, Mary, that 'nearly all of us wear smiles that a Cheshire cat would envy and our remarks to each other are full of wit, of a kind'. And there was plenty of joking about death.

'Don't get a shock if you read in the papers before you get this that Nos 66 and 67 of the 8th have stopped a Turkish bullet or shell,' Ernie continued, referring to his and his brother Stan's service numbers, 'because I am sure we will have died with a beautiful smile on our faces … Tom (Austin) says that Jack, when he is killed, is going to turn into confetti.' He chatted on about the 'very happy family in our Troop and all are doing well', and especially mentioned his friends Torn Austin, Lex Borthwick and Roger Palmer.

Sergeant Roger Palmer, the all-round athlete and citizen of the world, was very well liked. He seemed a devil-may-care sort of fellow who liked a practical joke – like the time he collapsed the boys' tent at four in the morning.

Lex Borthwick and his tent-mates – the three Macks, Jacky Dale and Austin – were now busy making up 'a small parcel of medicines which might be useful in case of colds and things like that'. Tom was being teased about losing the boxing match title by his mates but Stan Mack told his father: 'He now says he is good enough for three Macks and as many more as like to come along. We have some good scruffs and the tidy tent always suffers. He still objects to being wakened up with hot candle grease being dropped on him.'

Stan had been away in hospital again for a few days, this time with tonsillitis, during which he'd been alarmed at the possibility of being left behind in Egypt with the horses. The other brothers worried about him, but Ernie and Jack had been sick themselves – although, as Lex Borthwick wrote home, 'they won't go near the doctor as [they're] afraid they will not be able to go with us'.

Underneath the sometimes black humour and the mostly cheerful letters, there were now some serious undertones. There were instructions about wills to fathers, and messages of comfort for mothers who sat waiting at home, desperate for news of their loved ones.

Captain Sid Campbell wrote to his father, Hugh, at home in 'Maretimo', high on the hill overlooking Portland Bay. Written on the engraved notepaper of the 8th Light Horse, with its proud prancing horse emblem, the letter read:

Heliopolis
May 13, 1915
Dear Father:

The first part of this letter will be business. I want to remind you of various arrangements I have made and also tell you of some new ones.

I had my money all transferred to the Commonwealth Bank in London. I have opened an account in the Anglo-Egyptian Bank, Cairo, and transferred most of my money there but there is still some in the London Branch of the C. Bank. My wage is 26 shillings per diem. Of this I am drawing only one shilling and sixpence a day. Three shillings and sixpence of the remainder is known as deferred pay and is paid at the end of the war or on death or discharge. The remainder is paid into the account in the Commonwealth Bank, I presume in London, by the Paymaster, Melbourne, and is accumulating there. This is known as allotted money.

Next, my will is in the possession of N. Shankly, solicitor, Temple Court, Melbourne, and, finally when I go to the front, my heavy baggage will be stored with Thos Cook & Sons, Cairo. The charge is one shilling a month on each parcel and possibly insurance; the money is paid when the baggage is taken away.

If I am killed they, having found out officially that I am a goner, notify you and you can get the luggage, which will be simply clothing and books, on payment of the charges. I shall write another letter giving the reasons for their disposition but you will no doubt guess them …

It is less than a week since I wrote home and now we are told all mail closes at 10 pm tonight. Perhaps my last letter will go along with this one.

Yesterday I got two Portland papers, a letter from George, one from Chris and also a letter from Janet … I did not get any letters from home, which was a great disappointment. Perhaps they will turn up tomorrow. They will be the first to have gone astray. I want particularly to get them, as it may be very difficult to get letters after this.

Instead of 'England' or 'Egypt' address them 'On Service'.

I am sending some more photos, some of which were taken at Luxor and some out riding near here. I wish you could come and have a look at this interesting country some day.

Well, I don't think there is anything more to say except I hope you are all well and send you all love and hope I shall get the letters alright. My letters will possibly be few and far between, but don't worry at the gaps, no news is good news.

Well, good-bye for the present
Your affec. Son
Sid

Ernie Mack explained how the light horse lines were now 'upside down getting everything packed and all is bustle and confusion, caused by the numerous questions fired at the NCOs in regards to things to be taken'.

First the men were issued with a black kitbag and told they could only pack one pair of breeches, one tunic, one pair of boots, one pair of underpants, one hairbrush, one shirt and one towel. This was to be left at Alexandria for shipment. The rest they would carry on their backs.

They were next issued with a special 'Dardanelles' knapsack and haversack, which would fit with their leather ammunition bandoliers. On their shoulders they would have to carry the pack containing a cap, towel, shirt, 'comforter', spare pair of socks, razor and a 'housewife' mending kit. They would also carry a mess tin, overcoat, blanket, two waterproof sheets and a full water bottle.

And then there was the ammunition. All up, they would hefting a kit weighing 62 pounds. Not a comfortable load, if other words, as Corporal George Rayment complained:

> Unfortunately there was a shortage of web equipment in Egypt and we had to be content with our existing leather equipment with a rucksack in lieu of a pack. These were brutal to fit on as they were only made of heavy calico, something in shape like a sugar bag, the straps by which they were slung from the shoulders were merely pieces of thin canvas which immediately rolled themselves into a string and cut into the shoulders, while it was a work of art to pack in the articles we were supposed to carry.

In his usual methodical way and tidy handwriting, Trooper David McGarvie noted that he had been issued with 130 rounds of .303 ammunition, together with new boots and puttees. The stirrups and leather leggings of the light horse were to be left behind, along with the slouch hats. Everyone would be wearing the high-domed British-issue pith helmet to ward off the sun.

Everybody – including the officers – would be dressed the same. Experience during the first days of the landing had suggested that Turkish snipers had been picking off officers because of their distinctive uniforms, which had contributed to the initial chaos and confusion. So now the officers of the light horse would have to abandon their smart, tailored uniforms, which, together with swords and evening dress, were packed away now for storage in leather trunks and locked hold-alls.

'We dress like the men and carry rifles and bayonets,' wrote Colonel White, 'no silly swords. Now that we have helmets I thought it would be the end of the plumes but no, we are to wear them still in the helmet; it is such rot and spoils the look of the show.'

Many of the troopers were concerned about what exactly they should do with the kit items that were to be left behind, for, in Ernie Mack's words, 'we have been to some pains to collect a good supply'. Sending them to Thomas Cook for storage was the best option, he believed. This would be a great help to the wounded, who could have the international travel company forward their clothes to a hospital.

Alternatively, the personal belongings were packed away in kitbags and sent to the base depot, where, as Tom Austin noted later, 'most of the best stuff was subsequently thieved'.

Orders had now been given that all three light horse squadrons in each regiment would be marching out at full strength – six officers and 148 other ranks. To allow for this, some reinforcements who had been quartered elsewhere joined the 3rd Light Horse Brigade as it suddenly moved into last-minute urgent, *relevant* training for the close-quarters fighting that lay ahead.

There were other important changes. Brigadier Hughes' 'Shell Formation' on horseback was abandoned; reveille was moved earlier, to 3 am; and an experienced British captain was attached to the brigade staff. 'Decent training seems to have started,' Sid Campbell reported, considerably calmer than during his written tirade earlier in the month. '8th out doing trench digging – very interesting – instruction by an Imperial Officer, Captain Pelham. 9th doing battle firing. Going to do a lot of night work.'

The doctor had received a briefing from Jack Antill about his views on the early days on Gallipoli. There is a sense that the Bullant, Boer War veteran, was itching to get there and show the amateur soldiers how to fight. Sid recorded what he'd learned during their chat: 'Casualties were very heavy – 5,500 – men and officers were too impetuous, could not take advantage of cover, could not keep cool. The general conditions and nature of the country increased the general muddle and confusion. Just lately their position was a very precarious one and they had a difficult job to hang on.'

Meanwhile, the intense fieldwork continued. The men of the 8th were now doing the 'battle firing', while it was the 10th's turn to dig a pattern of trenches, under Captain Pelham. As for the 9th under Colonel Miell, they conducted a mock attack on a position, leaving 'casualties' behind for the 3rd Light Horse Field Ambulance to practise on.

Then there was bayonet practice, an early session of which was an uncanny rehearsal of what would happen on the battlefield in less than three months time. Colonel White described how at 3 am on 12 May the regiment had marched out into the desert, where he led an attack by the whole of his regiment, 'ending up with a bayonet charge, the trumpeters sounding the charge like mad and the fellows rushing along and cheering like fun. It was quite exciting but running over the sandy desert is no joke. We fell in at 7 and marched home to the bugles playing marches and the men singing.'

The light horsemen had been issued with the British 1907 Pattern Sword Bayonet. It had a single cutting edge and was 17 inches long, made from toughened steel. It was long, sharp and deadly, and did not snap off when thrust into an enemy's body. At the bottom of its guard was a hook called a quillion. This would prove useful later on, when a bayonet could be stabbed into the side of a trench or a sandbag, and its quillion used as a convenient hanger for watches or clothes.

In the last week before the regiment left Egypt, Ernie Mack wrote to his father, commenting on the recent training:

> On Tuesday and Wednesday we had to get up at 2.30 am and got out marching into the desert on foot, when we had to go through a course of field firing and charging with the bayonet.
>
> The latter must be very interesting when it comes to the real thing but one wants a lot of wind as we were very blown by the time the charges were over and I don't think we had enough energy left to put a bayonet through a Turk if we were at the front.

Elsewhere in the desert, brother Jack was practising firing primitive trench mortars, or 'howitzer bomb guns' as he called them. The infantry had been issued with a machine called the Garland Mortar, but the light horse also took delivery of a Japanese trench mortar, a larger device. This had a short adjustable barrel mounted on a heavy, narrow triangular base. The operator pulled a cord to fire a large mortar shell, which went high into the air and landed, somewhat inaccurately, on top of the enemy. On Gallipoli the Turks would call these shells 'black cats' because of the shrieking whine they made overhead before bursting.

Jack would later tell his sister, Mary: 'Sounds rather a big thing but two men can carry it and takes three to work it. Has a range of 400 yards throwing a 4lb bomb of high explosives.' There was so much for these new infantrymen to learn in the short time before they sailed.

Late in the afternoon on 15 May, the three light horse regiments marched to their parade ground. Following this, at 6.30 pm, the 8th and the 9th marched out to the railway station, and, 'amid much bustle and dust', climbed aboard a train made up of crowded old cattle trucks. The 10th left later, after a short farewell parade for Colonel Noel Brazier, who would be staying behind at Heliopolis, of course. The Western Australians gave three cheers for the CO, sang *Go Alone*, and then marched off cheerfully to the station, with Major Love at their head. A glowering Brazier wrote later: 'Oh Lord. How rotten things are in general.'

At 4.10 am the next morning, the first two regiments arrived in Alexandria, the large Egyptian port on the Mediterranean Sea. The train was shunted on to the wharf, where the long business of packing a ship for war began. Men were assigned to early fatigue duty to carry the ammunition on board.

The 8th and the 9th regiments were to embark in transport *X2*, a ship that had been formerly used in the American cattle trade under the name *Menominee*. Packed in with these light horsemen, there were other Australian troops (those who had been wounded but were now rejoining their units on Gallipoli), together with a number of British officers, many of whom were also returning to action. Delays followed as searches were made for missing men, and stowaways – trying to smuggle themselves aboard to go to the front – were removed.

Conditions on the transport were far from ideal, according to Corporal George Rayment:

> Altogether we had about 1,600 troops on board made up from 55 units. Australians New Zealanders and English. The accommodation was both insufficient and dirty; the boat had evidently been used for the transport of mules and horses and had never properly been cleaned out. I had only one meal 'tween decks, the rest of the voyage I managed to get my food from the Warrant Officers Mess and at night I slept on a couch in the office, for which I was heartily thankful as conditions down below were very bad.

'Some of the Imperial officers have very swagger kits,' wrote Sid Campbell, always one for detail. 'They are chiefly, I think, on their first visit.'

By 4.30 pm, twelve hours after arriving at Alexandria, all of the 8th Light Horse Regiment had embarked. There was a last-minute roll call – a total of 23 officers and 453 other ranks reported, 'Here!'

Meanwhile, the 10th had left Helmieh station in Cairo after 10 pm, but had been delayed by an accident. As the train left a siding called Benha, a Sergeant Hubert Hall had his arm sticking out of a window, and a train going in the opposite direction had torn it off.

After this unfortunate incident, the regiment eventually reached Alexandria and at midday began embarking aboard a captured German steamer, transport A25, *Lützow*. They found themselves crammed in with the whole of the 2nd Light Horse Brigade and the 4th Light Horse Regiment. The ship had already been used several times on the Gallipoli run, but had never been cleaned up. It was both overcrowded and filthy. On this voyage *Lützow* would be carrying 106 officers and 2,250 men in addition to the ship's company.

Writing afterwards, regimental historian Lieutenant Colonel Olden described one activity that kept the Western Australians occupied during the 48-hour journey:

> One incident which lasted the whole voyage to Gallipoli and which caused endless amusement was the appearance of numerous small rotary grindstones in every nook and cranny of the crowded decks.
>
> The men utilised them for sharpening their bayonets, and they were unceasing in motion from early morning until late at night. Many were the arguments around each wheel as to the best method of sharpening a bayonet, and each man put on the edge that he considered the most serviceable.
>
> Before going ashore, a church service was held, to which, of course, only a small portion of the troops could gain access, but the bayonet sharpening was continued by the remainder, and the old hymn 'Oh God, Our Help in Ages Past' was thus accompanied by the hiss of revolving grindstones.

Aboard *Menominee* when it sailed on the morning of 17 May, the mood was upbeat. Even Jack Antill was approachable – 'amusing ship's inspection, the Brigade Major being in good form,' wrote Sid Campbell, who was busy, since he was one of only two doctors aboard. As the ship steamed on its north-westerly course, past Crete and into the Aegean Sea, threading a passage through the Greek islands, land was rarely out of sight. A guard was posted day and night aboard the crowded ship to watch for submarines, while the doctor noted he slept in the music room.

'Everyone cheerful,' Sid reported the next day. 'Strange how casually one views the possibility of being shot in a few days time. Issued with maps. Several officers on board returning have given us good idea of what to expect. Sewed pockets on tail of tunic.'

The 8th's commanding officer confirmed that the mood was good during the crossing: 'The chaps are very keen, are cleaning up rifles and sharpening up bayonets.'

On 19 May, suddenly, the 8th Light Horse was at war: *Menominee* had arrived off Cape Helles. This was where the British force of some 18,000 men had made the main landings of 25 April, at five different sites. Four weeks later, the ships with the light horse aboard dropped anchor about three-quarters of a mile off the site known as V Beach – a small sandy beach below the tiny red-tiled town nestled alongside an old, battered grey stone Turkish fort at Seddülbahir.

Just offshore was the grounded *River Clyde*, a collier that had been used as a primitive landing craft on 25 April and was the scene of an annihilation of British troops as they had tried to storm ashore here. Six Victoria Crosses were awarded to Royal Navy sailors during this action; another three were awarded the next day to soldiers as they stormed the old fort and eventually secured this tip of the Gallipoli peninsula.

And now, as Tom Austin, the 8th's unofficial historian, wrote, another big fight was in progress:

> We saw the first shots fired by enemies … everybody worked up to an intense state of curiosity and excitement and we could see aeroplanes and airships being engaged at high pressure. Our ship stood off from the shore … and our rigging and top decks were crowded with swarms of chattering sightseers. We could see, on our right front, a fair distance up the Narrows and this water was being busily patrolled by torpedo craft round which could be seen occasional spurts of water as the Chanak forts tried their gunnery.
>
> Further over was the Asiatic shore – we looked from a distance on the fabled fields of Troy. Immediately in front could be seen the enemy was subjecting the camp and dugouts on Helles beach and these to a fierce shellfire from Achi Baba. All over the landscape, as far inland as four to five miles could be seen puffs of smoke, here from a battery in action and there were shrapnel and high explosives kept incessantly bursting. Every few minutes, above all, roared the broadside of a battleship and a long line of these imposing vessels could be seen stretching away in the distance to Suvla Bay.

Sid Campbell quickly jotted down his observations on a sheet of his crested notepaper:

> Crowds of troopships, tugs, war boats. Can see Aci Baba the highest point on horizon about five miles away. Booming of guns in the distance and dust showing up on the hill and country to the west. Saw shells bursting around British aeroplane just now. Saw warships bombarding Turkish positions …

Even from this safe position offshore, even to these new soldiers untried in battle, it was obvious that a very big fight was going on ashore on Gallipoli. Climbing over the upper parts of the ship, the men on board *Menominee* were desperately trying to get a better view of the action – a breach of discipline that resulted in an eruption from the brigade major. 'Col. Antill … ordered them all off the upper decks,' George Rayment recalled, 'then put the Sgt Major under arrest and generally did his block, but it was well nigh impossible to control the men when the real thing was so close at hand'.

On 18 May, while the light horsemen were sailing through the Aegean, a curious silence had fallen over the hills and gullies of the Anzac position for the first time since the landing. There was scarcely a rifle shot in five minutes; the usual snipers seemed to have taken the day off.

George Fish, the 2nd Field Ambulance stretcher-bearer, wrote of an 'exceptionally quiet day' as he received several old letters from his girlfriend, Beryl. There was a sense of unease among the Australians and New Zealanders in their trenches, which were still a long way off from developing into the maze of trenches that would eventually criss-cross the slopes like a grid map of a modern inner city.

The Anzacs were right to feel unnerved by the silence. Airmen from the Royal Naval Air Service had already spotted enemy troops on the move, other movements had been sighted from ships, and this intelligence had been telegraphed to the headquarters on Anzac Cove.

At about the same time as a second aerial warning was received, the Turks opened up with the heaviest bombardment of artillery yet experienced at Anzac. The shells crashed in from the north, south and east. 'Two men belonging to the 5th Battalion were struck by one of the Turks' big shells,' George recorded. 'A Sgt Major was blown to atoms, the biggest part found of him was as big as my hand. It was a terrible sight. Hole in ground was a great depth. We had a lively time from 6 until 8 pm, shells landing all round us.'

The commanders on the ground were now prepared for an imminent night or dawn attack, and all troops were ordered to stand to arms at 3 am instead of the usual 3.30 am.

The Turkish battle plan was simple enough: assemble four divisions of between 30,000 and 40,000 men, and attack about 12,500 Anzacs, right along the battle line on the heights. Then chase them down – and throw the infidel invaders off the soil of the motherland and into the sea. But, as Charles Bean later wrote, the Australians were ready:

[While] the Turkish troops were being silently crowded into the rear of their front trenches in preparation for their secret attack before dawn, on the other side of the same crests the rifles had been carefully cleaned and oiled and officers and orderlies were now hurrying among the sleeping supports to ensure that everything should be in readiness to meet the expected assault.

Shortly before 3 am, the Australians, wearing greatcoats against the pre-dawn chill, stood ready with bayonets fixed in their trenches, while the reserves formed up and waited in the valleys. The sky was clear and the light could be seen, in Bean's words, 'reflected from the sheaves of long, thin, Turkish bayonets'.

There were two warning shots from the Australian line, then a shout. The alarm was given and the Turks began charging, wave after wave, into withering fire from the Anzacs. It was the Turks who were surprised in this surprise attack.

Shouting 'Allah! Allah!' and with blaring bugles and wild martial music, the Turks kept on charging – and the Australians kept on firing, as fast as they could ram down five more rounds into their rifle magazines from the metal clips they carried in their pouches.

There was no covering fire, no artillery support for the charging Turks. Soon realising this, the Australians climbed fearlessly up above their trenches onto the parapets. They fired until their rifles were hot. They yelled with excitement. They waved their hats and shouted slang words they'd learned in Egypt – 'Eggs-a-cook' and 'Baksheesh' and one taunted, 'Saida-play you again next Saturday!' It was bloodthirsty and intoxicating. One man said it was better than a wallaby hunt back home.

In all that day, the Anzac rifles and machine-guns would fire 948,000 rounds.

Albert Jacka, a 22-year-old forestry worker from Victoria, with the help of three mates, decided on a quick plan. While the three distracted some of the Turks, Jacka climbed out into No Man's Land, jumped into a Turkish trench, shot five and bayoneted two. An officer found him afterwards preparing to have a quiet smoke, surrounded by the dead. 'I managed to get the beggars, sir,' said Jacka. They gave him the Victoria Cross, the first to be won by an Australian on Gallipoli.

Afterwards, the military commanders agreed that if the Turks had concentrated their attack at one place, instead of spreading it all along the battle line, they would probably have burst through.

One of the weakest-defended points was considered to be on top of the ridge called Russell's Top, where it joins another, Walker's Ridge, at a narrow strip of land at the head of Monash Valley they called The Nek.

On 19 May, the defences here were in their infancy. One trench had been dug along the width of the strip of land and three narrow, deep trenches (called saps) had been pushed out towards the enemy. On this night, the area was being defended by the Auckland Regiment of the New Zealand Mounted Rifles, in position in the trenches.

When the Turks charged, the New Zealanders fired at them but couldn't stop the advance. But, once the Turks began to run past the saps, the New Zealanders in them could turn and fire at them as they went past. One after another, three rushes by the enemy were swept away by rifle fire and one machine-gun that stuttered into action.

The first charge at The Nek had failed and, by 5 am, the attempt by the Turks to smash their way through the Anzac lines had turned into a terrible carnage.

Bean summarised this achievement and provided a moving description of the fate of those lying helpless on the battlefield:

> The slaughter was sufficiently great to secure the complete safety of Anzac. Of the 42,000 Turkish troops who had hemmed in the position at dawn, some 10,000 had before noon been killed or wounded.
>
> Not all who lay in No Man's Land after this fight were killed or wounded; a proportion, as normally happens, were feigning death and eventually crept away. Any disused trench or pothole in No Man's Land was crowded with survivors, mostly wounded. Here and there in the scrub some staunch veteran continued to fire at the Anzac line throughout the day.
>
> But while some thus survived between the opposing trenches, the dead and wounded lay everywhere in hundreds. Many of those nearest to the Anzac line had been shattered by the terrible wounds inflicted by modern bullets at short ranges.
>
> No sound came from that dreadful space; but here and there some wounded or dying man, silently lying without help or any hope of it under the sun which glared from a cloudless sky, turned painfully from one side to the other, or silently raised an arm towards heaven.
>
> The Anzac troops had lost only 160 killed and 468 wounded. At last they had been fighting, not an invisible enemy, but one who came forward to be shot until the men shooting were almost tired of slaughter.

'Very busy morning in hospital,' George Fish wrote on 20 May; 'had a fair number of patients in. One fellow wanted his discharge as he had the funks. During lunch we had two of our men hit, one seriously wounded in four places and Bill Rudd was killed instantly, the bullet (shrapnel) pierced his heart …'

The day before, Private John Simpson Kirkpatrick, a stretcher-bearer with the 3rd Field Ambulance, had been shot through the heart in Shrapnel Valley. He became immortalised in Australian history and legend as 'Simpson, the Man with the Donkey'.

Today, nobody remembers Bill Rudd. Private William Rudd of the 2nd Field Ambulance was just 27 years old, an ironworker from the Melbourne suburb of Albert Park. Harold Brentnall, George's mate, wrote that the shell had burst overhead a few feet from them, and they lifted Bill into their dugout, where he died. That night, at 9 pm, they buried Bill Rudd at the place where he lies today, in the Beach Cemetery in grave H7. It is just two rows from grave F1, where Simpson lies.

Then they went through his kit. The war went on.

Much later, Harold sent a letter home about that night on Gallipoli. 'The thing that cut me up most was when poor old Billy Rudd got knocked out,' the stretcher-bearer confessed. 'I have eaten my dinner heaps of times with my hands caked with blood but this time I had to wash poor old Bill's off and even had to shovel his gore out of my dugout before eating.'

At least they could bury Bill Rudd and John Simpson. Out in front of the firing line, there were now thousands of unburied corpses. The bodies of the fallen, mostly Turks but also Australians and New Zealanders, were turning grey-black and slowly bloating, splitting uniforms and being crawled over by fat, blue-green blowflies that laid their maggot eggs as they buzzed and hummed heavily through the shredded bushes.

A stink was growing past a stench, and into the sweet, yet gagging, cloying and clinging smell of rotting human flesh that would hang over Anzac and envelop it like a shroud of pestilent poison gas. Something, urgently, would have to be done about the problem.

Meanwhile, offshore, *Lützow* and *Menominee* had received orders to split up as the battle raged ashore. Quite why they had anchored off Cape Helles in the first place was a mystery – the 'authorities knew nothing about us,' noted Sid Campbell.

Menominee steamed off to the island of Lemnos, the base for the Gallipoli operation. *Lützow*, meanwhile, was ordered to sail north and anchor off Anzac Cove, where Colonel Olden recorded the scene:

> From the decks of the *Lützow* the 10th Regiment anxiously watched progress the whole night through. The rifle and machine gun fire was intense and the artillery duel continuous.

127

It was a thrilling, though disappointing, first experience for the Regiment, to watch this night battle and not be permitted to have a hand in it, and our hearts went out to our people ashore as we realised how hard they were being pressed and how gallantly they were fighting.

When the day broke the fire had slackened considerably and cheers went up from the *Lützow* as word came through that our line was unshaken, though the situation was still critical, as the Turks were apparently being heavily reinforced.

At 2.30 pm on 20 May, the 2nd Light Horse Brigade began to disembark and were all off the ship before dusk. As for the hungry 10th, they still had to wait impatiently for the rest of the 3rd Brigade to join them.

Menominee, with the 8th and 9th regiments, had, meanwhile, moved into the inner harbour of Mudros on Lemnos. It reminded those on board of their time in King George Sound on the first leg of the voyage to Egypt. There were over 70 vessels gathered there, from large warships and transport ships to busy tugs and torpedo boats carving white furrows in the still blue sea, as George Rayment explained:

> Dotted on the surface of the calm waters of the bay lay dozens of transports, warships of every description, hospital ships, trawlers and pinnaces, each taking in or discharging stores … There were three or four hospitals on shore where the slightly wounded cases from the Peninsula came for a short spell, the serious cases being taken by the hospital ships to Alexandria, Malta or England. The water in the harbour is deep enough to permit liners like the *Aquitania*, which was being used as a hospital ship, and battleships as large as the Queen Lizzie to navigate safely.

A boat delivered the latest British newspapers to *Menominee*, and these were posted up around the decks. Now the men could read weeks-old accounts of the original British landing at Cape Helles (of course, glorious and successful), together with the cautiously pessimistic view that the Allied forces were making no major progress on the western front and that a long war now loomed ahead.

At 7 am on 21 May, the men of the 8th were shaken awake. Orders had come for the 8th and 9th, the brigade headquarters staff and the signallers to transfer to three fast destroyers. Most of the 8th went aboard HMS *Foxhound*. Aub Callow, the 18-year-old signalman from Ballarat, precise as always, noted: 'Left Lemnos at 11.30, steamed along at the rate of 22 knots per hour arriving at Gallipoli at about 2pm.'

'Fortunately there was no sea running,' wrote Corporal Rayment, 'or we would have been drenched but as it was we received a good deal of the spray flung up by the bows'.

Tom Austin's account shows that the men were still upbeat:

'Twas a most exhilarating journey, the speed and motion of the boat being in great contrast to the slow going transports to which we had become so accustomed. The officers and crew were extremely generous and kind to all. Every man was served with hot chocolate; many secured a liberal supply of good tobacco, which proved a great boon during the next few weeks.

On arrival off Anzac the boats spent an hour or two cruising slowly up and down between Suvla and Anzac Cove. This was evidently to gull the enemy into the belief that the vessels were merely performing a patrol. Several warships nearby fired broadsides at intervals, serving to keep enemy heads down.

A cruiser was leisurely shelling the slopes of Hill 971 as the light horsemen got their rifles and packs together. 'Between the roaring of the artillery and the guns of the cruisers we could hear the sharp crackle of rifle fire and the splutter of machine guns,' said George Rayment.

Lützow had already been under Turkish fire during the day, he wrote:

[Shrapnel] had been bursting uncomfortably close. At the first salvo, the men realising that they were under directed fire for the first time climbed the masts and rigging to get a better view of it! Such was the spirit they were in as they descended from the troopship's side and went ashore for their first taste of the 'Real Thing'.

The 8th and 9th would be first ashore, at 4 pm transferring down the scramble nets hanging from the side of HMS *Foxhound* into the waiting barges and pinnaces. The 10th would transfer at 4 pm from *Lützow* to two other destroyers, HMS *Chelmer* and HMS *Rattlesnake*, for the quick dash close to shore and the transfer to the landing craft.

The 8th's Tom Austin described the landing:

Toward the early afternoon we were rushed close in towards shore, launches were immediately alongside, the landing was effected without mishap, though a few shrapnel were sent among us. Some of the other launches bringing other portions of the Brigade ashore had slight casualties, but nothing considering what could have been done had the naval people dawdled. Their arrangements were excellent and splendidly carried out, the little middies [teenage midshipmen] causing us all to gape with amusement and wonder at their power in handling men.

They had arrived at Anzac Cove. At one period, up to 600 shells a day fell along its short length and around the barges, the pinnaces and lighters ferrying men and supplies ashore. The beach, barely 10 metres wide and 600 metres long, and shaped like a new moon, was like an ants' nest, thick with piled stores and constantly moving men and mules.

As the 3rd Brigade arrived, there were some 30,000 men being fed, supplied and watered through the tiny bay. Fresh troops arrived in a never-ending procession as the wounded and the ill were being taken off. George Rayment recorded his version of the landing:

> From the destroyers we jumped aboard the barges, great unwieldy things like those used on the canals in England and France, but drawing very little water. Threw in our packs, rifles, tools and baggage and then with hearts beating faster than usual waited for the pinnaces to move shorewards. It did not take us long to reach the small pier formed of stones and bags and barges and out of the best part of one thousand men not a single one was hit coming ashore.
>
> We could not understand why the naval officers were in such a desperate hurry to get us off the barges and away from the beach, but we had landed in daylight in full view of the Turks and it was a wonder that we were not severely shelled.

First impressions came fast as the regiments of the 3rd Brigade formed up on the beach in the late springtime, in their new pith helmets and fresh uniforms. 'Anzac Cove ... pontoons, tugs, Australians, NZs, Indians, mules, dugouts everywhere,' scribbled Sid Campbell.

Some troopers, like the men of the 2nd Light Horse Brigade who had landed on the beach earlier, quickly took advantage of a dump of equipment left behind by wounded infantrymen. In particular they got rid of the flimsy drill haversacks, which they called 'pillowslip'', which they had been issued with in Egypt, and replaced them with discarded regulation infantry web equipment.

Their landing complete, the 3rd Brigade men were then ordered to march up off the beach to a temporary bivouac site at the foot of Plugge's Plateau, which rises up immediately to the left of Anzac Cove. Rayment's account continues:

We were loaded up like mules and as the day was late we did not feel inclined to hurry but took our time – had a shell burst near us we would have got a move on. After roughly forming up on the beach we wended our way past stacks of ammunition and stores, over a bit of a rise and then down into what we later called Light Horse Gully. When we arrived there were no dug-outs but after having been allotted an area we began to dig.

'There was a great deal of rhododendron scrub about,' Tom Austin wrote of the first bivouac, 'and digging in consisted of each man burrowing a hole slightly bigger than his body and two feet deep, covering it with waterproof sheet and some branches. Squadrons and troops were kept together as much as possible but all had to fit into the nature of the ground.' The soil was easy to dig when dry – soft, yellow-brown and crumbly with little pebbles. But it had a glue of clay under-neath and when wet would stick to boots like an extra-thick tractor tyre.

Suddenly, as the men dug, the famous 'Anafarta Annie', a Turkish gun sited in the hills to the north of Anzac, opened up. It was firing shrapnel, as usual, to cause maximum casualties to anyone in the open, on or near the beach.

Shrapnel, the ever-present killer that would stalk Gallipoli, was named after its inventor, General Henry Shrapnel. The British general pioneered its use on such battlefields as Waterloo. It was basically an artillery shell provided with a bursting charge and filled with lead balls, exploded in flight by a time fuze.

Each projectile was almost like a shotgun, fired by means of the time fuze, ideally at a height that would cause the maximum damage on the enemy. A 75-millimetre shrapnel projectile contained 270 lead balls, each about a half-inch in diameter, in a smoke-producing matrix; 155-millimetre shrapnel packed a lethal load of 800 balls. Some First World War shrapnel shells contained a mixture of small and larger balls – the smaller designed to kill or maim humans, the larger to disable or kill horses. At the moment of burst, these balls shot forward with increased velocity, normally without fracturing the case, and the result was a cone of bullets that could sweep an area generally much larger than that covered by the burst of a high-explosive shell of the same calibre.

Trooper Austin described the light horsemen's reaction:

As the first shell screamed towards us, nearly every man straightened himself and looked to see what would come of it.

'Twas beautifully ranged and landed right in our midst, but luckily proved a 'dud'. Everyone rushed to secure what, at that time, was considered a trophy. But curiosity was cut short by another shell bursting in our midst with a murderous shriek and a run was made for cover.

The gun, after firing a few more shots, switched further down the beach and we all came out again. There were no casualties, but we were all considerably wiser – the tragedy of the huddled bundles and wrecked barges up along the beach towards Suvla came home to us then.

The men now dug in with increased urgency and soon had built a sweat up, as Tom's account continues:

After the digging had been completed, nearly every one found time for a swim at the beach below. Anafarta Annie fired a few ineffective shots, but somehow one felt safe in the water and little notice was taken of her.

Towards sundown we were all gathered into the dugouts. Being under the cliff we were safe from rifle fire, which went directly over our heads and into the sea some distance out. Each bullet made a sharp snap-crack as it went over, and this noise was incessant during the night. No fires were permitted after dark and, despite the noises of real war which we were hearing for the first time, everybody went to bunk early and slept soundly.

'Digging ourselves in until 9 pm,' wrote Dr Campbell, 'bully beef, biscuits and tea. Shells and bullets passing overhead.'

After only a few hours ashore on Gallipoli, the men of the light horse were acting like veterans.

Chapter 11

Face Off

The first night on Gallipoli was hardly a peaceful one for the newly arrived light horsemen. Rifle fire crackled incessantly in the darkness, the bullets zipping high overhead, droning off the ridges in ricochets or pattering down, like spent hailstones.

Trooper Redge Mathers was a 23-year-old bookkeeper from the tiny town of Cohuna, on Gunbower Creek in northern Victoria, serving with the 9th Light Horse. He wrote home to his sister, Effie:

> After having a bit of tea in the dark we crawled into bed, four of us in a little hole in the ground. Sleep of course was out of the question, but I managed to snatch a little now and then between the scares I had when the fire would increase. Early the following morning we were all called out to Stand to Arms until daylight, then it commenced to rain and we were all most uncomfortable.

The men had been called out at 3 am – perhaps as a training drill at the instigation of the Bullant, as they were still not yet manning the trenches. The 'stand-to' would become a regular feature of their life, and on Gallipoli the times varied according to the time of the year, but generally averaged between 3.30 and 4.40 in the morning and between 6 and 9 in the evenings.

'It is most annoying being awakened on a raw morning, standing about shivering and groaning,' wrote Tom Austin, 'never, throughout our service, did the enemy choose to attack during the hour of standing-to and everyone was required to sleep with his gear on in the trenches, it struck us as rather unnecessary to wake us up when a good extra hour or two of sleep would have been much more beneficial.' On that next day, after digging deeper and enlarging their dugouts, 'most of us were allowed to wander round a bit, use our eyes and become familiar with the lay of the land.'

Their first bivouac was just above Ari Burnu, the northern tip of Anzac Cove, in the foothills of the sharply rising slopes of Plugge's Plateau. Ari Burnu was named by the Turks after the fat bumblebees that still nest and drone in the crevices of a rise that had itself been named on the first day of the landing after Colonel Arthur Plugge, commanding the Auckland Battalion. He had established his headquarters there.

Facing inland from Ari Burnu, another wider beach can be seen, North Beach, which sweeps away to the left of Plugge's Plateau. High above this beach is Russell's Top, named after another New Zealander, Brigadier General Andrew Russell, commander of the Mounted Rifles.

Russell's Top is towards the end of the main Sari Bair ridge, where the Turks and the Anzacs faced off across narrow strips of No Man's Land. This ridge – the commanding height – comes down to North Beach by way of three spurs. On the right are the steep slopes of Plugge's Plateau. Next, separated by a deep gully, is the bare, eroded and forbidding feature that the Anzacs named the Sphinx, after the ancient ruin they had got to know so well when they were camped at Mena in Egypt. Hardly less rugged, with steep slopes and a ridge that sometimes narrows to a wedge you can stand astride, is Walker's Ridge, separated from the Sphinx by another deep ravine, Mule Gully. The ridge got its name from Brigadier General Harold Walker, who commanded the New Zealand Infantry Brigade on the first day of the landing.

Today, it can still take a good hour to struggle and puff your way up or slither and slide down Walker's Ridge, grabbing at exposed roots for support and to stop you falling. It has always been tough going. Redge Mathers told Effie: 'I can vouch for the thorns and prickles in the scrub for as I slid down a hill, the best part of the back of my pants and also a portion of me came away.

From where Walker's Ridge joins Russell's Top, you go on today through scrub and thorn bushes, up and down indentations that were once trenches, to a saddle called The Nek, about 30 metres wide at its narrowest point, with sheer drops to the valleys on either side. Boer War veterans gave The Nek its name, from the Afrikaans word meaning 'mountain pass'.

This thin neck of land is really a bridge from Russell's Top to the Sari Bair ridge, which then rises rapidly upwards to a round-backed hill dubbed Baby 700, and then onwards and upwards to Battleship Hill and the commanding position of Chunuk Bair. Back in 1915, each of these rises was patterned with trenches and saps. The Turks held this high ground, could see down on all before them, and so dominated North Beach below.

Just across to the right of The Nek, they created a maze of defensive trenches known as the Chessboard. These were laid out in a methodical pattern so that one trench commanded another, and another, in a systematic plan that would repulse any Anzac attempt to try to seize the Turkish front lines. In addition, about a dozen of the German-made Maxim machine-guns, fixed at different points, could concentrate fire to protect the Chessboard, sweeping back and forth, spewing 8 millimetre rounds, if there was an emergency. In short, it was a well-planned death trap.

Walker's Ridge was the northern flank of the Anzac position, up which the light horse reinforcements would scramble and into deep communication trenches to the short series of trenches that led off on either side of the ridge at Russell's Top, which were then held by the New Zealanders. These trenches – with saps dug cautiously extending forwards – ended at The Nek and faced the enemy lines, rising upwards, no more than 50 metres away across No Man's Land.

The soil was crumbly here on Russell's Top, easily dug. The trenches were deep enough so that soldiers could stand without their heads appearing above ground, with traverses interposed so that the enemy could not fire straight down a trench. Because a trench was deeper than a man was tall, fire steps were cut for men to stand on to fire over the parapet, which was formed from the trench soil piled up in front. The soil piled at the back was called the parados. These mounds of soil had to be reinforced with sandbags to withstand the searching fire of Turkish artillery, from guns the Australians would call '75s' – guns that had been captured by the Turks in a Balkan war fought against the Serbs.

For the new reinforcements, there was little time to wait. On that first day on Gallipoli, some of the light horsemen were sent on outpost duty to some of the lower trenches running down to the beach from Walker's Ridge. Standing orders required six men for every 12 metres of trench. Redge Mathers was one of those sent on outpost duty:

> Talk about a trip up the hills, the track up being most slippery after the rain. And none of us were feeling too joyful as we passed some wounded New Zealanders being carried down.
>
> We had not long been in the firing line when the shells began to buzz around again, none of our men were hit, we were all too careful, but I saw two New Zealanders knocked out with shrapnel – their own fault, they would not take cover.

After hearing the shells screeching overhead a few times one gets used to the direction they are taking. A man on observation on hearing or seeing the smoke from a big gun gives the alarm and on hearing the noise knows whether they are coming close or going over to the beach.

Corporal George Rayment appears to have been a quick learner in some of the finer points of trench warfare:

The Turks were adept at placing guns and a ruse they adopted to mislead us to the exact position of a gun was by the use of a flash or smoke bomb some distance away from the gun positions. Sometimes I have seen a slight puff of smoke followed a few seconds later by the boom of a gun, but sometimes I saw the puff of smoke and no gun was fired. Thus we knew we were being deceived about the position of the gun but the deception saved many lives as the Brigadier had a lookout posted on Plugge's Plateau who sounded a whistle whenever the smoke was seen, giving us four or five seconds to dash for cover.

It was usually laughable when we came to think of it later on the way we used to duck for shelter instinctively when we heard a shell coming – usually a small howitzer. I have often seen men – and I've done it myself – crouch behind a bush that might happen to be close by and which would afford no cover whatsoever, while one day I tried to hide myself among some mail as a shell from Beachy Bill roared by a couple of feet above my head.

Further north along the beach were two more outposts, established and garrisoned by New Zealanders. To protect the men coming and going from the outposts, a deep trench, 3 kilometres long and known as the Long Sap or Big Sap, was dug all the way behind North Beach, from the northern end of Anzac Cove. Soon the light horsemen would toil alongside Maoris from the New Zealand Expeditionary Force to widen the Big Sap so that both men and mules could bring supplies and ammunition along the deep trench and feed into another deep supply route that was cut up along the top of Walker's Ridge. All the time they were under incessant fire. And all the time there were grim reminders of what had gone before as they dug and dug and dug.

Trooper Dave McGarvie told his grand-daughter in 1976: 'Quite often we'd be digging a trench to join this one up with that one and we'd come across a man who had been buried in one.'

What would you do then? the old man was asked.

'Oh, we'd put him in a bag and put him out somewhere else.'

For most of the 8th and 9th, the first day on Gallipoli was a reasonably peaceful one. Their bivouac beneath Plugge's was only temporary and within a few days they would move further north and camp on the side of Walker's Ridge, facing the crumbly sheer sides of the Sphinx.

Sid Campbell would draw a pencil sketch of the scene, with an arrow showing where a Turkish sniper had hidden for several days, in a cleft on Cathedral Face. Undeterred, the men scooped out their dugouts into the side of the ridge and made little ledges where they could sit and watch the sinking of the sun behind the hills of Samothrace – as Sid put it, the 'island refuge of ancient oracles across the sea, with deeper shades darkening the island of Imbros'.

There can be no more extraordinary experience today, no more direct link to this past, than to follow Dr Campbell's pencilled map, climb up the side of the ridge from the gully, and there, under the thorns of the gorse bushes discover such a terrace marked with the shards of a broken stoneware rum jar, the bone handle of a 1915 toothbrush, a brass buckle and a tiny button from a uniform tunic.

This is where the 8th lived and rested 90 years ago before going on and upwards to the firing line. Today a pair of hawks have made their nest in the cleft where the Turkish sniper once hid; they hover on the thermals rising up the sides of the Sphinx and wheel above the eroded and hidden terraces. Heavy black bumblebees drone over a trickling creek that runs through the gully that was once thronged with men and mules. The twitter of tiny birds darting through the dark green tangle of bushes on the creek banks is the only sound to break the long silence.

But almost a century ago, Corporal George Rayment wrote of the many noises he heard here from his 'office' dugout, measuring 5 feet by 4 feet, covered with just a waterproof sheet:

> The noises made by bullets and shells are wonderful in their variety. The nickel casing of the bullets used by the Turks is extremely thin and bursts when it ricochets off the ground or a sandbag and then as it sped along we could hear it humming or whistling. Sometimes a bullet high overhead would be heard like a boy whistling, starting on a low note, and getting higher and higher, then gradually sinking lower and lower until it died away. Others would be like the droning of a bee, the whimper of a whipped dog, the crack of a whip, or a faint zipp as a sniper's bullet flew close to one's head. When a 75 burst the pieces flew through the air at a terrific velocity, humming louder and

louder as they approached and hit the ground with a dull thud, or growing fainter as the fragment went out into space.

Sid Campbell wrote of his first day on the peninsula:

> Have good dug out, 3rd LH Field Ambulance staff alongside Dale and C Squadron. A Troop's sergeants on other side. Occasional bursts of shelling during day passing overhead and bursting at landing place where trawler destroyed.
>
> Had swim and change of socks, etc. at 5 pm. Swimming place shelled three-quarters of an hour later and one man killed … fed well at midday on stew of bully beef, fried potatoes, bacon and biscuits. Tonight cheese, jam and biscuits with tea.

But after just one day ashore the doctor would be imploring, 'Oh! For a case of apples or oranges.' On the subject of supplies, Dave McGarvie remembered:

> The men didn't get much at all … we were supposed to get rum twice a week and lime juice twice a week. Our quartermaster sergeant [Sergeant Leo Molony, a tough old Boer War veteran of the Canadian Scouts and Marshall's Horse who later died of wounds] used to drink most of the rum ration – you'd always smell rum every time he went past your dugout. Well, I used to give him my rum and he'd give me his lime juice.

Stan Mack often swapped sugar for 'Johnny cakes' and curry cooked by the Indians tending the transport mules near the Cove. Twice a week, if all went well, each man received half a loaf of bread, baked on the island of Imbros and delivered at Anzac Cove by a daily trawler service. All too soon, though, the appalling and monotonous diet would be taking its toll on the men.

Although adequate in calories, the absence of fresh fruit and vegetables meant that the men suffered deficiencies in vitamins B1 (thiamine) and C. Soon they would begin suffering from a form of scurvy, ulcers they called 'the Barcoo Rot'. Scurvy had been the scourge of the sea and of armies for centuries, kept at bay from the middle of the nineteenth century by the mass production of lime juice from British plantations in the West Indies. Lime juice was only about a third as effective as fresh orange or lemon juice, however, and in the absence of either, the Barcoo Rot meant that even the smallest scratches or sores on Gallipoli often became infected. It was not until the First World War that scientists even began to raise the possibility of a negative factor for scurvy – that it was actually caused by the lack of something – and it would not be until 1932 that the active antiscorbutic compound in fresh food and citrus juice was isolated. On Gallipoli, the men ate dreadful food. Nutritionists and dieticians were a world away.

'I have a great longing for a big green cabbage, anything fresh,' Colonel White wrote only a few days after arriving, 'one gets so fed up with bully beef and biscuits'. The rusty remains of the bully beef cans still crumble away on the Anzac battlefield. They can be found under the thorn bushes on the ledges, along with the pottery shards of Quartermaster Sergeant Molony's rum jars.

Major Arthur Deeble of the 8th was also busy digging in, pausing only to note professionally in his diary: 'Shell fire on our position, poor shooting by the enemy.'

As the 8th dug in, with one squadron deployed at the foot of Walker's Ridge, the South Australians and Victorians of the 9th had already been sent on further up the hill, to take over some of the trenches from the Auckland Mounted Rifles. It was a quick learning experience. 'These trenches were extremely narrow, it being quite impossible for men to pass each other except by one man stooping down while the other stepped over,' wrote Major Darley, the 9th's historian. 'The widening of the trenches was therefore immediately started and a week later was completed.'

Visiting British officers would soon admire the depth of the trenches, especially the main communications trenches, which were well over 6 feet deep, and wide in proportion as well. One at the top of Walker's Ridge was called Broadway. But the digging always came at human cost, as Major Darley recalled:

> Enemy snipers were very energetic, causing many casualties. Special men were therefore set to work, with periscopic rifles, to quieten them down. A certain officer succeeded in shooting one, and reported his success, but his elation was short lived as it was discovered that this particular Turk had already been dead for over a week before he succeeded in hitting him.

Each night the troops stood to arms from 7.30 to 9 and from 3.30 am until daybreak. As soon as it got dark, the enemy appeared to get a trifle nervous and would blaze away thousands of rounds without apparent reason. As this appeared a good way of making them waste their ammunition, it was decided to help them in the good work. Dummies were therefore made from sacks filled with straw, dressed in jackets and helmets, and mounted on poles. In the waning light, these were shown over the top of the trenches each night, when they would immediately draw a heavy fire from the enemy – who no doubt reported in their next communiqué that another attack had been abandoned owing to their heavy fire.

Gallipoli was still fresh and green at this stage, with heavy rain falling mostly at night and in the early mornings, when the temperature dropped sharply. There were wildflowers on the hills, white and purple anemones, the red and black poppies the Turks called *gelinciks* ('little brides'), on the flat land north and south of Anzac Cove, and a delicate flower that would soon be dubbed 'the Gallipoli Rose'.

Gallipoli is a beautiful place, even more so in springtime, when the Anzacs first arrived, but now the shrapnel was shredding the golden patches of gorse on the hillsides, the brush was being burnt in camp fires and the temperature began to rise. The browning grass now merged with the sienna hillsides that were being ploughed by the constant shellfire.

For the newly arrived light horsemen it was a strangely beguiling place. On those first few days on the peninsula they were innocents abroad, and the battle-hardened infantry often made fun of them as they marched off to take up positions in their smart uniforms and sun helmets. Before long the light horsemen would be as tanned and their clothes as stained and grubby as any of the other Anzacs.

The 2nd Light Horse Brigade had been sent off up Shrapnel Valley – the main communication line leading up to the front line from Anzac Cove – to relieve the 13th Infantry Battalion. Their Anglican chaplain, Padre George Green, says Joan Starr in her book, *From the Saddlebags at War*, noted:

> We rested in all innocence at points in the road which I later knew were no safe abiding places. Shells were bursting along the valley – 'ours or theirs?' was the naive concern.
>
> We were subject to innocent banter from passing infantrymen – 'Struth! It's the bally Light Horse, what a come down!'
>
> 'Where are your gee-gees? Find the pack a bit hard, don't yer?'
>
> We could stand this chiak. Proud we were, to belong to the Light Horse. In a few weeks original members of the 4th Infantry Brigade acknowledged us worthy to fight by them – and that is high praise.
>
> Indeed, for all their talk, they were more than glad to see us coming to reinforce them.

The Western Australians of the 10th Regiment had also been sent up Shrapnel Valley, to the trenches at Monash Valley. Here they came under

New recruits for the light horse arrive at the Broadmeadows camp in 1914. An outbreak of measles meant that some were quarantined in a remote corner of the camp where they spent the time skylarking. (Mr Noel Callow)

A group of light horse signallers including Aub Callow pose with their new semaphore flags at Broadmeadows camp. They have yet to be issued with their uniforms. (Mr Noel Callow)

The 8th Light Horse troopers practise firing at the Williamstown rifle range, watched by their commanding officer Lieutenant Colonel Alexander White (left) and his adjutant, Captain Terry Crowl, before the regiment sails for Egypt. (Australian War Memorial; J2D11)

Troopers from the 8th Light Horse rest between mounted drills at Broadmeadows camp in Australia. (Australian War Memorial; H03027)

The commanding officer of the 8th Light Horse, Lieutenant Colonel Alexander White, at home in Elsternwick, Victoria, with his wife Myrtle, and their son, affectionately called 'button mouth'. (Mrs Marjorie McPherson, Mr Alex White)

Trooper David McGarvie of the 8th Light Horse, a gentle dairy farmer who became a deadly sniper on Gallipoli and had a miraculous escape from death at The Nek. (Mr David Collyer)

Captain Sydney 'Sid' Campbell, the medical officer with the 8th Light Horse who was described as the 'best loved man in the regiment'. (Australian War Memorial; PR88/102)

Private George Fish, a 23-year-old stretcher bearer with the 2nd Field Ambulance and a good mate of Harold Brentnall. (Mrs Beryl Fowler)

Private Harold 'Brenty' Brentnall, a 19-year-old stretcher bearer with the 2nd Field Ambulance and one of the first ashore at Gallipoli. (Mrs Beryl Fowler)

The boys from 'Berry Bank'. The three Mack brothers, from left to right, Ernie, Stan and Jack, before they rode off to war. (Mr Greg Gillespie, Mr Bill Mack)

Lieutenant Edward Ted Henty of the 8th Light Horse from Hamilton in Victoria. (Henty family collection)

Henty brothers, Wilf and Ted (right), pose proudly in their light horse uniforms at the family farm, 'The Caves', near Hamilton in Victoria in 1914. (Henty family collection)

The Bullant – Brigade Major Jack Antill – second in command of the 3rd Light Horse Brigade, the man who gave the order to 'Push On!'. (Australian War Memorial; G01330)

The miserable life of the 'rest' trenches. Light horsemen with trench and dugouts carved into the cliff face of Walker's Ridge. (Photo J. Campbell in National Library of Australia; nla.pic-an23297151)

Three soldiers take shelter in a shallow dugout during a Turkish shelling of Walker's Ridge. (Photo J. Campbell. National Library of Australia; nla.pic-an23297150)

This extraordinary photograph is believed to show two surviving unwounded officers of the 8th Light Horse after the charge at The Nek sitting with the regiment's new medical officer, Captain Frank Beamish (centre) in his dugout. Major Arthur Deeble is identified as being on the right, Captain Mervyn Higgins on the left. (Photo J. Campbell in collection Mr Greg Gillespie)

Manning the trenches on Russell's Top. Light horsemen wait warily, with their rifles bayonet-fixed. Water has been carried up to them in the containers and rum jars in the foreground. (Photo J. Campbell in collection Mr Greg Gillespie)

A lull in the fighting. Soldiers in the trenches take time out to write home or bring their diaries up to date. (Photo J. Campbell in National Library of Australia; nla.pic-an23297142)

the immediate command of Brigadier General Harry Chauvel, leader of the 1st Light Horse Brigade. At Monash Valley, the soldiers looked up to Quinn's Post, said Bean, 'as a man looks at a haunted house'.

Soon they would be involved in desperate hand-to-hand fighting with bombs and bayonets at a place where the Australians and Turks were only 15 metres apart. The men from the 10th called it 'a dirty spot, one of the dirtiest on Gallipoli', before they marched back down the valleys to Anzac Cove and around Ari Burnu to rejoin the Victorians and South Australians of the 3rd Brigade early in June.

But two days after arriving at the end of May, the most pervasive impression for the newly arrived light horsemen was the reek of decaying corpses. The prevailing wind at Anzac blows from the north-west, and the smell was worse for the Australians than the Turks.

'Our men gave the Turks hell on Tuesday night,' Sid Campbell noted, 'hundreds or thousands found in front of our trenches and stinking horribly. Am told there are several Australian bodies half exposed in trenches, some covered with lime.'

'The stench of decaying flesh threatened terrible calamity on both armies,' wrote Phillip Schuler. 'For two days the Turkish dead in thousands lay rotting in the sun, their swollen corpses in some places on our very parapets.'

After an informal truce in which stretcher-bearers brought in some wounded, the Turks sued for an armistice to bury the dead. Following initial negotiations, on the afternoon of 22 May, a Turkish officer on a handsome horse, uniform glittering with gold lace, and carrying a white flag of truce, rode down the beach towards Anzac Cove to complete the formalities. He was checked by barbed-wire entanglements, where he halted, dismounted and was blindfolded. Four Australian soldiers then stripped off their uniforms and, quite naked, placed the officer on a stretcher and carried him out into the sea and around the wire barrier to the other side, where he remounted his horse and was led to a dugout containing the Anzac leaders. It took two days to thrash out the terms, which were then written down and signed in duplicate by both army's leaders.

On 24 May – Empire Day, as it was being celebrated back home in Australia, with parades, Union Jacks and choruses of *God Save the King* – the armistice to bury the dead on Gallipoli began. It lasted from 7.30 am to 4.30 pm on a cold grey day with falling rain, both sides facing each other off nervously. The burial parties wore white armbands and were forbidden to use field glasses or look into opposition trenches. Rifles were to be collected and handed back to the respective armies to which they belonged (minus the rifle bolts).

In his little diary with the snapshot of the horse he had left behind in Egypt, Trooper William McGregor described what he saw:

> After stationing men with white flags midway between each other's trenches, both sides proceeded to collect their dead.
>
> The Turks buried all their side of the white flags and we did likewise on our side. It was the most awful sight anyone could witness. There must have been thousands to bury and we placed Turks and Australians in the same trenches and covered them in. Some had been lying there for three weeks and some for three days. In patches of about half an acre they were almost touching.

Near Quinn's Post, the 10th supplied a large burial party. The dead were piled up immediately in front of their trenches in the ratio of twelve to one. Nearer the enemy trenches, the proportion of Turkish to Australian corpses was even greater. Many were still kneeling, clutching rifles with fixed bayonets, frozen where they had sunk down after being shot during their wild charge on 19 May. 'Talk about dead – there were thousands lying in all positions,' Redge Mathers remembered. 'One sight I shall never forget – an Australian and a Turk dead together, the Australian's bayonet through the Turk's body and the Australian still clutching his rifle The smell of course was most awful.

Chaplain Green also wrote about the day:

> Jacko the Sniper was dealing out death and destruction until the last second. Indeed it seemed to me some two or three minutes after 7.30 when the cry 'stretcher bearer!' arose from a spot opposite my dugout. Two of those who responded to the cry were wounded – one I believe fatally.
>
> Then peace. What a relief! Burial parties, doctors, padres, scrambled up the slopes into No Man's Land, there to behold an unforgettable sight and to scent a stench indescribable. Dead in all stages of decomposition were strewn over the ground.
>
> In the valley opposite Quinn's and Courtney's, the Turkish dead lay as a battalion in open bivouac and one was assured that the accounts expecting the enemy loses on May 19 had not been exaggerated.
>
> But overall, the stench! It was in one's system for days. My job was the burying. Cotton wool in the nostrils and occasional nips of rum and water fortified me for the ordeal.
>
> There was a line of demarcation equidistant between our respective trenches. This was marked by guards, so that friend and foe stood face to face and neither could trespass.

All military equipment was stacked on the dividing line.

In most cases the only identification on bodies were their boots, and thus one distinguished Australian, New Zealander or Tommy.

The chaplain also described how he had buried a newly commissioned officer with three others in a communications trench 'interred with more earth and ceremony than was possible with some'. Many more were buried in mass graves, dug close to where they fell in No Man's Land. Burial places were marked out with stones or rough wooden crosses.

'I was pleased to get away from the scene and the stench early in the afternoon,' Green concluded, 'although the taste of the latter didn't leave one for days … It was a day of general visitation and everyone was very cheery and brave.'

Ernie Mack wrote of the sector in front of the trenches on Russell's Top: 'It was estimated that the AIF buried over 4,000 Turks, so you can get some idea of the slaughter on one piece of cultivated ground 80 yards by 60 yards. Just over 600 Turks' bodies were found. These were just buried in one big pit.'

The usually upbeat Tom Austin was understandably reserved when writing his account:

> There were so many in certain places that they were just pushed over the cliff face and loose earth broken down over them. Wherever possible services were read over our own dead. Many men whose fate up to now had been uncertain were found, their wounds undressed, in the shrubbery where they had died fighting to the end.
>
> In some cases our boys and the Turks were found close together, evidence of the bitter struggle each little party had fought out.
>
> One wounded Turk had been lying out for nine days. He was brought in but died almost immediately. It seemed pitiful that a man should thus die after giving his all for his home and country.

The chance to see the enemy at close quarters proved irresistible. As George Fish's diary entry shows:

> After the major had finished with the patients I went up to the trenches to have a look at the burials. I had the experience of being right out in the battlefield – was looking through the glasses at their lines when a Turk spotted me and called out to his officer. I had to push the glasses away lively or I would have soon been picked off by a sniper.

Trooper Dave McGarvie went up for a look, too, but with a different view in mind. He wanted to get an exact lie of the land for when he took up sniping. He noted in his pocket diary the range of the nearest enemy trench: 50 yards.

The next day, 25 May, the 8th Light Horse Regiment set out in strength with full packs and ammunition pouches for their first two weeks in the trenches, on Sector 4 of Walker's Ridge, relieving the Wellington Mounted Rifles. The pattern for each regiment would become two weeks on the firing line and then two weeks back down in rest areas near the beach.

'Rest' was really a misnomer. On Gallipoli everybody was within range of the Turks. The men were under fire constantly – and there was no real rest. If they were not up on the firing line they would be put to work enlarging trenches or helping miners tunnel under the enemy's positions.

Being in the trenches meant periods of higher anxiety and sleepless nights manning the firing line, interspersed with the constant wearying climbs down and up Walker's Ridge when on fatigue duties carrying water and supplies.

The men left their beach bivouac at noon for their first climb up the ridge, which would take some of them nearly two hours to complete, slipping and sliding with their heavy packs, grabbing at exposed grey roots for leverage, and stopping frequently for rest. They were halfway up the ridge and sitting down taking a rest break when there was a huge explosion out to sea. An enormous column of water spurted into the air. A torpedo from a German submarine, *U-21*, had hit HMS *Triumph*, a twelve-year-old battleship of 11,800 tons.

'Our view was as from the gallery of a picture theatre,' wrote Tom Austin.

'The saddest sight I ever want to see,' Ernie Mack lamented.

The huge battleship took on an immediate list and for eight minutes remained at an angle of 45 degrees as her crew leapt or were spilled into the sea. 'Destroyers, tugs, trawlers, dashed to her assistance,' wrote Sid Campbell, 'the list gradually increased and in minutes she heeled right over ... then her port side which had till then been above the water gradually sank and the stern and propellers tilted up – and down she went.'

'I saw a magnificent sight and that was the number of destroyers racing up to the rescue,' Ernie continued, 'seven of them came from Cape Helles way, they just looked like splashes of foam travelling over the sea and out of the foam belched forth a great black line of smoke, each boat was going over 35 miles per hour.'

The crews on neighbouring ships stood to attention as HMS *Triumph* went down. The destroyers saved most of the crew, although 71 men were lost.

Two days later, *U-21* struck again, sinking the battleship HMS *Majestic*. When the light horsemen heard the news, said Tom Austin, 'most of us began to realise we were up against it, both on land or sea'. There was a small consolation prize. Later on, butts of wine from the *Triumph*'s cellar were washed up, shared around, and Tom's troop 'enjoyed a little beano'.

There was initial excitement as the men of the 8th took their positions in the trenches, heads below the sandbags on the parapets as a cold rain began to fall. Here they were, at last, on the front line. 'Baptism of fire. No man to sleep. Bayonets fixed,' McGarvie recorded in his diary.

Tom Austin's observations:

> On the 26 May we were in it up to our necks, everyone was most anxious to do some shooting. Throughout the whole day each loophole in the sandbags was manned by men as keen to secure a Turk as a schoolboy armed with a shanghai is to shoot a sparrow.
>
> Whether any enemy did get shot it is difficult to say, as they made no complaints to us, but if their casualties were half as numerous as our shooters claimed, they must have suffered severely.
>
> One Sergeant was extra keen and he used to discover and kill Turks where not another man could see any sign of one either before or after he was shot. The notches to his credit would have filled up three or four gunstocks inside a week. The rumour was started that the Turks were offering five hundred pounds for him, dead or alive, and his keenness seemed to fade right away.
>
> As the days wore on, we soon learned to conserve our ammunition until it was wanted, and after suffering seven casualties our heads were kept a little lower below the parapet.

One of those wounded on 26 May was the Macks' friend Sergeant Roger Palmer, the former captain of the King's College Taunton cricket team. Another was Aub Callow's friend, Signaller Edgar Kent, with a shrapnel wound to his shoulder that penetrated a lung. Roger Palmer was luckier; he had received a shrapnel pellet to the hip. Both were evacuated to hospital back in Heliopolis.

But while Edgar Kent was repatriated back to Australia (there to take up a career as purser on interstate steamers), Roger Palmer had different ideas, as Stan Mack outlined later in a letter home:

It was shrapnel that brought poor old Roger Palmer down first time we were in the trenches. He heard the gun go off and made a dive for a small dugout but fat Q.M. Fry [Lieutenant Hubert Fry, quartermaster and a Melbourne merchant] got in before him ... Roger did not get the bullet taken out of him but was quite all right and did not affect him in any way. For all that, he was supposed to go to England to have it removed.

He was pining to get back to the front so one day ... he stowed away on a train which was taking some of the 8th reinforcements and walked back into the middle of A Troop while they were having breakfast.

You can imagine the cheer ... but he will be getting hurt for sure, he's so game – but not careless like some others who have been wounded and killed.

Sid Campbell had hurried to tend the first wounded. He had been sent for at 5.30 am, when a bullet had shattered after piercing a sandbag and injuring the men nearby. Trooper Hugh Wright, who had studied as a dentist, had received scratches to his head; Trooper Bill Moodie, a horsebreaker and Boer War veteran, had been hit in the ear and lower temple, which had 'bled furiously'.

Four more men were wounded the next day by shrapnel, fired from a gun 5 or more kilometres away, which concentrated its fire on Anzac Cove, but occasionally shortened its range to fire a few shells over Walker's Ridge.

The increasing strain soon took its toll. Within a few days a trooper from Benalla had to be sent away after suffering from a nervous breakdown. At first the men laughed, then pitied him as he began constantly bobbing his head up and down like a nervous fowl as he dodged imaginary shells and bullets.

As the casualties grew, Sid Campbell abandoned his long descriptive diary entries and began another diary, a red-covered book. The entries were no longer in a flowing hand but in tight urgent notes and soon the words would be as small as sutures.

There was a shortage of writing paper, too, and little time when on guard in the trenches to write long diary entries, or letters home (which were still scanned by an officer acting as censor). Yet the men managed to keep records and a sense of humour. There was always big Tom Austin, for example:

We used to manage a little diversion each night towards about 8 pm. Word would be passed along the trench to do five minutes rapid fire, and this – with a few cheers and shots thrown in – seemed to put the fear of death right up the Johnny Turk.

Every rifle and machine gun in his trenches would open up with an awful din and this fire would be kept going for a full 20 minutes.

He never made the slightest attempt at hitting us, as we could often see his rifles pointed straight up to the sky and being fired.

We had no casualties through this and besides giving us a good laugh it must have cost them an enormous amount of ammunition … it took them many weeks before they desisted from replying to our demonstrations.

'We were only a few yards from their trenches,' Redge Mathers told his sister, 'it was sudden death to show our heads and they kept firing at our shovels as we made trenches. When they missed we used to wave a miss like on the rifle range. One of the 9th out of A Squadron had his shovel hit and was rather severely injured by the splinters.'

Dave McGarvie had spent a miserable cold first night in the trenches before making two trips down and back up Walker's Ridge carrying water. His diary entries for the next three days are typically phlegmatic:

Thursday 27th: Had good sleep last night. Stood to arms at 3 am. Had an easy day on firing line. Detailed for 24 hours sniping duty. Got ready, drew rations then Colonel decided not to send out any snipers.

Friday 28th: Stood to arms 3 am. No sleep all night. Went down, brought up a bundle of wood, had swim. Slept for two hours then had to go on fatigue carrying water. Stood to arms 7.30, on guard 9 to 10.

Saturday 29th: To arms 3 am. Sniping … fired 16 shots … went into firing line again 9 am. Heavy firing from 3.30 to 8.30pm … very hot in trenches. Jim Cameron wounded with shrapnel … only one hour sleep … firing commenced to keep down enemy fire.

On the 28th, Redge Mathers was also busy with the dangerous task of collecting water:

There is now a well with fairly good water about a quarter of a mile from the beach but the Turks have spotted it and have snipers on the watch and it is rather risky going for water but one must take risks. Have to carry rifle and ammunition when going there and hand name and regiment in to a sentry before leaving. I went to the well this evening but was disappointed it being dry. Also four men shot there during day.

147

Even the beach itself was something of a danger zone, according to George Rayment:

> During our leisure hours our favourite and only pastime was swimming. The first week we were ashore we were able to use the beach at the foot of Light Horse Gully but one morning a member of the Brigade staff and an interpreter were having a wash at the water's edge when a sniper commenced firing at them. Thinking they were spent bullets they took no notice until the interpreter got one through the shoulder, but a few minutes later another man was shot through the neck, death being almost instantaneous. The sniper was located in what was known later as Sniper's Nest about fifteen hundred yards from Light Horse Gully and he used to wait until a man was at a certain spot before firing. Until about the middle of August it was courting death to walk along this part of the beach in the day time.

The true turning point for the 8th was 29 May. Suddenly the full horror of war burst among the young men who had ridden through Melbourne so full of such idealism and hope only three months before, riding off through the cheering crowds to do their duty with honour and glory for King and Country. Now they were frightened foot soldiers, standing in squalid trenches stinking of blood and death on a hilltop at the other end of the world, being killed and maimed and wounded.

Early in the morning the Turks blew up part of Quinn's Post with mines and began an attack, which was repulsed after heavy fighting by the 10th Light Horse. The 10th launched a counterattack the next day and of the 46 men who took part, three were killed and only fourteen came out unscathed.

The 8th gave supporting fire from Walker's Ridge, with trench mortars and an Indian artillery piece that was sited in their trenches. Jack Mack was working his Japanese mortar and as George Fish observed: 'The Turks are very afraid of the Japanese mortar … after one goes off you can hear a terrible squealing amongst them, then a fusillade of bullets.'

The mortars attracted the fire of two Turkish guns, which plastered the 8th's and 9th's trenches with high-explosive shells.

'The gun that fires and shells us so often we have christened Tucker Time Liz for she only seems to fire at meal times,' Redge Mathers would write. 'Another gun which fires from a different position and we know nothing about it until the shells burst is called Screech Annie. This gun gives no warning whatever.'

148

Sid Campbell's tiny, frantic notes tell the story of that day: 'We have had hell to do this morning. Furious rifle and shrapnel fire started about 3 am. Was called up to attend wounded men in our part and thence to 9LH trenches to see man with both feet shot away and left arm broken and right hand peppered ... grenade.' He then scrawled, in capitals, 'VERY FRIGHTENED', before going on:

> Another grenade came over and the man I left in charge of the wounded case was himself wounded later by bomb.
>
> A few yards up trench man dying with bullet through head – large exit wound.
>
> Some yards further back a similar but worse case in our C Squadron. Dead. Coe dropped dead on blanket.

Trooper Charles Coe, a 27-year-old engine driver from Nagambie, had been shot dead while firing over the sandbag. He was the 8th Light Horse's first battle fatality. The doctor continued:

> All [the] time bullets and shells screeching. Had breakfast about 5 am and relieved between 6 and 8. Kept busy helping Follit with 9LH wounded – three killed in all.
>
> Turks blew up, attacked, bombed and took Quinn's Post but lost it again when we counter-attacked.
>
> Saw my chaps shoot dead 8 of the Turks attempting to regain the trench.
>
> Now 8 am. Hope no more today.
>
> 7 pm: We lost 1 dead 3 wounded; 9LH 4 killed 11 wounded. I had a look at Quinn's from top of sap across gully. Could see pile of dead which had been collected from the trench.
>
> Trench badly torn about sandbags scattered. Turkish trenches opposite knocked about. Our artillery gave them a doing. Turks lost heavily.

The doctor's work was not finished, though:

> Sunday 30th: Called at 5.20 to Leonard killed by bullet through heart while going for water just below here. Must have been bullet from engagement which has been proceeding all morning near No.3 Outpost. [Trooper John Leonard was a 28-year-old labourer from Brunswick in inner Melbourne.]
>
> The CO and I watched for some time until too many bullets came our way.

Machine guns putting in a burst now and again and Gentle Annie sending along a few. Our own artillery kicking up a hell of a row.

Just saw 9LH Sgt shot through head. Lt McWilliams (9LH Duntroon boy) shot today thro' head and died a few hours later. Very sad business.

May 31: V. quiet day, the quietest day we have had. No.3 proved too hot and our men retired during night bringing their wounded. It was a bad position, under fire from almost all sides.

Turks in possession when we woke this morning. They tossed a naked body out of the trench, evidently have taken uniform. They have had a bad time today from our boys' howitzers and mountain guns ...

Redge Mathers described the aftermath:

On day breaking we could plainly see three bodies stripped of all clothing and thrown over the cliffs (ours) by the Turks, while attacking they have a most mournful wail (Allah Allah) reminded me of hounds baying.

Tonight on duty in communications trenches – had to call our troop out three times from support trenches to support fire trenches.

His diary entry for the following day: 'Tuesday 1st June: My 24th birthday today and I can tell you I never expected to see it.'

Trooper Arthur Gay, a driver from South Melbourne, had his life saved on 1 June by Sid Campbell. Lieutenant Charles Carthew helped the doctor with the wounded man, who later wrote a letter to Carthew's family describing his gratitude for what had happened:

On the morning of June 1st the day I was shot our troop were relieved in the firing line after 48 hours work to take our turn in the rest trenches just behind the firing line for 48 hours – that is the way we used to work, 2 days in and 2 days out, the ones who are out doing the fatigue work for the others.

Well, in the afternoon after we had finished work I thought that I would take a rifle and go into the first trench to see if I could get a sniper who had been troubling us a bit so I took up a position at a new loophole where I could enfilade a small section of trench running up the hill from the place where the snipers used to work from.

I watched there from 12 o'clock until about 4 pm when I saw the top of a man's hat start to move towards this piece I was watching and as soon as his head appeared I got in one shot which missed, I think, for he ran – but stopped him with a second.

It was getting late then and the sun getting behind us throwing my shadow across the loophole.

I saw the danger of it but thought I would just take one more look. (I knew they had located me, as you only had to pass your hat over the loophole to draw their fire.)

Well, I had just moved sideways over the loophole until I could see out with one eye only, but that was enough – for then two or three bullets came through the hole and got me in the top lip just under the nose and the bullet striking the top teeth broke up and travelled along the jaw and down the throat after shattering the lower jaw and cutting two arteries in my throat, so you can see what a narrow escape I had. Captain Campbell, our Medical Officer saved my life ... poor Charlie helped to carry me out on a blanket and when I felt myself going from loss of blood and the morphia that they had injected into my arm I thought I was dying. I shook hands with him and poor old man he nearly broke down – I think it hurt him more than it hurt me – he couldn't stand to see anyone suffering, even the Turks.

Sid Campbell made no mention of saving Trooper Gay in his entry for 1 June. Instead he noted:

Nearly 8 months since my military career started. Another quiet day.

Had a swim. Interesting picture for *Melbourne Punch* for our families. Lt. Col. White and his Medical Officer on beach at Anzac Cove, naked, and carefully examining their underclothing for unwelcome intruders. A background of Australians and New Zealanders engaged in the same occupation.

The lice had arrived on Gallipoli, along with the first of the other summer insects. The men called the lice 'the Scots Greys' or 'Greybacks'. They began breeding in the warm, fetid trenches, scuttled across bare skin, biting and laying their eggs in the seams of the filthy, sweaty uniforms. The only thing to do was strip off whenever possible, burn the eggs and exposed insects with lighted cigarette butts, and go for a swim.

George Rayment described the pests:

Greybacks, a mammoth species of louse, a fully grown one being about three sixteenths of an inch long and in the grey army shirts and singlets they almost defy detection. The only thing that gave us a bit of comfort was that the officers were as badly off as we were for the

151

louse is no respecter of persons and very few officers or men were fortunate enough to be on the Peninsula any length of time without carrying 'live stock' with them. After a tiresome night in the trenches and when sleep appeared to be the best thing on earth, one would lie down but ere dozing off a multitude – or so it seemed – of lice commenced an attack, and after advancing and retreating several times they would 'dig in'.

The only way to get any relief was to go through one's clothing every day and never trust to luck as they are a thousand times worse than rabbits at breeding.

Sometimes we would be free – or thought we were – but whilst down having a swim we had put our clothes where someone had previously been 'lousing' or 'depopulating' himself and then the merry hunt would begin again. Later on we were given small bags of sulphur as a preventative but the species bred on the Turk takes more than sulphur to make them sick.

Chaplain Green told the story of two men engaged in the search for lice:

Snowy: 'I don't reckon this does any good, yer know, Ginger – just picking 'em out. They only breed again.'

Ginger: 'Of course it does no good. What yer want to do is turn yer shirt inside out immediately yer feel the first nip. Yer see, reverse yer shirt every time yer get the first bite from one of the blighters.'

Snowy: 'What the — does that do? It doesn't kill 'em, does it?'

Ginger: 'No – but it makes 'em damned tired of marching. It breaks their 'earts!'

From Friday 4 June the weary troopers were relieved from the forward trenches and began the long climb down Walker's Ridge. But the guns could still reach them. Especially the one they called Anafarta Annie. The Reverend Ernest Northcroft Merrington, a Presbyterian, was senior chaplain with the 1st Light Horse.

On Sunday 6 June he obtained permission from his commanding officer to hold the first church service at Anzac – provided there was no singing to attract the enemy's attention. With three other chaplains he did the rounds to attract a congregation, and at 9 am 'a goodly crowd of Australians and New Zealanders gathered', although 'some dead bodies lying by the side of the road had to be removed to the mortuary before the service began'.

The altar was made from two Red Cross wooden boxes borrowed from a nearby New Zealand dressing station and placed one on top of the other.

All four chaplains – two Australians and two New Zealanders – took part in the service, with Chaplain Merrington delivering a homily based on Galatians, chapter 5, verse 1: 'Stand fast therefore in the liberty wherewith Christ has made us free.'

He wrote in his journal afterwards:

> A communion service followed and 40 of our lads knelt in the blood stained track from the trenches and received in their rough hewed hands the elements which set forth the Supreme Sacrifice for the sinful world and the food of the human spirit in the battle of life.
>
> The service passed without any mishap although the snipers' bullets were singing over our heads and we had the clatter and din of war as our choral accompaniment … we were all refreshed and strengthened by the touch of God's hand and felt more ready to face the duties and dangers of the uncertain future.

But the Turks managed to hurt the congregation as it returned to its dugouts after another service a week later. Anafarta Annie roared and two men were injured. By the time the men of the 8th had returned up the hill to occupy the fire trenches again, on the weekend of the 20th, they had suffered another 25 casualties from Annie, with Tom Austin noting that 'she was a source of great annoyance all round – rarely a day going by but what she obtained 40 to 50 victims on the beaches and on the tracks leading thereto'.

With the arrival of the summer insects, so the springtime wildflowers had faded away. Only the dry wild thyme was useful, for seasoning the bully beef rissoles and stews. Gallipoli was becoming a shimmering dusty brown, with a glare that made the men's eyes squint almost shut.

There was no shade, save for the rough roofs of bagging, blankets and scrap iron over the shallow dugouts, and as the temperature began to rise, the sun beat down on a human warren where pestilence would begin to suppurate, then spread rapidly with the droning of the breeding blowflies.

Chapter 12

Hell on the Heights

Now began two months of terrible physical and mental attrition among the light horsemen on Gallipoli. They were now stuck, becoming increasingly ill and traumatised, growing gaunt and thin, in a noisome, burning hell on earth. It stank like the open grave that it was. A place where there was no real rest and where the strain caused by the ever-present threat of being killed or wounded, by shrapnel or a sniper's bullet, was compounded by the exhaustion caused by diet, disease and overwork.

As the full force of summer turned the peninsula into a shimmering, dusty furnace, millions upon millions of flies began to breed. They bred in the dung of the transport mules and horses crowded into narrow gullies; they bred in the human faeces dumped wherever men squatted; they bred in the rubbish tossed over trench walls; they bred in the fat of bacon rinds and the crusty slop from bully beef cans and in the abandoned homemade stews and rissoles flavoured with wild thyme that were thrown aside because they were so bad.

Above all, the flies bred in corpses. Maggots made the dead heave and move again. The brief May armistice had seen thousands of bodies covered with a thin layer of dirt, but many more human parts had taken their place in No Man's Land. And as men dug fresh tunnels and saps, they uncovered more rotting remains, more food for the already bloated blowflies, as the 8th's Trooper Tom Austin confirmed: 'It was quite a common sight to pass through portions of the saps and see a pair of boots, the feet of a dead man, or his hands, or else some boards passing through the sides and holding the bodies in place.'

Back in Australia the men's loved ones had little idea of what the conditions were really like. Letters sent home were censored and, in any case, the troopers tended often to make light or gloss over what they were enduring. One example is this letter from Trooper John McGlade, of the 8th, an architect who had been born in Belfast:

The tucker bill is simple. Bully beef and biscuits and jam, with a little rice once a week. The bully is so salt you could drink the sea dry.

Then to add to the comfort of our meals we have FLIES. Little flies, big flies, young flies, old flies and dead flies. Keep waving a biscuit and jam with one hand and with the other keep rescuing flies who are trying to drown themselves in the tea.

Suddenly you make a dive at the biscuit and jam with your mouth and, all going well and you happen to be quick enough, you may not get more than two or three flies in a mouthfull.

Of course you must remember that these flies have very likely been taking a little gentle exercise over the body of a Turk who has been laying outside the trenches about two months.

Correspondents' reports on conditions on Gallipoli were also censored, and otherwise delayed. This account, by a special correspondent for a British press agency, managed to sneak into *The Age* – but only on 17 September, by which time it was early autumn on Gallipoli, after the worst of the fly plague:

Some of us came here fully prepared against the mosquito, only to find there is no trace of him. But the fly abounds in millions. From dawn to sunset he comes to torment your life. He swoops down in brigades upon your meals and altogether obliterates your plate. You make an effort to proceed with your meal by eating with one hand and driving the hordes away with the other. They completely predominate. How the men manage to remain of good temper I fail to understand.

They came to my table at lunch when I was hungry and thirsty after many hours in the sun. But they would not let me proceed with my meal. Finally I gave over my dishes and moved away with some light beer. The dishes were soon one living mass of flies; the rest followed me to take my beer. In the firing line where the dead and dying cannot be brought in till night the sky is black with these winged pests.

As usual with Gallipoli, efforts to try to fight the fly menace were bungled. These efforts were described by Chaplain George Green, with his usual good humour:

The medics who knew that they couldn't be killed thought at least the evil might be mitigated by a supply of chloride of lime and paraffin to sprinkle on the infected ground. They therefore requisitioned for these articles, but were refused!

155

Some Surgeon-General on headquarters staff at Imbros refused sanction in a letter which, for infantile futility, was the climax of red-tape stupidity! The document should be preserved to explain the sort of things that make some of us lose faith in the Army regime. Here was a man, away from the conditions, having the final word against experts on the spot.

And he recommended 'tangle foot papers and string' to combat the evil!

Fact! – Why, if the whole of Anzac was plastered and festooned with them, there would have been enough uncaptured flies left to blacken Imbros!

With the flies came the spread of disease. First came diarrhoea, then amoebic dysentery, then the disease they called 'the enteric' – typhoid fever. Jaundice was also prevalent. Respiratory complaints that were lumped together under 'pneumonia' were another common ailment.

In *Gallipoli: The Medical War*, Dr Michael Tyquin wrote that there was extraordinary ignorance as to the cause of disease. One senior British medical officer, for instance, noted, 'A good deal of diarrhoea among Australians – possibly due to sea bathing.' While a field ambulance diary suggested the outbreak was 'possibly due to the wholemeal biscuits and large supply of onions & limited vegetables'.

Incredibly, the first improvised fly-proof latrine was not built until August. For the rest of the time men strained in agony, perched on rough boards over foul holes in the ground as the flies crawled and hummed overall. Unpredictable bursts of shrapnel overhead added to the men's misery. Of course, they were literally sitting ducks for snipers.

From June 1915 the number of men reporting sick kept on doubling. Many of those who stayed on duty were almost as sick as those sent away. In July the number of men evacuated from Anzac averaged 1,400 a week – three-quarters of them ill, not wounded. The tall, fit young men who had ridden away to war were now becoming exhausted shadows, doubled up with internal pain due to dysentery, lying down utterly exhausted every few hundred metres they went and with many troopers covered by masses of septic sores.

On 5 July, Captain Sid Campbell, the 8th Light Horse's medical officer, would report his regiment casualty list to date as: '108 sick (33 returned); 73 wounded (5 returned), 21 deaths. Shortage is 163.'

Enteric fever was given its name because a key feature of the disease is enterocolitis – inflammation of the colon. The small, densely populated Anzac area of Gallipoli, swarming with flies and no sanitation, was an ideal incubation chamber. Early symptoms included fever, sickness and abdominal pain. With no modern-day agents like antibiotics or intravenous fluids to treat the disease, the troopers could easily slip into delirium and unconsciousness. Complications could include psychosis.

But there was another effect of the enteric, which may well have had a bearing on decision making when exhausted officers and troopers were considered fit enough to return to the firing line. For while the incubation period for enteric fever was one to three weeks, the effects of the illness could last for six, and could easily re-occur.

Medical advice today suggests that the soldiers' ability to make basic day-to-day decisions would have been severely affected, and that their situational awareness would have been poor, dramatically increasing the likelihood of their straying into a sniper's sights or into other deadly situations. In other words, *unreality* had set in, and a lot of the mistakes that were to be made later might well have been due to decisions made by officers and men still ill with the disease.

From the CO down, the 3rd Light Horse Brigade soon fell victim to exhaustion, disease and stress. Colonel White, commanding officer of the 8th Regiment, soon admitted to a weariness of life on the front:

> Everything is so unsettled, am always expecting things to happen; this sort of thing gets on one's nerves. I do all night work and am writing this at 6 am. Am just off to bed. Dear little wife and kiddie I seem so very far away from you all; I do not want to speak about the war; it's horrible. If I let myself think too much about it my nerves would go. Have seen things and done things I want to forget.
>
> We get very well fed but water is very short. 1 lb biscuits, 1 lb bully beef, 3 oz bacon, and 2 oz cheese a day. We are all getting a bit thin. Thank goodness when it's over.

White's young officers like Ted Henty tried to keep the men's spirits up with a cheery word and pitching in with a spade to fill sandbags for the trench defences. But Ted, too, would go down with gastroenteritis so severe that he was evacuated back to a general hospital in Egypt for treatment. (He would return to Gallipoli two weeks later.)

The older men just couldn't handle the conditions. Major James O'Brien, the Irish veteran and second-in-command of the 8th, was among the first to go. ('Have arranged for Major O'Brien to go back, he is cracking up,' Colonel White noted on 4 June.)

His place was taken by a popular and experienced officer, Major Ernest Gregory, the commander of 'A' Squadron, who was nearing his thirty-third birthday. Gregory was a Geelong College boy from the town of Murchison in Victoria, well known to the Mack brothers. The town had presented him with a sword and binoculars in a public farewell before he sailed. A keen soldier, he had joined the Victorian Mounted Rifles before he'd turned eighteen and was later selected for military training in India, where he served on the North West Frontier and the Khyber Pass with illustrious units like the 13th Hussars, the 18th, 19th and 21st Lancers, and the Bengal Native Cavalry.

The brigade major, Lieutenant Colonel Jack Antill, had already taken a shine to Gregory, complimenting him on the way he took charge of the embarkation of the 8th at Alexandria and the regiment's disembarkation at Anzac Cove. Gregory seemed marked for further promotion.

Meanwhile, Brigadier Hughes, who was 57 and stout, must have found the constant climbing of Walker's Ridge in the heat very difficult indeed. The cold nights got to him, too, and he was evacuated in June, suffering from pneumonia; he spent some time back in Egypt and much of the month on a hospital ship. Hughes returned but soon became ill again and would be away for another week in July. When he came back again, Colonel White noted: 'Poor old chap is sticking it out well – do not know how he keeps going up hill and down dale.'

Brigade Major Jack Antill fitted easily into the role of acting commanding officer of the brigade when Hughes was away. There was no need for the Bullant to white-ant Hughes for command – the old peacetime general was self-destructing anyhow.

The greater pity was that, rather than being replaced and repatriated by higher command, Hughes was allowed to return – in time to make critical decisions involving the lives of most of his men. In 1924 Lieutenant Wilfred Robinson, one of the survivors of The Nek, would write to official historian C.E.W. Bean and give this damning summation of Hughes and the top command of the 3rd Light Horse Brigade on Gallipoli:

> In time of war as in peace, our Brigadier's idea of soldiering was to salute smartly, roll a great coat correctly and note the march discipline. Our B.M. [Antill] talked volubly about getting over 'with rifle butts and pick handles' and chasing the other fellow out. Our acting staff captain, Billy Kent Hughes was a mere boy, very good-natured and thoroughly inexperienced. Like the Brigadier, he left most things to the Brigade Major, who largely trusted to luck and countermanded his own orders.

Similarly, Trooper David McGarvie, the sharpshooting dairy farmer with the cleft palate, and another one of the survivors of The Nek, would tell his grand-daughter: 'Our Brigadier K.G. Hughes was an old man … he was too old for the job.'

Instead of being retired, Hughes' promotion to brigadier general would come through on 25 July, with White remarking: 'I am very pleased. He has done a lot of work and it's wonderful how the old chap can get round the way he does.'

Even without the trench warfare and illness, there was no respite when the men came down from the front line. Ernie Mack wrote of the 8th's first 'rest break':

> On June 7 we came down the hill into rest trenches where we did fatigue duties till the 20th. These fatigues are the worst things you ever heard of and are simply caused by lack of men. Anybody would think that when we did a fortnight in the firing line we would be entitled to a spell. But no, as soon as we came down parties had to go all over the place day & night digging trenches & lanes & roads.
>
> It was absolute murder for the men & they had to go without sleep during night after night & were told they could sleep during the day. Well you have only to go to the Peninsula during the summer and try and sleep in the daytime, it is pretty well impossible as the heat is terrific and the flies are there by the million.
>
> Well, it did not take long before men were being sent away sick and until now the wastage in sick alone among the troops at Anzac is awful.
>
> Another thing while you are in these so called rest camps which are on the side of the hill just behind the firing line, you are always subject to shell fire & during the quiet time fifty per cent more men are killed or wounded in these camps than there are in the firing line.

Redge Mathers had a similar tale:

> I have been continually sapping working day and night & feel most utterly worn out and have a very bad cold. Have sapped through dead Turks, round them and the stink of them is awful.
>
> Friday 18th: … spent 24 hours guarding prisoners and had to shift everything about dinner time – Tucker Time Liz let loose killing 8 or 9 men of our Regt, 2 Indians and wounding several and 20 mules killed and many more wounded and several of them had to be killed.

The next day Redge left for the firing line again with the 9th Light Horse. The writing in his diary grows noticeably weaker:

Saturday 19th: Left here for firing line again. The heat is now becoming intense and the flies are awful and much sickness is breaking out. Dysentery is the main trouble but fever cannot be far off now.

Sunday 20th: Our section on guard of a gully for the night – cannot see two yards in front for thick scrub.

Monday 21st: Too crook for anything today had a day off.

Tuesday 22nd: Went into fire trench again today. Our section had to guard a secret sap; it is only 3 ft deep and only 15 & 20 yards from Turks trench. Dead men all round & the smell is something damnable. Some were supposed to be buried, but the way the Turks bury their dead is this. They put enough dirt on the overcoat to stop the wind from blowing the coat off.

Wednesday 23rd: Went to support trenches again and we got particular hell for nearly 2 hours, shells coming, dirt, stumps, sandbags, kitbags and things of all description flying everywhere. Four of our men killed and several wounded. Swagger Long was knocked over by the explosion of a shell and had some shell splinters in his back. One shell landed on a grave and unearthed two 3 weeks old corpses and the smell was most awful.

Thursday 24th: Feeling very ill today and was put off duty again. Turkish guns shelled the beach considerably all day, one shell accounted for 7 wounded & 2 killed, in all 52 in an hour.

Friday 25th: Turks artillery still very active stirring us up a treat and put one of our mountain battery guns out of action.

Saturday 26th: Had to go into fire trench again and take on the secret sap by the dead Turks again & had to wear my respirator the smell was terrible.

Sunday 27th: Early this morning Turks artillery very active & for about an hour we got particular hell. How two sections of us escaped is a miracle. One shell landing in the trench behind us (not 2 ft from one man) and exploding, we were only smothered in dirt not one being hurt.

Monday 28th: Too ill to do anything. Put off duty. Had my 7-week beard shaved off, it was not a bad one at all.

Tuesday 29th: Went to Dr this morning and he sent me to hospital. At night went down to hospital base at beach and found I had bronchitis and pneumonia.

On 1 July, Trooper Redge Mathers left Anzac Cove. By way of hospitals on Lemnos and Malta, and then in Britain, the bookkeeper from Cohuna would be coming home. The last line of his letter to his sister, Effie, reads: 'I feel most awful grateful to be alive and cannot now tell how I was never hit.'

Sid Campbell, the 8th's doctor, was also writing to his sister, from the regiment's headquarters, five officers' dugouts in a row fronting onto a levelled terrace, carved 150 feet up the side of Walker's Ridge and facing out to sea. More informative than his short diary entries at the time, there was no hiding the obvious war-weariness in his words to Hetty:

We have seen enough and lost enough to realise what a horrible, disgraceful thing war is.

Sometimes when one sees some fine young chap with a ghastly wound one wonders whether any quarrel between any nations is worth bothering over to the extent of killing even one human being.

The majority of wounds are of course slight but when one sees splendid fellows killed or disfigured and maimed for life it is hard to see how any good can come out of such things.

I saw some Turkish prisoners the other day, bathing in the sea, there were 5 of them, only one appeared young, the others middle aged, and some showing grey hairs, or getting bald. They were almost as white as us, certainly not so dark as Italians and looking inoffensive ordinary family men whom one could easily imagine sitting in an office or behind a counter or running a farm and bringing up a family in a respectable manner.

And here are the two armies busily engaged in shooting each other as fast as possible, and inflicting horrible disfiguring injuries on each other with shells and bombs and mines.

What awful foolishness it seems, and the individual only counts as an instrument to direct and pull the trigger of a rifle or some other machines.

Of course, although I have been writing this, our thoughts don't wander in that direction often. Most of the time one hardly gives a thought to the horrors of war and one is delighted to hear of Turkish losses and good work by our gunners in downing a few of them, [we jump] up and enjoy watching through a periscope to see whether a man using a rifle alongside in the trenches is potting anyone in the opposite trench. There is the added excitement of keeping your head down behind the sandbag so that you do not get potted yourself ...

The only real moment of relief for the men was with the issue of the rum ration from the big stoneware jars that they lugged up the slopes. Occasionally there was also a scene of total unreality.

Friday 18 June marked the centennial of Napoleon's defeat by the Duke of Wellington at the Battle of Waterloo. That night in the dugouts of Gallipoli, mugs were solemnly raised in a toast, as Colonel White recorded: 'There was an issue of rum in honour of Waterloo day. It was good, all hands do enjoy the rum issue.'

On 20 June the troopers of the 8th made the long climb back up Walker's Ridge for their next tour of duty in the firing line. This time they took over trenches a little to the left of their old position, directly facing the enemy trenches on the hillock called Baby 700 across The Nek. 'The shellfire and bombing had greatly increased on the part of the enemy since our last turn,' Tom Austin noted, 'and it was very evident that this portion of the line had been greatly strengthened by them since the armistice.'

With any spare time they had, the boys would more often than not write to their families back in Australia. Sid Campbell, in his letter to his elder sister, Hetty, told her that he was writing on a beautiful morning, looking out to sea:

> It is all very beautiful. There are no big guns firing this morning and the rifle fire is very quiet. You would hardly know there is a war on. The C.O. is sitting a foot or two away smoking; the adjutant is washing his clothes.
>
> It makes one think of the good old times we used to have at home when we were kids and how one longs for home and all of us together. There is plenty of time to sit and think here and naturally my thoughts turn to Maretimo and all sorts of simple things crop up in my mind and make me wish for it all to come back again.
>
> It is funny they are nearly always the things that used to happen when we were young before we went to boarding school, mostly of the winter time, the water on the flat, the drains, horses getting bogged, stilts, tramping along the roads, mushrooming the 78 acres on Sunday afternoons, waiting at the gate for Father, school, bread and dripping in the afternoons, fried fish in breadcrumbs (oh how

my mouth waters) on a winter's evening in the cosy breakfast room, the blustering wet days, the Sou' Easters, the Friday afternoon's trip to town – behind old Blossom with Mother driving – the driving and waiting on visiting days, or collecting for the P.M.U. And so on ...

Mother in her old hat and sunbonnets, pottering round with the fowls and pigs and vegetables. You will be amused at my using up so much space on this sort of thing, but there is no one to talk about these things over here and at this distance, home and everything connected with it has a tremendous grip on one.

I feel – and I know the others do also – that when I get home to Australia again I won't budge, and lead the quietest of lives (a farmer's life for preference with frosty mornings and milking and ploughing will suit me).

Just think of milk and cream and homemade butter and toast and scones – you know we often talk of food like this when we are eating our hard biscuits and cheese and bully beef and tea without milk ...

We are fed extraordinarily well all the same. Parker, our cook, has been excelling himself lately as we have had frozen meat on two or three days with this and some dried potatoes, and once or twice dried vegetables. He has made us delicious stews – the fame of which has gone abroad so that officers passing our dugout where we eat often drop in and partake of a mess can full.

The ration of water (half a gallon per man per day) is small, but we supplement it with water from a well, which is all right when boiled. We drink about one and three-quarter pints of tea, without milk of course, at each meal.

You should see me consuming slices of fat bacon at breakfast time; would turn up my nose at it at home.

It was only four months since he had probably last been to the family property, 'Maretimo', and life was now so very different. Here on Gallipoli, he continued:

I am in splendid health, climbing up the long steep ridge, swimming nearly every day, tramping along the trenches and occasional pick and shovel work are making me very fit.

We are now living in dugouts on one of the lower spurs in a very safe spot. Even now, however, we are only 300 yards in a direct line over the brow of the cliff from the firing line. Alb and Hugh [his brothers] will know what the shots sound like when one is marking on a rifle butt – sitting under the mound the sound of the bullets going overhead is very sharp and loud.

Well, here the cliff is the mound and we are on a ridge 100 ft below, the sound of the bullets is therefore exaggerated – the sound is like a huge stock whip being cracked.

The Mack boys also wrote home, to the family on 'Berry Bank'. Ernie made light of recent artillery activity in his letter to Nell:

On June 21 a new Turkish shell made its first appearance amongst us & this was a great big ugly 10-inch high explosive. The second one that landed practically buried Jack and myself & the former was much annoyed as a stew that he had been at much pains in making for his tea was also buried. This shell was christened Jack Johnston as it made a tremendous noise when it exploded.

While Jack described the same incident to his father, Joseph:

Turks played a rotten trick. I had been a bit off and gone without breakfast or lunch but feeling very fit, set out to cook an extra good tea. Just made the tea and giving a final stir to a lovely stew when a shell landed about three yards behind me and when I scrambled out of the dust and debris a minute later found tea, stew & fire buried 2 feet deep and had to be content with biscuits and water. Stan's comment was as usual humorous but will keep that until we return.

Everyone takes things in a very matter of fact way here, I haven't seen anyone frightened and no one worries; a fellow gets shot, someone remarks 'bad luck', a couple more carry him away & the rest go on without interruption.

On 23 June at 6 pm the Turks began a heavy bombardment of the 8th's trenches, as described by Signaller Aub Callow:

Shelling lasted for about an hour. Several of our Brigade were killed and many wounded. A shell burst in our trench with a deafening crash. A piece of shell or stone grazed my head, ripping the puggaree off the side of my helmet and another small piece caught me on the inside of the right thigh causing a slight wound.

That day Dave McGarvie was on fatigue duty again and having a row with his sergeant, the football umpire, Henry 'Bunny' Nugent. 'My sergeant and I didn't get on very well together,' Dave later told his grand-daughter. 'He had no time for me and I didn't have much for him. He had me on every fatigue party you could possibly get ... no sooner off one than I'd be on another.'

One of the trooper's duties on 23 June saw him delivering rations up Walker's Ridge from Anzac Cove to Ted Henty's troop; there, he reported to another sergeant, David Crawford, a big man with a bushy handlebar moustache, who had served in the Boer War. Crawford then ordered Dave and Trooper Ralph Reeves to collect water bottles and fill them up, back down at the beach. This they did and, on the return climb up the ridge, both men heavily laden, 'We noticed a shelling going on in our position on The Nek'.

The two water carriers arrived back at the troop's trenches to find 'a row of stretchers along the side of the trench with blankets over them, and this Dave Crawford was one of them'. The result was that Trooper McGarvie was now detailed for a burial party.

Slipping and stumbling downhill, the party reached Ari Burnu (Bee Point) and the rough cemetery there. 'We had to dig a grave and it was all through the scrub ... It was pretty tough going,' Dave remembered. It was about midnight by the time they'd finished digging, after which the men had to return to the beach and wash the stretcher in the sea. But there was no letting up from Bunny Nugent: 'He just carried on with his usual swearing and cursing.' On this occasion, though, Nugent's keenness to keep the young man from Pomborneit on the go probably saved his life.

In the trenches during the bombardment, Colonel White scrawled a pencilled note to his brother:

Dear Old Joe:

I am quite well and fit and doing our bit – at times things fairly busy. The row is tremendous and all is very awful but one gets quite indifferent and callous, sees and does things you would have thought impossible. When all is quiet again you come back to a huge feed of bread and jam,

I do all the night work. O'Brien cracked up.

At present we are both looking at each other waiting for the other to attack. My trenches are only 15 yards away from theirs so you see all hands must be awake. Some times we hear them singing, our chaps roar with laughter over some funny yarn so the Turk must wonder what on earth is happening.

The bomb plays a most important part – they hurl them in at us – we chuck back, two to every one.

The sniper is a devil, but now we have just about cleaned them up. They are dead shots and scarcely miss.

Our food is very good – tinned beef, biscuits, jam, cheese, bacon and lime juice.

It's wonderful to see the numbers that bath in the sea each day – hundreds in spite of shrapnel and rifle bullets. It's a Godsend to have it. I can't go in while in the trenches but when we rest, go in every day – it's grand.

Two nights after the burial party for Sergeant Crawford, on 26 June, Dave McGarvie and three other troopers stood to arms as they always did, an hour before daylight and an hour after dark. They settled down for the night in a space in a trench half the width of a normal bedroom and, in Dave's own words: 'There was a man buried in that corner and another one buried in this corner, and the juice was coming down into the trench and there were blankets there that were lousy … we got in touch with the lice. Couldn't get rid of them.'

Shivering and itching they got to their feet to stand to arms again the next morning. Then all hell broke loose. 'An awful morning' is how Major Arthur Deeble began his description of the attack:

At 5 am awakened by shells flying everywhere. I'll never forget the hail of death with the roaring of shells and the hiss of rifle bullets. On our front of about 50 ft, hundreds of shells were falling. I get to the firing line and await attack with hundreds around my head and my eye fixed to a periscope. The parapet is broken in many places. Earth is flying about and filling our dugouts. Kits are on fire, flares and ammunition scattering.

At about 6 a messenger brings me word that the commanding officer is wounded and Major Gregory [second-in-command of the 8th] is killed. I assume command of the Regiment. A few minutes later word is brought that the Adjutant, Captain Crowl is killed.

This was devastating news to the 8th Light Horse, even more shattering to morale than that first day on the climb to Walker's Ridge when they'd seen HMS *Triumph* sunk before their own eyes. This time the loss was close and much more personal. Colonel White was only saved from death by the peak of his cap slowing and deflecting a piece of shrapnel. He would later write home:

I was hit at 5.30, Crowl and Gregory within a few minutes of each other, poor chaps they never knew what killed them. Seven killed and 15 wounded, for half hour's shelling it was horrible. It was Gregory's birthday, too. They put me on the hospital ship where the piece of shell was taken out, a hot bath, pyjamas and sleep. Monday they inoculated me for septic as the thing had been in my head for eight and a half hours before they got it out. Such a beautiful black eye.

Like White, Corporal William Scarff, a miner from Snake Valley, was one of the lucky ones:

I don't know how I escaped being killed as the shell passed over my shoulder and burst about 4 feet in front of me. The flame of the shell came right back in my face, burning the skin from the chin right up round my left eye and ear, and bursting in the ear drum. A splinter of shell entered by eye, but thank goodness it missed the sight. Another splinter entered my left leg.

I did look a beauty but I managed to walk down to the beach, as there were more serious cases than mine needing stretcher-bearers. Lt Colonel A.H. White sustained a bullet wound in the forehead. Lt Col. White is from Ballarat and one of the finest men I ever met. He is one of Nature's gentlemen and our boys would go through fire and water for him.

Major 'Ern' Gregory had been killed on his thirty-third birthday when he broke cover from his trench to help a stretcher party with the wounded. As he returned to his trench, a 6-inch shell lobbed, killing him instantly.

And then there was Captain Joseph 'Terry' Crowl, the popular stock auctioneer from Geelong, whose family would now mourn his death. Dave McGarvie witnessed the adjutant's death. He'd also been wounded himself. Dave's eyewitness account with him standing to arms that morning with his mate Trooper Ralph Lee, a horse dealer from Corryong:

My mate Ralph Lee – he came from Banjo Paterson country in the Snowy Mountains area – he took over watch. You see, we had a periscope with us in our section. We took it in turns to be on watch. Well, I sat down with the rifle between my knees and went to sleep, of course, and the next thing I heard this terrific bombardment and a shell burst out in front.

The Turks had a French gun – the 75 – which they used pretty frequently. It used to go whiz-bang and then blow out the whole thing ... well, one landed here and blew our trench in.

Ralph Lee was knocked down and he's lying down there, and a sandbag had burst and the dirt was pouring down his throat. The fellow on the other side started getting him clear and I picked up the periscope.

Just at that time our adjutant came along and he said: 'Keep that periscope up, keep it up!' It was all bent out of shape and I was just wondering what I would do with it … I stood up but I couldn't see anything out of it because it was bent. He (Crowl) went about 10 yards and he was killed. He had his head blown off.

The next thing, another shell burst and the whole of the trench came in and you could have walked straight out. I was knocked about 8 yards down this way. I had a gravel rash, a cut on the head.

Dave made his way back from the destroyed front trench, his head covered in blood. An officer instructed him: 'You better go round to the dressing station, lad!'

There he found several other walking wounded and two stretcher cases. One of them was his old friend and swapper of lime juice for rum rations, Squadron Quartermaster Leo Molony. 'He was in a bad way,' Dave recalled. 'Much of his leg was just shattered pulp. He was worried because he'd left his paybook in his dugout and he got me to write a note to the OC to go back with the stretcher-bearer. But he was on the way out. He died next day.'

Ralph Lee, Dave McGarvie and Colonel White were all evacuated to Lemnos. But while Colonel White rested in pyjamas aboard a hospital ship, Dave McGarvie remembered different treatment at the field hospital:

Had wound dressed and was put into one of the RAMC hospital tents, head feeling very heavy. Lying in tent all day, very sultry, not feeling too well.

We just had a bare stretcher to lie on – no blankets or anything – and I was there for several days, best part of a week I think it was, and then we went back on another minesweeper, back to Gallipoli.

Ernie, Stan and Jack Mack had escaped injury. Like the rest of the men, except for those manning periscopes, they had lain on the bottom of the trenches as shells landed around them – fifteen shells a minute for well over an hour. After the bombardment, they had expected the Turks to charge, but this attack did not eventuate.

The Macks felt the death of Major Gregory most keenly. Only the night before the shelling Ernie had been talking to him about news of other Old Geelong Collegians who were serving, to relay in a letter he was writing home. Now Lance Corporal Ernie Mack was sent for and put in charge of the burial party for Gregory and Crowl. They stood guard over the bodies during the day and passed the word around that there would be a funeral service that night.

In the evening they carried the bodies down Walker's Ridge to the point by the sea at Ari Burnu. It was 8.30 pm, a time when the threat of snipers and random shelling was least likely. There was, wrote Ernie, a 'great muster' of troopers who had been to school together at Geelong College and two old Melbourne Grammar School boys joined them as well by the graveside. These were the ties that bind.

'We three with another Collegian acted as coffin bearers,' Ernie continued, in a letter to Nell, 'very impressive funeral in the dark and the parson read the service with the aid of an electric torch'. Today, Major Gregory and Captain Crowl still lie side by side, three rows from the sea in Ari Burnu Cemetery, just the way they were laid to rest by torchlight by their old schoolmates 90 years ago.

Sid Campbell noted it was 9.30 pm when the service finished: 'A rotten business. Had swim in the moonlight afterwards.'

Stan Mack had a narrow escape that day. He had gone into the firing-line trenches to relieve Trooper Robert Halahan, aged just 21. As Halahan took cover in Stan's dugout, an 11.4-inch shell landed at the entrance and blew one of his legs off. He died of his wounds a week later in hospital in Cairo, in what was once the luxurious Palace Hotel.

Soon Stan would be in hospital in Egypt himself. Dogged by illness, he would be sent off Gallipoli for the second time. Now it was the enteric. He would be on his way home.

He wrote to his mother Helen from his hospital bed:

> Well, I've come to the conclusion that I am – to use a military expression – a rum sort of ragtime soldier. I've been sick again. I'd been feeling a bit run down over on the Penin. And got the usual complaint after feeding on bully beef and biscuits so went to the Dr for some medicine. He told me to pack up and be ready in the morn, for a trip to Lemnos where the hospitals are. Had been there for a few days and with a change of tucker and a few comforts felt much better and ready to return to the firing line. If the Dr had let me return then it would have been all right but he said to stay with him for a few more days and get stronger. I did stay and got weaker.
>
> Anyway I couldn't have been very bad, as I didn't get unconscious but temp was up pretty high.
>
> The brutes starved me! Fed me on milk. I liked it at first as I had not tasted it for months but I got it every way, hot, cold, sweet and sour and now I'm off milk diet.

They carted me round to four different hospitals and a week ago told me to pack up for base. This was the biggest shock for me of the lot but I had to go a lot of us sick and wounded got on a cargo boat, *Ionian,* and arrived in Alexandria.

We got straight off the boat onto a hospital train. By this time I was off milk diet, there being no one to deny it, so on the train I had beef tea, cakes, cold chicken, bread and butter and lime juice.

It was a five hours trip – an express train – and here I am at Heliopolis and being treated like a lord too.

Last night I slept in a bed with sheets and for the first half hour could do nothing but rub my feet up and down and wriggle my toes about. Also a pair of pyjamas, and I had a bath in clean fresh water as well.

I can tell you that after doing without those things for a little while you appreciate them when you get them again. Nurses came along and pressed some cigarettes and chocolates on to those of us who were well enough for them. When they have time they sit on the foot of the beds and ask about the fighting ...

The shelling of the trenches on Russell's Top continued as the Turks prepared to launch a major attack across The Nek. They realised that if they advanced just 300 yards into the Australian trenches on Russell's Top and held them, they would have the Anzacs at their mercy. On the one side they would have North Beach and the Anzac anchorage within range, and on the other they would be able to fire into the backs of all the posts facing them along the eastern back of Monash Gully. The Turkish military chiefs believed that if they held the captured trenches they would force the Australians and New Zealanders from the peninsula or destroy them when they tried to evacuate.

A new Turkish regiment, the 18th, was placed in line on Baby 700 and the Chessboard, facing the trenches then occupied by the light horse's 8th and 9th regiments. The original plan called for the attack to be launched on 28 June, but the Australians had attacked the Turks elsewhere on that day, so the Turkish regiment decided to postpone their charge until the next day.

It was to be an absolute disaster. There had been a charge here before by the Turks, at the beginning of the Gallipoli campaign, but this was to be the first terrible massacre at The Nek.

The night of 29 June was very dark and at 9.30 pm a wild squall preceding a thunderstorm roared in from the sea. The wind whipped up clouds of dust from the powdery tracks and shelves behind the lines and scooped up bits of rubbish, including dozens of pages from well-read newspapers. The storm burst around the Turks while at the same time a destroyer offshore and an Indian mountain battery began firing star shells overhead. Elsewhere the Australians had been told to confuse the enemy by throwing homemade flares (pieces of hemp dipped in kerosene), and shouting and cheering.

The whole largely unplanned disturbance led the Turks to believe that it was *they* who were being attacked. They opened up a heavy artillery barrage on Russell's Top, which went on for about half an hour. This was followed by a fierce rifle fusillade lasting another hour before dying away altogether.

The light horsemen were now fully alerted that a mass attack was imminent. Small parties of troopers in the most forward saps reported that there was movement in the trenches across the strip of No Man's Land in front of them. The men in the reserve trenches were stood to, while in the forward trenches the men stood waiting, shoulder to shoulder, with rifles and fixed bayonets. Elsewhere, the ammunition belts were being fed into the Vickers and Maxim .303 machine-guns, which would fire at eight rounds a second.

It was dark with a black cloud over the moon. Suddenly there were cries of 'Allah! Allah!' from the soldiers, and shouts of *'Taaruz! Taaruz!'* ('Charge! Charge!') from their officers. What happened next was described by more than one trooper as a rabbit shoot.

The 8th's unofficial historian recorded:

> At a quarter of an hour after midnight the Turks sprang out of their trenches and made a fierce rush, but were immediately met with a withering fire. Their numbers must have been 1,000 strong and in such a small area were tightly massed. Our hail of bullets wrought great execution and had the effect of making the line swerve to the left. This pressure forced those on the right into some of our secret saps where they were promptly accounted for by bayonets and bombs. A terrific din went on and flares lit up the scene, making all as plain as day.

Major Arthur Deeble was now temporary commanding officer of the 8th. His diary entry reads:

> At 12.15 the Turks attack the position held by the 8th and 9th with a whole regiment. 12.30: Our fellows take up a vigorous defence. They meet them with rifle fire, flares (100) and bombs (150).
>
> Some bombs injure some of our fellows in the saps and about eight Turks enter ... wounded or dead in a minute. Not a single Turk reaches our fire trench, nor do we lose a sap for a second.

171

3.40: Machine gun fire indicate enemy had given up the enterprise. A number of wounded crawl out of our trenches and a few prisoners are taken.

There are about 250 dead in front of our position and our casualties are 6 killed and 12 wounded. Glad to have success as the Colonel is away. (500 killed on a front of about 200 ft.)

Ernie Mack was another to provide an account of the action:

They attacked by getting out of their trenches and trying to charge us with the bayonet. Our men sat right up on the parapets of our trenches & when not firing were all the time calling out for the Turks to come along and hooting & barracking them. In fact most of our chaps took the whole attack as a real good joke.

As soon as they stopped the first rush they jumped out of the fire trench & sat up on the parapets and yelled and cursed at the top of their voices calling out to the Turks to come on they would finish them, etc. etc.

About a dozen Turks towards morning tried to creep round on our flank but were at once observed, but instead of firing our chaps let them come on & then started to chuck off at them all manner of names for coming so slowly & it was not until a voice answered them and said 'We will finish you Australian hopping kangaroos' that one of our chaps said 'We can't stand that – so into them boys', which the boys did, with the result [that] those Turks still lie here.

Ernie also described the thick of battle in a letter to his sister, Mary:

You ought to hear the roar of rifles during an attack it is something tremendous & you can hardly realise how anything can live through the hail of bullets, as for the machine guns it is something wonderful to hear them when a few get going properly. I once saw about a dozen Turks come up onto a piece of ground where the M.G.s could get them & before you could speak they were all killed or wounded.

Lieutenant Ted Henty wrote to his father at 'The Caves', outside Hamilton:

We had a really good stand up fight on the night of the 29th which cost the Turks 260 killed and a large number wounded while our casualties were very small.

It was much more satisfactory than the infernal pot-shooting through loopholes though this is fair sport now as we are only about 60 yards apart at the widest and in some places much less than that.

To drop so many in that narrow space is not bad is it and speaks rather well for the alertness of everyone concerned as it was a night attack …

After the first massed attack, which appeared to come in three waves, the Turks had continued their attack all night, with small parties of ten or twelve men trying to get into the 8th's trenches. There was savage hand-to-hand fighting.

One heroic episode involved Trooper James Sheehy, a 33-year-old from the Wimmera who had been an engine driver at the Murtoa flour mill. That morning Jim went looking for a missing friend and found his dead body in a trench – just as the Turks found him. 'The Turks rushed Jim who smartly shot one, drove his bayonet through another, and with a backward sweep of the rifle-butt smashed the skull of a third – accounting for three in one act,' his local newspaper reported later.

Tom Austin described the whole attack as a disaster for the enemy. When daybreak came, the 8th counted 255 corpses in its trenches and on the parapets, while the ground in between was covered with dead and wounded equalling as many again.

'The sun gets mighty hot in these parts now,' wrote Ted Henty, 'and the trenches will be mighty unpleasant after a few days of heat on those dead Turks. We have been dragging in as many as we can reach with grappling irons and ropes but there are a lot left yet what can't be reached. Luckily for us we will soon be spelling again.'

The men were also busy recovering Turkish rifles and ammunition. Major Deeble noted: 'I take for use a revolver and cartridge belt from an officer killed and we got maps of the Turk trenches.' Ernie Mack put the total collected at 130 rifles and 8,000 rounds of ammunition.

Sergeant George Fuzzard, a farmer from Tatura, closely noted the appearance of the Turks as he collected their weapons. '[T]hey were rather roughly clad, some in uniform of various sorts, others in plain dress,' he wrote. 'Equipment was different in pattern, mostly poor and worn. Ammunition in plenty. We gathered 100 rifles.'

The brave but futile attack by the 18th Turkish Regiment had failed. The first awful carnage had been wreaked at The Nek.

Chapter 13

'Out of Our Trenches – Out for Good!'

On 2 July, the 9th Light Horse stumbled down Walker's Ridge from the firing line for a fortnight's 'rest', followed two days later by the men of the 8th. The two regiments were in terrible shape, both physically and mentally, as were the Western Australians of the 10th. The hospital ships were now taking 200 men a day off Anzac Cove, and the numbers going down with dysentery and diarrhoea just kept growing, seemingly in direct proportion to the swarming flies around them.

'The strength of the troops visibly declined,' Charles Bean observed. 'The great frames which had impressed beholders in Egypt now stood out gauntly; faces became lined, cheeks sunken. Several warnings were sent out by medical officers pointing out the increasing weakness of the men.'

Lieutenant Colonel Richardson, the historian of another light horse regiment, described the situation that July:

> Officers and men in great numbers had been evacuated to hospital sick or wounded and the remaining were often in the most wretched condition with diarrhoea or dysentery … some were so weak they could hardly stagger to their places in the firing line and men fainted where they stood at 'stand to' in the morning after a long night of watching.

By 14 July, an official return showed that a quarter of the men of the 9th were sick. As for the 8th, Tom Austin wrote:

> [The] men suffering very badly with a vomiting sickness and with septic sores. The latter is a kind of scurvy and is similar to the Australian scourge known as Barcoo Rot to every bushman west of the Darling. The flies and vermin becoming intolerable and the

174

Medical Officer at his wits end to know how to cope with disease owing to the very limited facilities at his disposal.

Aside from the obvious hazards of an appalling, monotonous diet and fly-borne diseases, modern medicine today says that the constant shortage of water in the furnace heat of the trenches would also have severely affected the men's health. It is known that even moderate dehydration can lead to serious problems with mental functions such as judgement, focus and clarity of thought.

The toll through sickness was so bad that the return of the 8th to the front line would have to be delayed to await reinforcements, as, by 22 July, Colonel White wrote that he was reorganising his regiment. Instead of the normal three squadrons he had 'just enough men and officers to make up 2 Squadrons, so now I have B and C'.

These men would stay in the rest camp until 29 July – but, of course, there was no rest. As Ernie Mack put it, they were 'absolutely killed by the quantity of work and everyone of us got as thin and weak as starved kittens'.

His commanding officer appears to have agreed: 'Although resting from the trenches we simply come out of the trenches and go straight on to road making, digging trenches, carry supplies, filling water tanks, cutting down hills, chopping down scrub and very often there are no men left in the rest camp at all.'

Up and down the men went, day and night, practising hill climbing or doing the fatigue duties. Dave McGarvie, with pick and shovel, was making roads, and carrying dirt from the miners busy tunnelling away at fresh trenches and saps.

In spite of the disease and exhaustion, huge plans were afoot and decisions were being made by the officers the men called 'the Heads'. Plans that would throw the sick and exhausted men on Gallipoli, together with new reinforcements, into a giant and ambitious offensive. The August Offensive was to be a highly complicated series of interlocking actions on neighbouring battlefields, with each action largely dependent on the success of the other, in order to break out of the trenches and put the Turks on the run.

As rumours of all descriptions began to spread, Lieutenant Colonel Miell of the 9th made a bet with his second-in-command, Major Carew Reynell: he wagered his issue of rum for three months that the regiment would be in Constantinople before Christmas. The Western Australians of the 10th, who at that time were holding a position on the northern spur of Walker's Ridge, could look down below and sense something big was in the offing, as the regiment's historian, Colonel Olden, explained:

It was evident from the huge preparations that were being made that a big offensive was contemplated. Ammunition was constantly being brought up to our positions from the beach by the Indian Mule Corps detachments and stowed as safely in the ground as possible. Water in sealed petrol cans was also carried up and dumped just in the rear of Russell's Top and jealously guarded. The scanty supply of bombs became augmented by numbers of homemade ones – the bully beef and jam tins being utilised as vehicles for the explosive charge.

More than 50 men worked on the beach at Anzac Cove making the bombs – packing the tins with gun cotton, shrapnel and varying lengths of fuse. A trooper in the 8th had invented a 'fuse stick' for easier lighting of the bombs, which had received wide approval for ingenuity. But otherwise, troopers in the trenches had smouldering lengths of rope hanging from their belts to easily touch off a five- or seven-second fuse. They would blow on the fuse to keep it alight before throwing the jam-tin grenades. The Turkish bombs were like black cricket balls and had striker fuses. Sometimes these bombs were caught and thrown back at the Turks by the Australians; at other times a man misjudged and his hand would be blown off.

Forty men, experienced miners from the goldfields of Western Australia, were put to work up on Russell's Top, digging new saps, edging their way forward cautiously, foot by foot, from the front-line trenches that faced The Nek.

As early as May, General Sir William Birdwood, the small and popular cock sparrow of a man in command of the Australians and New Zealanders, and his principal aide, Lieutenant Colonel Andrew Skeen, had come up with the first draft of a plan for a surprise movement from the north of the Anzacs' position against the Turks on the heights of Sari Bair. The key points to be captured on the heights would be Chunuk Bair and Hill 971, further along towards Suvla.

One approach to Chunuk Bair was up Walker's Ridge, along Russell's Top, across the land bridge called The Nek, and then on up the ridge by way of the hump called Baby 700. But this direct route from Anzac was blocked by the Turks at The Nek, which was barely 30 metres wide. And beyond was Baby 700, the strongest Turkish position on the heights above Anzac, its row upon row of trenches filled with soldiers who could fire down below and pick off targets, as easily as shooting rabbits around a dam.

The Nek was held by the Turks with two lines of trenches. Beyond was a maze of more trenches, while on either flank, slightly towards the

Turkish rear, were inaccessible spurs from which Turkish machine-guns, free of interference, could sweep back and forth across the tiny No Man's Land. As Bean described it, going forward here would be like trying to attack an inverted frying pan from the direction of its handle.

By July, Birdwood and Skeen would write: 'These trenches and convergences of communication trenches ... require considerable strength of force. The narrow Nek to be crossed ... make an unaided attack in this direction almost hopeless.'

But they had a better idea. Chunuk Bair would be attacked from another direction. A force of New Zealanders would climb up an almost sheer ridge where it was thought the Turks were few, and attack the enemy on top, where they least expected it. Further on, the planners decided that the capture of Hill 971 would be carried out by an Australian force, led by John Monash, a future general. This attack would follow a night march over terrain so rough that it would be known afterwards as 'the mad country'. Then, while the Turks were fully occupied with the New Zealanders, there would be a converging attack to capture Chunuk Bair. The 3rd Light Horse Brigade was chosen to make a frontal attack from its own home ground on top of Walker's Ridge.

But the new plan was very much a plan of 'ifs'. If Chunuk Bair was captured by the New Zealanders on time it would go ahead; if it was delayed, then a minor assault might be considered.

Because of the narrowness of The Nek, a force of 600 men was eventually decided upon to try to push through the funnel. They would be asked to capture nine lines of trenches to the front and several to the flank, totalling in all at least 40 separate trenches and saps. There would be other troops in reserve, standing by to help and to hold the trenches once they had been captured.

Birdwood and Skeen hedged their bets. The attack would occur 'at 4.30 am ... unless orders are given to the contrary'. First 'if', now 'unless'.

At the same time as the attack at The Nek, other light horse units to the right would attack the Turks at Quinn's Post and Pope's Hill, to keep the pressure on. And these attacks, all set for 7 August, would be preceded by a major infantry push at Lone Pine on the evening of 6 August, a feint designed to make the Turks believe that the breakthrough would be from the south. Another infantry attack was planned on the sector known as German Officer's Trench for midnight. This, it was hoped, would further confuse the Turks and help protect the light horsemen's flank.

The rest of the grand plan for the August Offensive was being developed and devised by Sir Ian Hamilton's generals, and seems to have remained something of a mystery to both Birdwood and Skeen. That was, until the arrival on 25 July of General Sir Frederick Stopford, who had been put in charge of operations overall. This ancient incompetent (who would later be sacked) told the no-doubt-astonished officers that a large force of troops would also be landing at Suvla to help in the capture of the Sari Bair range. When Anzac headquarters later tried to give general headquarters some local intelligence as to the location of guns and trenches on the range, they were politely told to mind their own business. It was that kind of high command.

Meanwhile, in faraway Egypt, Lieutenant Colonel Noel Brazier, left behind with the horses he had once personally selected from the farmlands of Western Australia, was packing his kit. At last he was to go to the front. His anger with the Bullant and Hughes had not subsided in the slightest and was still simmering away in the desert heat. He didn't bother to return letters from the 3rd Brigade headquarters at Anzac and was now insisting that he would take his orders only from the local commander in Egypt.

There had been a fierce row over four motor cars that had been left behind when the three regiments sailed. Antill heard that Brazier was using one of the cars and wrote insisting they all be locked up and the keys sent to him at Anzac. Brazier appealed to his local commander, who ruled that he could keep the keys and the cars. More ill will festered with the brigade's commanders, for it was by now essentially a divided command, with a sick Hughes and a compliant Antill in the wings.

When Brigadier Hughes returned to Egypt, exhausted, for a short rest, he had stayed the night at Brazier's camp. The colonel thought Hughes looked 'a wreck'.

The next day the old brigadier tried to outflank him by ordering the four cars to accompany him to Cairo to pick up comforts for the troops. Once there he dismissed the drivers and arranged for the cars to be sent to a motor company. But, after Hughes had left, Brazier simply went again to his local commander, who gave authority for the cars to be returned to him. Hughes was furious. He and Antill decided that Brazier had to be brought under their control on Gallipoli and replace Major Alan Love, the 10th's acting CO, who was also falling out of favour.

Major Love wrote back to Heliopolis on 1 July:

> My dear Brazier: I have just received a communication from Bgde HQrs that the Brigadier proposes bringing you over here and putting some other officer in your place. They casually tell me that they have

written to you for several reports and such like on 2 or 3 occasions
but rec'd no reply from you, or in fact a single line since we left …

Love asked Brazier to bring him a luminous watch that he had ordered,
and then enquired after six officers who also had not been in touch with
him:

I felt very annoyed. You can imagine with all these officers away I am
having a rough passage … the 8th and 9th have recently been in the
thick of it. Col. White was wounded and Major Gregory and Capt.
Crowl killed. The 10th considering the work & engagements has been
very lucky – although suffering big casualties there are only 6 killed.
We are holding our end up and I don't think you will have cause to
be ashamed of your command.

I hope the end of our trench fighting will soon be over as it is most
nerve racking. A fellow wants a spell every 5 or 6 weeks. When you
arrive I will apply for a week's trip and get away from dodging shells
and bullets which lately has been a very difficult job as they have
pelted them in at times like hail. I am told that 500 shells fell in 3 hours
in 170 yards perimeter of our trenches, but we not only held on but
repelled a heavy after attack with great slaughter, hundreds of whom
are still lying outside of our trenches.

Two weeks later, Love wrote again:

I am informed by Brigade HQrs that you are expected here any
day and the sooner the better for they are worrying the life out of me.

A CO has not only to fight the enemy but the staff as well … the
Brigadier and myself had a long yarn this morning and he finally
agreed with me that there were 4 vacancies for commissions in the
Reg't. But he suggests a competitive examination and that the matter
should await your arrival.

I have been bad with diarrhoea for about 14 days and am just
about played out and intended, as soon as you arrived, having a
week's spell on the hospital ship or in Lemnos.

You can imagine I have had a rough passage with so many officers
knocked out and can appreciate the urgency of getting others
appointed.

Olden and McDonald arrived this morning with 51 men. I understand the Brigadier was very annoyed with you over something
[Brazier's handwritten note alongside: 'Motor cars. He got kicked!']
hence his decision to relieve you and get you over here.

> Antill is as great a bully as ever and leads us a cat and dog life [Brazier: 'Wait awhile'.] I understand there is a possibility of his getting command of the brigade if the Brigadier again breaks down. What ho then! [Brazier: 'Never'.]

Brazier would arrive on Gallipoli on 30 July, just eight days before the charge. In all the events that followed, his loathing for Antill never subsided.

The men of the 8th came down from the trenches on 11 July to find their colonel, head bandaged, back with them again. Jones, his batman, had made his dugout comfortable, and Sid Campbell was changing the dressing every day. The wound was healing nicely, but White thought it would leave a big scar. He looked forward to being able to swim again. Meanwhile, he busied himself with other duties.

A couple of days later, the popular CO received a request from Brigadier Hughes to visit him on his hospital ship. White described the trip:

> I went out with a large load of wounded, the old chap was very glad to see me, had lunch on board with him, a good feed – soup, fish, beet (fresh), apple pie and milk. Gee, I did stuff, then some afternoon tea, with cake and bread and butter. Was hoping the trawler would not come alongside until after dinner, but she put in an appearance at 4 pm so I had to go. Was in the trawler for three hours waiting for a launch to come from shore. They are good chaps, all naval fellows, they gave me a huge bowl of tea and some bread and dripping.

Colonel Miell of the 9th ('blooming old humbug') also called in. But White was always thinking of his own officers and men. He organised a concert for the 8th – 'it will do them good' – although he acknowledged the lack of facilities: 'Of course there is no campfire, wood is very scarce, so we will just sit on the hillside and sing songs, etc.'

And he was insisting that some of his officers, including Ted Henty and Keith Borthwick, go offshore for a spell on Lemnos, as they were 'all very sick and tired out'. After fighting influenza and a high temperature for three days, Aub Callow, the signaller, was also to be sent off. Young Aub was much sicker than he thought, and would end up in hospital in Malta.

In the evenings Colonel White played bridge with Sid Campbell and the two young Duntroon graduates, Lieutenants Leo Anderson and Charles Dale, high up on the terrace outside their dugouts. From here they looked down on the beach and around the bluff of Ari Burnu to Anzac Cove.

On the evening of 12 July, Colonel White decided to go swimming again – 'Can't swim until dark, the snipers are getting brisk again, several chaps have been hit so it's not worth the risk'. Afterwards he pronounced it a success: 'It was grand, such a wash.'

Phillip Schuler was later to tell the readers of *The Age* of the scene at the Cove, near the wooden Watson's Pier that had been built out from the sharply shelving shoreline:

> Like the other piers that lie around it is stoutly built and broad enough for stretchers to pass along it. It is riddled with the enemy's shrapnel, yet the pier is one of the favourite bathing resorts of those who live on or near the beach. Generally in the vicinity are some naval launches and barges – some stranded, others just afloat.
>
> The toll taken by the enemy's guns on the beach is amazingly small, it seems to me, for the amount of ammunition they fling over. Bathing is carried on at all times during the day, and it must not be supposed that one is safe at night.
>
> You can see hundreds of men in the water; the greatest treat that can be given to the infantryman from the trenches is to bring him down to the sea.
>
> They undress behind the piles of stores and they have so little to shed that it takes but a second. Then they are diving from the pier or off a barge, and the Turks commence to 'pot'.
>
> Immediately the sound of a shell is heard there is a scatter. Many men dive at once into the water; those in the water dive deep down. It is hard to believe, but I have seen a man swimming out of the circle caused by the disappearance of an unburst shell into the deep.

Everyone knew that swimming was a dangerous business but it seemed to be a risk worth taking, as Sid Campbell explained on 12 July to his sister Hetty: 'We are singularly free from the effects of dirt and filth here chiefly because the sea is so close and the weather good. The beach is not the safest place to loiter on though, except late in the evening.'

Two nights later Colonel White, accompanied by the medical officer and Charles Dale, climbed down from the terrace outside their adjoining dugouts and went down together for a swim in the dark again. It had been a quiet day with little shooting and White had enjoyed reading a book as well as consuming 'a feast' of rice and golden syrup. Like their men, the officers were now wearing their trousers cut off at the knee and were mentioning in their letters home how very tanned they were becoming. 'We are a rough looking crowd now, short pants, boots and singlets and plenty of beards," the colonel admitted to his brother, Joe.

Senior Chaplain Merrington, attached to the 1st Light Horse, had been visiting patients aboard a hospital ship moored off Anzac Cove that day. On returning ashore the Presbyterian minister dropped in to see his friend Chaplain McPhee in his dugout, on the heights above the beach:

> After tea, we were sitting in front for some time talking and watching the bathers who were very numerous on the beach below. It was getting quite dark when, suddenly, we saw the flash of a shell burst amid the forms of bathers who were dressing on a barge.
>
> Stretcher bearers were called for at once and we saw four of those who had been enjoying a bathe a few minutes before carried along the beach towards the hospital … We went down and found Captain Campbell, a medical officer, lying on the operating table with his feet shot away. McPhee, who had known him at Ormond College, Melbourne, stood beside him and spoke to him. I understand there is no hope of his recovery.

Sid Campbell, described by officers and troopers alike as being the best-loved man in the 8th Light Horse Regiment, was dying.

Another of Sid's old friends from those happy, far-off days, ten years before at Ormond College, was Captain Mervyn Higgins, the young man they had called 'Buggins' at university. Two days later, Merv wrote what had occurred, in pencil, on the last sheets he had of the 8th's fine notepaper with the raised engraving of the regiment's emblem, the prancing horse. The letter was addressed to Sid's father at 'Maretimo', the grand house on the hilltop near Portland in Victoria:

> This is how it happened. The evening before last Sid left our rest camp here with the CO and adjutant to have a swim down by the base, about a mile away. They undressed on a barge and were just ready to go into the sea.
>
> The CO had stepped off on to another barge and Dale, the adjutant, was bending down about two feet in front of Sid, who was standing. An 8-inch shell came along and caught Sid sideways on, cutting off both legs below the knee, before it burst at the bottom of the barge, where it wounded three or four others.
>
> There was a field ambulance within a few yards and he was brought in in less than a minute.

He was conscious for a few seconds and gave the stretcher-bearers instructions as to tying him up, but he was unconscious by the time he got into the ambulance hospital from which he was soon removed to the hospital ship.

He died about one o'clock yesterday morning.

I know how agonising these details must be to you but I thought you would prefer to know exactly how it happened and I have given them to you just as Dale gave them to me …

Colonel White was distraught as he wrote home to Myrtle:

A sad, sad, day, poor dear Campbell, how we all loved him. The best and most honoured of men. Doctor, soldier, gentleman, friend, how I shall miss him. I was very, very fond of Campbell, how he worked; he was always so gentle, sympathetic and kind. The men loved him; the officers called him a man.

He was my own special friend, dear, straight upright clean living Campbell, cut off just as your splendid young life and career was just beginning, why should it be so? You who could so ill be spared to us. God comfort your parents; the whole Regiment mourns for you. Oh war is horrible.

I don't feel much like writing, it was so horrible. Campbell and I always bathed together; we went as usual to the safest place, and all the adjutants with us, undressed on a barge. I was undressed first and about to plunge in when the shell came by where I had been sitting beside Campbell, missed Dale and me by inches and caught Campbell – it was horrible.

Poor chap, the last shell of the night, it made a tremendous row and my clothes were blown to bits, not a stitch left. I managed to borrow something from the Hospital people to come home in.

Perhaps I should not have mentioned this, it will make you sad and troubled and anxious – but remember this, I could not have been closer to death than I was and quite untouched. I said at the first I would come back to you all and I now say it more fully than ever – but no more bathing for me, except at dead of night, it's not safe, I have learned my lesson; no more.

The grief that swept the regiment as they learned of Campbell's death was palpable. Major Tom Redford said he was 'beloved by all who knew him'; Lieutenant Charles Carthew wrote how 'very cut up' he was, 'we miss him sorely – he was a splendid fellow – nothing was too much trouble and he was one of my closest friends'. The doctor was 'very well liked and his loss is sorely felt' were Aub Callow's words.

It was the third major blow to the men's morale. The doctor's death ranked alongside the sinking of the battleship *Triumph* and the loss of Gregory and Crowl in the bloody shelling on the heights in June.

Merv Higgins' letter would take many weeks to arrive in Australia, of course, and the Campbell family would hear of the tragedy through official channels. Back in Melbourne, the Defence Department arranged for the Premier of Victoria, Sir Alexander Peacock, to break the news of Sid's death to his father, the Member for Glenelg, Mr Hugh Campbell. Sir Alexander got the message on 21 July. It was just two days after the Campbells would have been unwittingly celebrating Sid's twenty-eighth birthday.

Captain Campbell was buried at sea off Gallipoli on 15 July. Today his name is inscribed at Lone Pine among the 960 Australians who incurred mortal wounds or sickness and were buried at sea. If you search at the other end of the world you can also find his name in weathered script, black on white marble – in the windswept front porch of the RSL in Portland, Victoria, just a few kilometres from Maretimo, the family house.

From his dugout on Walker's Ridge, Frederick Hughes also wrote to Hugh Campbell, grieving at 'Maretimo'. The brigadier was writing on scraps of grid-lined mapping paper now, not crested notepaper:

> Your son was not only wrapped up in his work which he performed with great skill and care whether in the Trenches or Field Hospital but in addition his charming manner and personality endeared himself to everyone who came in contact with him ... thus ended the life of one of our finest young men in the service of the Empire and one whose life gave every promise of a very brilliant professional career.

The *Speculum* magazine of October 1915 had the finest epitaph: 'Poor Sid. A faithful, gentle, stalwart soul.' But life went on. A new medical officer, Captain Frank Beamish – 'a nice chap ... glad to come to us', wrote White – had joined the 8th. Beamish, who had also studied medicine while at Ormond College, was seconded from the 13th Infantry Battalion to take Sid's place.

Meanwhile, the planning for the August Offensive was continuing apace. On 21 July, Brigadier (soon to be Brigadier General) Hughes, Brigade Major Antill, and the three regimental commanding officers –

White, Miell and Brazier – went out to sea aboard the British torpedo-boat destroyer HMS *Chelmer*, 'to have a look at the Turkish position'.

Quite what the officers saw of the Turkish position, even through the best field glasses, is open to conjecture. Cruising down the same stretch of sea today, the jagged skyline which is the Sari Bair range reveals little to the naked eye. Details of trench lines on the summits would have been almost impossible to pick up. However, reconnaissance by British aircraft was continuing over the Turkish lines along the ridge and beyond.

Still, the officers enjoyed the day's outing, White would write:

> It was very nice out at sea – a cool wind – no dust and no flies. The officers were very decent to us. Had a good lunch, Irish stew made from fresh mutton, spuds and onions, also some mazena pudding, also some bread and butter – it was grand to see a table cloth again. We also had some afternoon tea with some toast and butter. Just think of it. I was quite sorry when we had to come home again.

The discussions continued between the senior officers. After breakfast on 26 July, White had to attend 'a pow-wow of C.O.s that took all the morning', where the topic was the 'great preparations for the supposed attack that is to come'. While one can detect a tone of indifference in those words, there is no mistaking the faith he had in his men:

> I am certain my chaps will do well. It will be a pleasure to lead them – good old 8th. The numbers are going down but they are still full of grit and go yet. I am very fortunate in my officers, could not have a finer lot of men, and all loyal to the backbone. I love them all but it does seem a waste of troops doing this work – such a bonnie Regiment of Light Horse.
>
> Anyhow we have done what we can and relieved the Infantry a lot, we could not do more. I believe our horses are looking very fine and well – only wish we had them – no chance here for mounted work.

This light horseman was still looking ahead to glorious days fighting on horseback. 'In Austria we should have our chance and do something,' he enthused.

But, just three days later, the troopers were ordered to hand in their leather light horse bandoliers and exchange them for the ordinary webbing equipment of the infantryman. 'It appeared to us we were parting with our last link with the horses and as a consequence we were not too pleased,' wrote Tom Austin, who also noted that it took the men a while to put the new equipment together.

At about the same time, reinforcements began arriving. White said he was 'dashed glad' to get two officers and 70 other ranks from Egypt, which enabled him to get the regiment up to three squadrons again. More men would arrive on 3 August, four days before the grand offensive.

The light horsemen were being readied for an extraordinarily impossible infantry feat of arms. As Peter Burness wrote, 'Godley was proposing to use the light horsemen in a massed bayonet attack of a kind which had been rendered ineffective by weapon developments back at the time of the American Civil War'.

But according to the brigade major, Jack Antill – writing after the war to Charles Bean, as the latter prepared the final draft of his *Official History* – the officers of the 3rd Light Horse Brigade had opposed the idea from the start:

> From the initial intimation of the proposed operations and right through the subsequent discussions and conferences, in the definite and reiterated judgment of the brigadier, his brigade-major and of regimental commanders, the projected attack on The Nek was fore-doomed to failure.
>
> On the contrary, and in opposition to this view, both Anzac and divisional headquarters were confident of success.
>
> The brigade had been in occupation of this narrow and contracted frontage since its arrival on the Peninsula and from the advantage of close contact and constant observation might be assumed to be competent judges of the situation.
>
> Except for their attack on the 29th June, the Turks, while fairly quiescent after their disastrous failure on that occasion, were intensely active in strengthening their positions on the sloping open area in rear.
>
> The Chessboard now somewhat resembled a mining camp. Line after line of close parallel and deeply dug trenches, inter-connected with innumerable inter-links as far as the crest of the hill; and, during the week or so immediately preceding the attack on The Nek, every morning disclosed large quantities of fresh earth thrown up during the night, thus indicating feverish anxiety, in undoubted anticipation of attack.
>
> All these preparations were fully know to headquarters; notwith-standing, superior authority thought this frontage was comparatively

lightly held, and contrary to brigade estimation, discounted and waved aside their views.

In this, Colonel Skeen (representing headquarters), who took a prominent part in the discussions, was particularly optimistic and confident. Headquarters decided the attack should proceed and the necessary preparations and orders drafted accordingly. This was done. Brigade orders were drafted and duly examined and approved by division.

But as Major General Sir Brudenall White wrote to Bean after it was all over: 'Skeen's plan was quite a brilliant conception and was sound from a military point of view, but it totally disregarded the almost impossible nature of the country.'

The Bullant sent a later handwritten note to Bean in 1931. In it he said: 'Skeen and the other superiors always seemed to pooh-pooh the idea of any serious opposition at The Nek – we realised and pressed it from the very outset.' But Antill was writing long after the disaster. He wanted to lay the blame squarely on divisional headquarters and distance himself from the decisions that he would make that day on 7 August. Perhaps, nearly sixteen years later, he had convinced himself in his own mind, because he scrawled to Bean: 'I regard the launching of that attack as a callous and unforgivable blunder and the massacre, for it was nothing else, must rest with higher authority.'

However, in those last, fatal days of July 1915, a higher authority ruled and reassured Hughes and the Bullant. They should prepare their orders for a successful charge on 7 August because they would not be acting in isolation. Other attacks would be going on at the same time, they were told. The 1st Light Horse Brigade would be attacking the Chessboard from Pope's opposite, and others from the 1st Brigade would break out of Quinn's in four waves of 50 men. The infantry at Steele's Post would be attacking German Officer's Trench and knocking out the machine-guns that enfiladed the ground in front of The Nek. And meanwhile, the successful New Zealanders would have captured Chunuk Bair and now would be coming down Battleship Hill, firing into the back trenches of Baby 700, as the light horsemen attacked those in the front from The Nek.

The plan for the charge at The Nek seemed simple enough: in essence, four lines, limited to 150 men each because of the width of the sloping ground, would charge across a narrowing hillcrest between steep gullies in quick succession.

The first two lines would be made up of men from the 8th Light Horse, the next two lines from the 10th Light Horse, while the 9th Light

Horse would also be on Russell's Top in reserve. A battalion of the British Cheshire Regiment would help to consolidate while two companies of the 8th Royal Welch Fusiliers were to climb up Monash Valley in support as well.

The first line would attack the Turkish trenches across The Nek using just handmade bombs and bayonets. They were to charge with no bullets in their magazines, not even a single round up the spout. This was an instruction from Godley, a literal interpretation of a Birdwood instruction that the rifles be unloaded. The presumption is that these British officers believed the bayonet charge up a hill might be slowed if the men stopped at any stage to aim and fire their rifles.

The second line was to pass over the first and take the nearest saps on Baby 700. The third line would capture the farther trenches, while the fourth, armed with picks and shovels, would either fight or dig in as required.

The actual brigade orders were more elaborate, more astounding. Brazier said after the war: 'If you want to know how NOT to write an operational order you will find it in that order for the attack; as the Brigadier called it a "comprehensive order". It took my adjutant an hour or two to copy it and almost detailed individual men to take specified machine guns!'

The orders included capital letters and numbers identifying Turkish trenches that had been marked on British maps from aerial reconnaissance. 'Y' and 'Z' referred to centres or junctions of several trenches. The basic orders read:

> 8th L.H. 1st Line – First line will consist of troops already in firing trenches and saps. On a given signal, silently and without rifle-fire, it will rush The Nek (A1) and with bayonet and bomb engage the enemy, taking possession of the flank, communicating and advanced trenches (A9, A5, A8, A11) paying special attention to the machine guns, which must be sought for and rushed, and to the trenches to the north of The Nek and to those on the southern flank of same, so as to prevent flank interposition by the enemy – mine fuses and 'phone wires to be sought for and cut.

> 8th L.H. 2nd Line – Second line (already on banquette) will immediately follow. Jumping advanced trenches (already engaged by first line) it will sweep on and attack, supporting and subsidiary trenches (A12, C1, C4). Its action will be forward, ignoring trenches behind, but accounting for those to right and left (C6a, B1, B2, B3). Bayonet and bomb without fire. Note – As soon as first line has moved from

our trenches, second line will take the position vacated in order to make room for third line. In passing over intervening space officers will take post in the ranks so as not to make themselves a conspicuous target.

10th L.H. 3rd Line – Having moved up communicating trenches, third line will in like manner be prepared and follow on at once. Its objective will be the next line of trenches (C2, C3, C5, C7, C8) and, if possible, Z, Y, C10, C11 to C12-13. With bomb and bayonet only, the enemy will be driven back and out without turning back, and avenues blocked. Once in the trenches the enemy will not be able to make effective use of his machine guns. When the extreme limit of advance has been reached the gain must be made good and safe against machine gun fire and against counter attack. Here fourth line plays its part.

10th L.H. 4th Line – Fourth line will in like manner follow and act in concert with 2 and 3. It must endeavour to join up with the latter. Every second man will carry digging tools in the proportion of one pick to two shovels. It is impossible to define precisely what this line may be called upon to do. This must in necessity depend upon the progress of its predecessors. It may have to down tools and assist, but it must make every effort to join up with third line and block the approaches. This is its role.

The orders did warn that the enemy's garrison at The Nek was believed to be 'not light' or that machine-guns were believed to exist in five positions, all commanding the approach to The Nek, or that, with the exception of one, all these positions were around 200 metres beyond the Turkish front. All the attackers were told was that the fighting might disclose other machine-guns.

While these weapons might not be silenced at the first rush, the light horsemen were assured in their orders that the attackers would have 'the full assistance of naval guns and high explosive fire from the full strength of our howitzer and other guns'.

In the few remaining days of July, as these orders were being finalised, the men of the 8th were aware of rumours of a big attack to be launched soon at Suvla, and by the time they returned to the trenches, on 29 July, they knew something big was afoot, as they were put to work supplying parties to haul artillery pieces up onto Russell's Top.

There had been a false alarm.

On 25 July, Ted Henty and Keith Borthwick had returned from sick leave and called on their colonel who said they were 'both looking much better'. Ted had brought White some big packets of chocolates and some writing paper and envelopes, which were well received.

The next day, White had attended the 'Pow-wow of Cos' which had lasted all morning.

White then held a meeting with his own officers where 'I passed on the information and made my own plans, so now feel that everything is attended to'. It was now also suspected that the Turkish were planning a concentrated attack on 27 July and Aub Callow wrote that:

> General Birdwood has written to the troops here saying the Turks have brought up 100,000 reinforcements and are going to make a final attempt and wish everyone to be on the alert and hold the position.

The Turkish had been expected to attack again at any time and there was a new fear. This time the enemy might use asphyxiating gasses and the troops had been issued with respirators in an attempt to combat this new menace. They stood to arms fearfully in their rest trenches waiting – but nothing happened.

This false alarm meant White and his men were not called to the trenches until two days later to wait anxiously for further orders. 'It will be great when the advance comes,' wrote the colonel, 'what a yelling and a shouting there will be'.

Meanwhile, Jack Mack had been taken from his troop to join Lance Corporal Don Oliver's 'howitzer bomb gun' crew, where he replaced a man who was sick. It was a decision that probably saved the Berrybank man's life.

Don Oliver would play a critical role in what was to come. Each line in the charge would carry four small red-and-yellow marker flags. As soon as he saw one waved from the first line of the Turkish trenches, Don was to hurry across with his trench mortar crew.

On 29 July both the 8th and the 10th were on Russell's Top. The 10th's historian, Colonel Olden, described how the average distance separating them from the front line Turkish trenches was no more than around 35 metres, while a sap running from the main trench line came as close as 10 metres. The Turks with machine-guns, rifles, bombs and shells were constantly harassing the whole position. Observation was only possible by periscope, but these were frequently shattered in the hands of observers on being raised above the parapets. Olden continued:

Only the most fleeting glance, consequently, could be had of the enemy works, but even these disclosed the tremendous advantage he still held as to ground. Everywhere one looked, the gradient was with him and his spherical bombs would often roll of their own accord for yards after being hurled, to eventually find lodgement in one of our saps.

The 10th made a 'demonstration' on 3 August to test whether this section of the Turkish line was as strong as suspected. It was. The feint drew forth 'such a hurricane of machine gun and rifle fire, supplemented by shells and bombs, as to leave no doubt as to the enemy's never-tiring vigilance'.

On the first day back, the 8th soon learned of this vigilance when they were shelled heavily and Trooper John Kane, a 41-year-old horse trainer from Castlemaine, was killed and two others injured just before tea time. It was a bad start, but not unexpected, according to White: 'It's always a rotten job changing over – one crowd going out, the other going in. It always takes some time to get them in their right positions and when they are, it's a job to get the blighters to keep a good look out.'

Less phlegmatically, perhaps, the commanding officer told his wife that he was still dreaming of what it would like to be at peace again and out of uniform, but that 'when I come home and a motor-tyre bursts, I shall make a rush to the nearest door for cover.' He was still recovering from his head wound, and would take time off to lie down and rest in a new dugout in the trenches, trying to escape the heat and the flies, while passing some of his duties on to his squadron leaders and his second-in-command, Major Deeble.

His last letter to his brother was written in pencil on scraps of paper, at twilight, three days before the charge. By then he knew what he would be facing, and his words are disjointed yet strangely fatalistic:

Trenches
4.8.15
Dear old Joe
Jolly glad to get your second letter from Tasmania yesterday and hear that you know now what is wrong; you can build up your system – swig all the claret you feel like.

Those blighters had no need to open your letter, it was already censored. I am wondering if Capt Hillard came over – it is up to him – all military chaps should come – did you notice in the casualties just what a lot of immigrants there were. Nearly half of this show is not very Australian after all.

We are still plugging away and I think that this show will soon end – by the time you get this we shall be just about finished. It is nearly autumn here and the early mornings have quite a nip in them now – but very beautiful days and calm sea. Sgt Parker went away sick tonight – he has not been too well for some time – thank goodness I am right and very fit.

I have just written the Mater, hope she is not worrying, a few wounds are sure to come but they soon heal up again. It will all come right. I often think of our meals in the office and how we used to make the average come down about 3d a bushel. It's good to hear that things are going right with you and only hope you are not just telling me so as you are always thinking of other people.

Pascoe you mention is a decent chap in the 9th. He has gone over to some dentist job in Egypt.

It's wonderful the work the mule does here, the loads they carry up the hills – all run by Indians. Sorry I cannot tell you military news – censor won't stand it.

It's a great pity the papers are not allowed to publish facts. We do not know what is happening here at all.

Any Germans we find will get short shrift. The Turk is all right and plays the game fair.

I get very home sick for you all at times. It will be a great home coming. Wait until – wedding we shall hit it up. Old Moll sends me long interesting letters, so do the others.

Of course I always keep yours and Myrtle's letters to the last, read them over about 10 times.

It's almost dark and no candles – so good-bye old chap – keep fit and well and don't get too lonely. Love to Rose and regards to old pals.

Always, your Alex

PS. Am very hot and dirty. Burn this when finished; it's not too clean.

Immediately before he wrote this, Colonel White and the other senior officers had met again over the first three days of August with the brigade staff to receive their final orders to pass on to the men. Lieutenant Wilfred Robinson, the tall farmer from the Wimmera, was particularly scathing afterwards in describing to Bean what he thought of the headquarters briefing: 'The work of the Brigade staff as far as arrangements for the attack of the 8th and 10th regiments were concerned was disgraceful. Beyond being given the time for the attack we officers were practically left to make our own arrangements. There was no cohesion.'

Antill's own written orders to the light horse troop leaders reflect his usual bluster:

> One thing must be clearly understood and appreciated – WE ARE OUT TO STAY – THERE IS NO COMING BACK – the surest means are DASH and DETERMINATION. No time to waste on prisoners – no notice of tricks of the enemy such as 'cease fire' and there is no RETIRE.
>
> ONCE OUT OF OUR TRENCHES – OUT FOR GOOD and the assault, once for all goes right home.

On Wednesday 4 August, the men received their final orders for the charge. It was, coincidentally, the first anniversary of the declaration of war. Back home in Melbourne, Prime Minister Andrew Fisher, amid cheers from both sides of the House of Representatives, had moved:

> That we, the Representatives of the Commonwealth of Australia, in parliament assembled, do, on the expiration of a year of war, present to His Majesty our most loyal service and record our unchanging determination to continue to a victorious end the struggle for the maintenance of the ideals of liberty and justice which are the common and sacred cause of the Allied Nations.

Seventy-five thousand Australian troops were now overseas and another 40,000 were in training. On the eve of the charge at The Nek, the 60th casualty list would be published in the newspapers. It would have nearly 200 new names to add to the one printed on 3 August, bringing the total so far to 12,469 men killed and wounded.

The list would soon grow much, much longer. At the end of August, Colonel C. St C. Cameron, Assistant Adjutant General to the Imperial Headquarters and adviser to General Birdwood, would arrive back in Australia to declare:

> Blood and bone and iron alone can win the present struggle ... although Australia has answered nobly to the call we must double our efforts. As yet we are only at the beginning of a great struggle for national existence and the Turks must be wiped out before we can hope for any successes that will lead to the final victory. I would like to see Australia get another 100,000 men ready for transport by Christmas and a third 100,000 men ready by the following June ...

On Walker's Ridge, the light horsemen were shivering in the dawn. Four days before the attack in a mistaken order they had been told to hand in their woollen tunics – a mistake because, despite the daytime heat, it was freezing cold in the trenches at night. All they had left to wear were their light sun helmets, flannel shirts, ragged torn-off shorts, wound-up puttees around their ankles, and their boots.

The order of the 3rd Light Horse Brigade was for: 'Shirt sleeves, web equipment, helmets, 200 rounds, field dressing pinned right side inside shirt, gas helmet, full waterbottle, 6 biscuits, 2 sandbags (4 periscopes per line and gas sprayers to be carried by fourth line), wire cutters, rifle (unloaded and uncharged) bayonet fixed.' Some would also carry planks and scaling ladders to help climb over barbed-wire entanglements and up over the parapets and into trenches.

Only bayonets and bombs were to be used. Each line would have 24 bomb throwers and carriers. Each squadron carried 48 bombs and a reserve of 400 bombs was to accompany each line.

No further water was to be issued, and whatever there was was to be conserved as much as possible. The men were told that all wounded were to be left to the stretcher-bearers, and any prisoners were to be sent to the rear. Nothing was to stop the impetus of the charge. Officers and men were ordered to stow all their spare belongings in kitbags, which were thrown into big heaps by the cliff edges at the rear of the trenches.

There were some exceptions, according to Bean: 'Most of the men crammed into some corner among their clothes certain specially-treasured mementoes – a fragment of Turkish shell, some coins bought off a prisoner, a home letter, a photograph or two. There was no chance of taking such treasures with them; they expected to bivouac on the open hills.'

Dave McGarvie noted in his diary that he had been issued with calico 'to sew on back and both arms', adding: 'No tunic to be worn. Spent very cold night in shirt sleeves.'

'Throughout the whole day everyone was busy and as soon as the work was done most of us sat down to pen a note of farewell home,' Tom Austin reported.

Ernie Mack wrote a cheery letter to his sister, Nell, in which he had news about a good friend of the Mack brothers: 'Roger Palmer who was wounded a few days after landing came back last week but he has the bullet still in his leg.' Then he added a postscript: 'Maybe this is the last note I may ever write so, if so, goodbye to all. Can't say more but am quite ready to do my share or so I feel at present.'

The Macks' other friend, Lex Borthwick, had to leave his farewell letter until the next day due to his being detailed for a burial party. Trooper Ernest Butcher, the errant milkman from Port Melbourne, was cooking his tea in the trenches when he'd been struck by a piece of flying shell fragment; Ernest died at the field dressing station, and they carried his body back down the ridge to Ari Burnu, where Lex dug the grave and helped bury him.

So, the following day, Lex sat down and wrote to his parents back in Sale of the task that lay ahead:

> We will be called upon to charge a strongly fortified hill opposite …
> it is a difficult job and the 8th will have a rough journey. I hope Keith
> and I pull through all right but if we don't you will know we have
> done our little bit. Poor old Mother must not worry too much, and I
> hope, if we should have the bad luck to get hit that Father will console
> both of you by remembering that we quitted ourselves like men.

The regiment's historian, Tom Austin, summed up the situation that the men of the light horse faced:

> All realised that ours was to be no light job. The difficulties and
> strength of the enemy position had long been known, not only to us
> but had practically become a bye-word to every Anzac on Gallipoli.
> However there was never a thought of hanging back, rather did each
> man look forward with expectancy to having a real try-out with Brer
> Turk.

The 3rd Light Horse Brigade had been stuck for eleven long weary weeks on the side of a rotten hill in Turkey, shot and shelled at, with never a major advance. Instead of glorious victories there had been only flies and filth, diarrhoea and enteric fever, Barcoo Rot and lice. The heroes who had jingled and jangled as they rode in style through the cities of Australia had been reduced to coolies toiling up and down the slopes of Walker's Ridge with their loads of tins and water bottles, digging away forever on roads and in holes with the picks and the shovels. They had been enveloped by the stink and the popping of dead men's tunics on the parapets, and splattered with the blood and brains of their mates in the trenches.

Now, here at last, was the chance to break free. To burst out of the trenches and shake off the ignominy of being enforced infantrymen. To become light horsemen again, to be reunited with their horses, their mates, and to do what they had been trained to do and ride away to glory. To dream, as Colonel Alexander White dreamed, of charging to fresh victories in Europe, among the white men where they really belonged. To be part of greater deeds for the empire, new adventures to thrill a fresh generation of schoolboys.

They would, wrote Charles Bean, be moving through the green and open country again. 'The prospect filled them with a longing akin to home-sickness.'

Chapter 14

'Damn it! I'll lead my regiment'

Thursday, 5 August 1915, 10 o'clock. A crisp early morning had given way to another still, burning day on Walker's Ridge as the men of the 8th Australian Light Horse filed into the forward trenches on Russell's Top, moving up the line from the major communications trenches they called Broadway and Main Street.

Despite the task ahead of them, the men were fired up by the challenge, as Chaplain Ernest Merrington would eloquently describe:

> The Light Horse were to make the biggest attacks they had ever made. There was an air of suppressed excitement and the thrill of manly spirits about to be engaged in a deadly but noble enterprise.
>
> 'After all, this is what we came to do and it's better than living like rabbits all the time' said one trooper to me and that expressed the innermost feelings of all our men.
>
> Each was busily preparing for his own particular duty. All packs were made up and everyone was ready to advance.
>
> If it was humanely possible to storm these heights, these were the men to do it.
>
> All hands knew that it was the most desperate business that had ever come our way.

All three brigades were to be involved in the Charge at The Nek. The 2nd Light Horse Brigade was preparing to attack the Turkish trenches at Quinn's, the 1st Light Horse Brigade would be attacking the Chessboard, and the 3rd Light Horse Brigade was to charge at The Nek.

'It was last Thursday the 5th that we got orders to pack up our spare belongings and get ready to advance early on Friday morning,' Trooper Alexander Meldrum told his mother, a week later. His letter was written from a hospital bed in Egypt, and went on:

197

We started by sewing white patches on our shirts, one on the back and each sleeve, as we had to attack in shirt sleeves. Our bundles were thrown into big heaps on the edge of the cliffs and we were issued our rations for 48 hours.

Then came our first disappointment. We were not to attack until Saturday morning so we sat in our saps and trenches all night and shivered. I can't say we slept. At any rate, I didn't.

The forward trench line was shaped roughly like a boomerang, about 180 metres long, with sheer drops from cliff faces at either end. The row of eight-main saps splayed out in front, like bony fingers towards the first line of the Turkish trenches across the small patch of brown dusty and uneven ground called The Nek. On the left was what was called 'the secret sap', a ditch hidden in the scrub without a parapet in front or parados behind, with some cover from the enemy.

This uneven forward line faced the dents and hollows, the patchy, thorny scrub, and the sun-dried corpses that made up No Man's Land, sloping upwards from left to right. The nearest Turkish trench was only about 20 metres or less, from the nearest sap, at the centre extending to about 65 metres at the wing. On the right the two sides faced each other across more or less flat ground with little or no cover.

As the Victorians of the 8th moved forward on Russell's Top, the Western Australians of the 10th who were being replaced at the front firing line moved quietly back to the reserve trenches to prepare for their roles in the third and fourth lines of the attack, when they would move up again.

The 9th Light Horse was also getting into position. Their job was to remain in reserve until needed and provide covering fire from machine guns when the 8th and 10th attacked, and then themselves to launch and attack the furthest-off trenches up Baby 700 once the forward lines had been secured.

Meanwhile Major Carew Reynell, second-in-command of the 9th, and another of his officers, Captain P.I. Callary, were to act as marshals. They would co-ordinate and direct the men of the 8th and 10th into position and liaise with Brigadier General Hughes, Antill and others from the brigade, which had moved its headquarters up from Walker's Ridge to a dugout at the rear of Number 8, one of the forward saps.

Reynell wrote in his diary a message directed to his home and his baby son:

I am looking forward to the attack very much as I am very hopeful that it may result in a glorious stroke. I think I have arranged for every

198

contingency as far as this regiment is concerned and hope we shall give a good account of ourselves and in case of accidents – goodbye and may it be a consolation to you to realize that I have been some use here and Dickaboo may grow up quick and be comfort to his Mother and Grandfather.

The 8th was to lead the attack with two lines 'each of 150 bayonets', but this was subsequently altered to read 'every available man', bringing the strength of each line to over 200. Exactly how many troopers charged that day is still open to conjecture. On top of Walker's Ridge there were at least 600 extraordinarily brave Australian dismounted light horsemen in dirty shirts, ragged shorts, badly wound puttees and scuffed boots. They stood ready with sharpened bayonets fixed to the end of empty rifles waiting for the order to charge from Australian officers.

They waited, crammed together, shoulder to shoulder in the trenches and the saps. A band of brothers. The men were so excited that some who were really too sick to be fighting either hid from the medical officers or begged to be allowed to take part, or otherwise inveigled their way up to the front line.

Three squadrons made up the 8th Regiment, and the men from each would be intermingled. The first line of the 8th was to be commanded by Major Thomas Redford, from Warrnambool, with 'B' Squadron – which included Lieutenant Ted Henty and so many of the men from his troop who had engraved their names on the silver salver in Hamilton, less than a year before. 'B' Squadron was to be supplemented by two officers and 50 men from 'A' Squadron. The second line would be commanded by Major Arthur Deeble and his 'C' Squadron, with a similar addition of men from 'A' Squadron.

But very late in the sequence of events, Colonel Alexander White made a startling discovery. The regimental commanders, he learned, were expected to remain in the trenches observing the battle through periscopes until the fourth line had been launched forward successfully. He made a characteristic decision.

'Damn it!' he told Brigadier General Hughes and the Bullant. 'I'll lead my regiment.'

Colonel White would indeed lead his men in the first line, from the front and centre, together with his new adjutant, Lieutenant Charles Dale, who had replaced the slain Captain Terry Crowl. Young Dale had graduated from the second entry into the Royal Military College, Duntroon. Another young Duntroon graduate, Lieutenant Leo Anderson, would be on his left in the front line, with Major Redford and Lieutenants Ted Henty and Keith Borthwick among the other officers taking up positions on the right.

Behind these squadron and troop leaders came the troopers, of course, who had their own preparations to make. Corporal William McGrath, for instance, was a 27-year-old office clerk from South Melbourne, attached to the quartermaster's detail:

> B Squadron manned trenches on Thursday 5th all day and night. Relieved for meals one troop at a time. Major Redford and Mr Henty more serious than other officers and seemed to realise the gravity of operations more than the juniors. All were in good and bright spirits and so confidant [sic].
>
> Major [Redford] gave me several instructions but did not speak as if he expected the end and gave no instructions re disposal of his property.

McGrath went on to tell how young Sergeant Major Colin Cameron, formerly a Scotch College boy, had been 'very sober and gave me a letter to post as did several of the men'. Apart from these, 'each man either took all his valuables or had them packed in his kit'.

Dave McGarvie packed his Bible in the haversack on his back. He told his grand-daughter: 'Our fellows were as pleased as could be, but I wasn't very keen on it; not that I was afraid, but I knew that many who went out would never come back.'

McGrath was ordered to take six men who were on light duties and report to the Scottish Quartermaster Sergeant Jim Sproat. A double issue of rum was to be given to each troop to help them through the next long cold night before the attack was launched.

Throughout Friday, 6 August the troopers waited, baking in the trenches. As the day progressed they were allowed out in turns for a spell in the sparse shade at a spot named Shrapnel Terrace. Early in the morning they had heard the roar of artillery on the wind from Cape Helles, where a preliminary feint was in progress to try to draw Turkish forces away from the Anzac positions.

Antill would always insist that they'd been assured The Nek was 'very lightly held' and, in a diary entry from October that year, he added: 'A recent prisoner now says we were expected and prepared for since 2 pm 6th August, and that the whole of these trenches and Chessboard and Baby were heavily held and full of M.G's [machine-guns].'

The Bullant also claimed to have told an unnamed general that day that the enemy trenches were full of troops and machine-guns, and that a planned bombardment before the charge occurred would be 'worse than nothing (especially at night) as it was merely "ringing the bell" and telling the enemy we were coming'. These opinions were ignored, he said, 'but they were facts'.

Early on Friday afternoon, however, the troopers' attention was on the furious bombardment that had begun further down the main ridge to the right, on the enemy trenches at Lone Pine. Phillip Schuler, *The Age* correspondent, was there:

> At 5.30 came the avalanche. The artillery ceased. A whistle sharply blown was the signal prearranged. A score of more other whistles sounded almost simultaneously. The officers crouching each with his command under the parapets, were up then, and with some words like 'Come, lads, now for the trenches!' were over our parapets, and in a long, more or less regular line the heavily-laden men commenced the dash against the dead ground in between.

The great August Offensive had begun in earnest. In savage hand-to-hand fighting that would last for days at Lone Pine, some 2,200 Australians would be killed or wounded in the trenches, 7,000 Turks would be killed, and seven Victoria Crosses would be won. For two hours the light horsemen watched excitedly as group after group of distant khaki-clad figures ran forward into the yellow haze that covered the trenches at Lone Pine.

Most of the onlookers, said Bean, had not the least doubt that at dawn the next morning their attack upon Baby 700 would be equally successful. Throughout the night, wild bursts of rifle fire were heard, first comparatively close at hand, then more distant as the assaulting columns worked into the hills. 'Lastly, a little before daybreak, there came, far off and faint, a sound as of the bubbling of water in a cauldron. It was the rifle-fire at Suvla.' It was also the first sign of the new landing by a British force 8 kilometres to the north of The Nek.

While Schuler took eyewitness notes, Charles Bean, as official correspondent, could only listen for much of the night from his dugout. A stray bullet had hit him in the leg. But he kept making notes of the sounds he was hearing and would later pull together from eyewitnesses an extraordinary reconstruction of what actually happened then and later.

Sergeant Bunny Nugent, the football umpire, described his long wait in a letter to his mother:

We had to sit in the trenches all night and listen to the boys charging on both flanks. First they charged about nine o'clock on our left and then from our right at about midnight. We had to sit tight and wait as we were given the hardest job to do. All night long we sat and the strain was awful.

It is wonderful what you can do in such circumstances. About two o'clock I went to sleep. I slept for about an hour. Then I went and served out the rum to the men as the night was cold ... during the night I got the boys to dig with their bayonets, footholds in the trenches.

The word was passed down to stand by. We were told the order to advance would be given this way: 'Two minutes to go', 'One minute to go' and then 'Charge!'

As the sun went down over Imbros, Trooper Lex Borthwick caught his final glimpse of his brother. 'The last time I saw Keith,' he later told his parents, 'was on the evening of 6th August, just after dark, when Colonel White, with some of his officers, including Keith to assist him, was quietly – very quietly – moving the different troops thro' the saps into that particular part of the trench from which we were to attack the next morning.'

One of the men on the move was Trooper Meldrum, who said he was moved into the secret sap at 8 pm and waited through the night, about 35 metres from the nearest Turk trench. Most of the men just sat through the night, shivering, partly from the cold, partly from fear and apprehension.

Roger Palmer wasn't scared. He'd stowed away with reinforcements to get back to Gallipoli with the shrapnel pellet still in his thigh, and, according to Jack Mack, he'd had a bet of £5 that he would get into the Turkish trenches, alive or dead. 'Look at the example poor old Roger set us and we all knew he would,' said Stan later.

Behind the 8th, the Western Australians of the 10th were now getting ready in the rear, loading up with their picks and shovels, ready to file into the front trenches as soon as the two lines of the 8th had gone forward. Men from all ranks and stations of life joined together here. They described themselves, simply, as cobbers. They were all heroes, but when they rose from the trenches there would be no clarion calls from silver trumpets. When the time came, the charge would be sounded by shrill blasts on the nickel-plated regulation City Whistles (patented and 'Made in England') that had been issued to officers and NCOs from the army stores in Melbourne. And the men were expected to move forward, without hesitation.

At 9 pm a group of engineers arrived in the front lines and set to work to remove sections of barbed-wire entanglements so that there would be a clear passage through for the men in the charge. The Turks showed how vigilant they already were by shooting dead one sapper and wounding several others including the engineer in charge, who was shot through the foot. He caused some amusement to the troopers because he seemed more concerned about his damaged boot than his foot.

By now field guns and howitzers from Australian, New Zealand and British units had just begun a night-long bombardment of the Turkish trenches at The Nek and the Chessboard. They were each firing at the rate of a shell every two-and-a-half minutes. The enemy trenches facing the seaward slope could only be reached by the New Zealand howitzers, which were firing from Anzac Beach and soon were causing damage to the men of the Turkish 18th Regiment crowded into holding bays behind their front lines at The Nek. The 18th was the same regiment that had charged in the opposite direction – downhill – on 30 June, with massive casualties as the Australians shot them down as if it was a bush turkey shoot.

The artillery orders were to keep up this rate of fire until 4 am and then to increase the rate of fire to four shells a minute. This barrage would be supplemented by naval gunfire from the cruiser *Endymion*, the destroyers *Chelmer* and *Colne*, plus a naval monitor. Timing was critical for the success of the whole operation.

The barrage times in the artillery orders were changed twice but the final instructions were for the land batteries to fire slowly on The Nek from 10.30 pm on 6 August until 4 am on 7 August, then for a quick rate of fire from 4 to 4.30 am, before switching their fire to Battleship Hill, up the main ridge from Baby 700.

The navy's orders were also to fire at a quick rate from 4 to 4.30 am, before starting on new targets. So 4.30 am was the critical time. That was when the Charge at The Nek would commence.

But something went terribly wrong. On 7 August the guns would stop firing at 4.23 am, according to those on Walker's Ridge. Seven minutes early.

Subsequent investigations indicate that the artillery and naval gunfire was always going to stop at least three minutes early. On one hand, the navy wanted to allow some time to elapse between their ceasing fire and the start of the infantry attack. On the other, as Phillip Schuler would tell Charles Bean, some artillery officers had said they were ordered to fire 'much too close to their attacking troops on The Nek', so, because of the genuine concern that the gunners might hit one of their own, 'they were not going to take any risk'.

Even more curious was an inquiry afterwards into the role of the artillery, in which Australian and New Zealand commanders blamed each other and the claim was made that the Australian Field Artillery, then under the command of the New Zealanders, 'were never informed of the attack'.

In addition, Lieutenant Colonel Noel Brazier said that a fellow Western Australian, Colonel Bessell-Brown, commanding the WA field artillery, had told him he was not informed of the attack either. The officer apparently watched the light horse go into action feeling 'they could have been helped'.

The officer commanding the 1st Australian Division Artillery, Lieutenant Colonel J. Talbot Hobbs, told Bean later:

> I remember that General Hughes and Col. Antill endeavoured to saddle [the New Zealander] Johnstone's 2nd Field Artillery Brigade with the responsibility of the disaster, owing, as they said, to its failure to support or cover the Light Horse attack. I proved that these charges were unfounded and that Col. Johnstone was clearly and distinctly ordered to stop firing at 4.30 am.

Major General H.B. Walker, commanding the 1st Australian Division, had the last word: 'As Colonel Johnstone points out, he was not provided with a copy of General Hughes' operation order for the attack on The Nek and he was therefore not aware of the trenches to be attacked or the time.' Muddle and confusion.

But the question of the seven-minute time lag still hangs over the Charge at The Nek. It gave the Turks enough time to load up, cram their trenches and fully prepare for the full frontal charge.

Peter Burness, in his study of the battle, says the inescapable conclusion seems to be that there was a failure to synchronise watches somewhere along the command chain. Was regimental time correct? Did it agree with the watches that had been checked at 3rd Brigade level? According to Antill, when Colonel White visited brigade headquarters for the last time he 'said good-bye to the brigadier and brigade-major, compared watches, and rejoined his waiting command'.

Uncle Fred's nephew, Billy Kent Hughes, told Bean later that watches had definitely been synchronised here but 'how brigade time was synchronised with other times is a matter for higher command. As far as I remember the bombardment did stop early, but at a time when seconds are minutes and minutes seem like hours I should hardly like to hazard a guess at the length of the period.'

But what of divisional time? How were times checked off between Walker's Ridge, The Nek, the artillery and the navy? Burness advanced a theory that there could indeed have been two different local times on Gallipoli – Turkish time and British time – actually found to have been eight minutes apart back in May, when the two sides met to arrange times to bury their dead. Did these times sometimes get mixed up? These were the days, after all, when men checked their mechanical pocket watches, often giving them a tap just to make sure the second hand was working. Or did it all simply boil down to someone's watch running slow, or nobody double-checking?

Nine years afterwards, Lieutenant Wilfred Robinson of the 8th was quite sure of the seven-minute gap when he wrote to Bean, who was trying to check out the timing of the charge:

> I am quite certain that the discrepancy in the timing at The Nek on 7/8/15 was seven minutes.
>
> When the last shells burst in front I was standing with Col. White, Major Redford and Lt Dale.
>
> For a few moments no one spoke. Then the Col. said, 'Come along Dale' and then walked along the trench from the 'secret sap' and I remarked to Redford: 'What do you make of it. There is seven minutes to go.' He replied: 'They may give them a heavy burst to finish.'
>
> For three minutes hardly a shot came from the Turks and then a scattered rifle fire broke out above, which could be heard distinctly the rattle of about ten shots as each Turk machine gun was made ready for action.
>
> I got my men ready and shook hands with Major Redford a few seconds before he leaped out. He remarked as he did so: 'See you later Robbie.'
>
> His watch also showed the same time.
>
> We [the officers of 'C' Squadron] received our instructions and set our watches at 4.20 on the evening of the 6/8/15.
>
> Major Deeble remarked that he was not sure the time was correct but he would find out. Later when I asked him, he said it was correct but from his manner when I asked him I thought to myself that he had not made any inquiries.
>
> But evidently he had regimental time, as Redford belonged to B Squadron and his time was the same as mine.
>
> But I am sure that the bombardment ceased at 4.23 according to Redford's time and mine, and that the attack was launched seven minutes after the bombardment ceased and by that time the rifle and machine gun fire of the Turks had swelled to terrific fury and was

supplemented by shell fire from the French 75 guns with which they used to bombard us with before for some weeks.

Brazier wrote to Bean in 1931:

> Had the times been properly co-ordinated there was just a sporting chance that the job would have succeeded because some of our men could have reached the Turkish trenches before they manned their parapets. As it was, once the timing failed, I knew there was no possible hope and to push line after line on into it was absolute murder.

The men on Russell's Top had been awake all night as the shells shrieked overhead, whining, half whistling into a scream before exploding with a roar in the Turkish positions in front of them. The Australians had a secret red lamp right in their forward sap facing seawards so that the naval gunners, at least, knew that anything within 20 metres of the lamp would mean Allied casualties. The navy had been practising for weeks, using their searchlights for better observation, and the gunfire was accurate. Occasionally, however, a round fell short. Billy Kent Hughes said, for example, that brigade headquarters 'was very nearly blown up by one of our own shells'.

The Turks had responded at around midnight with a shower of high-explosive shell from their battery of French 75s situated further inland. The shells burst against the light horse parapets and in some places levelled them to the ground.

Sergeant Cliff St Pinnock, a Melbourne stockbroker, wrote later: 'The warships had been pounding their trenches with heavy guns. They kept it up for two hours. It was simply one continual roar and nerve racking to the extreme. You can't imagine the awful din of exploding shells, it was really awful.'

This is Ernie Mack's description:

> All we could do was watch spellbound as most of the shells were landing only thirty or forty yards in front of us on the first line of trenches. Nobody seeing such a bombardment for the first time would believe that anybody could be in and live – but we had often seen worse going on from Walker's Ridge down to Achi Baba and heard the results, which were always nil as far as the effects from the ships' guns were concerned as their position is too flat. Though it was a wonderful sight we were not much elated and as soon as the guns stopped firing and we got out of the trenches to wait for the signal to charge, our worst fears were realised …

Antill later dismissed it as a 'piffling' bombardment. It had certainly caused some enemy casualties and damaged part of the Turkish trench line to the right, but it had not destroyed the machine-guns.

The Turks were the first Balkan power to acquire the water-cooled Maxim machine-guns. Quite how many they had mounted on their tripods on the slope of Baby 700 covering the killing field at The Nek before dawn that day is still open to conjecture.

Sergeant St Pinnock thought there were about 30 firing 1,000 rounds a minute. But Bunny Nugent, a Boer War veteran, said afterwards that there were about 100 machine-guns playing onto about 65 metres of trenching.

They fired 7.92-millimetre sharp-pointed bullets, the kind of bullets compatible with the ammunition used in the Mauser rifles held by the Turkish infantry, who would cram two deep into the trenches from their holding bays once the Allied bombardment ceased.

A Mr G. Valentine Williams, war correspondent for the London *Daily Mail*, had already reported from the Western Front on the effectiveness of the machine-gun in a despatch that had been reprinted in the Australian newspapers when the light horsemen had been in camp at Broadmeadows.

> When you have blown away the enemy's barbed wire entanglements and parapets, his machine guns remain, either those which have survived the bombardment or others rushed up by hand from the rear. As an instance of the deadly swiftness of machine gun fire it may be mentioned that a man coming under fire of one of these weapons and shot through the head by the first bullet can be struck yet ten times more in the second or two that he takes in collapsing and falling to the ground.
>
> The British soldier is irresistible in the attack when he is man to man; but not all the valour of the British Isles can prevail against a machine that spits six hundred deaths in a minute, though the trench be blown to fragments and the barbed wire blasted away.

Things were not going well elsewhere as the night wore on. The preconditions for the Charge at The Nek were beginning to fall apart. The attack on German Officer's Trench had failed. The New Zealanders' planned attack from the rear on Chunuk Bair was disintegrating in the darkness. The officer in command, Brigadier General Francis Johnston, is now widely supposed to have been either drunk or suffering from some sort of physical or mental breakdown at the time. Whatever, the New Zealand force was running very late. Three battalions of Kiwis had clambered up one rugged ridge, then stopped and waited for another battalion, which became lost while trying to climb another. An order was misinterpreted and most of this force ended back where they had started from.

On Quinn's Post, Pope's Hill and in the trenches facing The Nek, the light horsemen all awaited their final orders. At Quinn's, Major G.H. Bourne of the 2nd Light Horse said afterwards that the orders from divisional headquarters were 'being changed all through the night'. It was symptomatic that it was here, at one of the most dangerous outposts, only after dark, and right before this most desperate operation, that infantry webbing equipment had been sent up to these Queenslanders on the heights, with orders to substitute it for their light horse bandoliers.

The spirit of the men the night before, said Major Bourne, was excellent. They were 'quite confident of their own and the whole big offensive'. But in the morning, as the preconditions evaporated, 'though grimly determined they knew the truth'.

Four lines of 50 men each set to charge here. When the first line was eventually ordered to move off, at 4.30 am: 'I saw my entire first wave mown down – apparently five machine guns were playing on the narrow front.' Forty-nine of his 50 men were either killed or wounded.

Bourne immediately gave an order to the second wave to 'stand fast'. 'To continue the operation would have been sheer murder,' he told Bean later.

At Pope's Hill, also at 4.30 am, another 200 light horsemen, this time from New South Wales, would also be ordered out in another joint action to the main attack by the 3rd Light Horse Brigade on Baby 700 through The Nek. At Pope's only 46 men returned uninjured. Every officer except one would be hit.

All this would pale – and is to a large extent forgotten – in the shadow of what was to happen at The Nek.

At divisional headquarters, General Birdwood and his ever-optimistic offsider and scheme architect Lieutenant Colonel Andrew Skeen had been in anxious communication over the primitive telephone system all night with the divisional commander, Major General Alexander Godley, the British parade-ground soldier whose gung-ho attitude had been echoed by Antill when he had issued his orders.

As the reports came in, Birdwood and Skeen knew that in the grand plan for the offensive, Monash and his men, operating further to the north in their attempt to take Hill 971, were now battling through the darkness and held up in the razorbacks of 'the mad country".

But they had heard that the New Zealanders had achieved an early success in the foothills in their crucial back-door climb up to Chunuk Bair to attack Baby 700 from the rear. The divisional headquarters pictured them struggling upwards in the night, needing all the help they could get.

This success was critical if the grand offensive was to succeed. So headquarters had no hesitation in ordering the light horse into action. The original idea of the converging attacks was thrown out the window. Now it was to be a full frontal assault. 'It is not the light horse I am anxious about,' said Skeen later when the fighting raged above him on the heights, 'I think they will be all right. What I hope is that they will help the New Zealanders.'

It was half an hour before zero hour on Russell's Top. Hughes, Antill and White were among the officers crowded into the crumbly, shell-battered earth dugout, which was forward brigade headquarters. It was only a few metres behind the front line trenches and fitted with a telephone. There were another half-dozen phone points towards the rear and the lines went on down the ridge. But the phone lines could not be relied on and were often destroyed once a battle commenced.

The orders for the day said that progress reports were to be furnished directly to headquarters from this forward phone point 'as occasion permits so that HQ is kept fully alive to all developments' and that 'In case of breakdown helios and lamp will be available'. Elsewhere the orders said, 'until then C.O. lines will keep Headquarters informed by orderlies of its fortunes and should unforeseen difficulties present themselves advise headquarters'.

In practice, once an action began, commanders had little direct control on what happened once their men had gone over the top.

Jack Antill said that at about 4 am there was suddenly an intense and continued fusillade of rifle and machine-gun fire aimed at the top of the parapets:

> There must have been a score or more (machine guns) in action at close quarters indicating a sure knowledge of our plans.
>
> Between the commencement of the fusillade, which never slackened a second, and zero [hour], two urgent telephone messages were sent to divisional headquarters describing the situation, which was stated to be a most serious development and urging the abandonment or postponement of the attack.
>
> The laconic reply was that the attack must proceed according to plan.

In the hand-written note he sent to Bean in 1931, Antill himself would claim he regarded that decision as a 'callous and unforgivable blunder'. (Whoever made the 'laconic reply' was never identified.)

Colonel Alexander White must also have known at this point that the order meant certain death. It was then that this most decent and honourable man decided he must make the ultimate sacrifice of leading his men from the front. It was a terrible but final decision.

Ten minutes before zero hour he held out his hand to the brigade major. 'Goodbye Antill,' he said.

Perhaps stung by the popular CO's earlier remark ('Damn it! I'll lead my regiment'), Antill the martinet, the disciplinarian, couldn't avoid sneering in the same note to the official historian as he described that moment.

> White's goodbye was pathetic – he had no coat on and round his neck was a chain and locket with his young wife and infant baby's photo.
>
> He insisted on leading his men – we did our best to persuade him otherwise.
>
> He certainly had the ultimate right to choose his own place.

With his faithful adjutant Charles Dale behind him, White walked back along the trenches, calmly talking to his men of the 8th. There were no shirkers.

'It was just before we went out,' remembered Dave McGarvie, 61 years later. 'He said, "How are you feeling?" and I said, "We'll do our best, sir." He said, "I'm sure you will." And then he went on. I didn't see him again.'

The officers went to their places along the line and looked down intently at their watches. At 4.23 am the artillery had suddenly, inexplicably, ceased firing and the naval guns shifted their aim to boom away at some of the more distant trenches.

Across The Nek, opposite the light horsemen, the Turks cautiously raised their heads. Then, not believing their luck as no more shooting followed, they began pouring into the front line trenches, two deep. One line seated themselves on the parapet, the others stood behind, all the soldiers nestling their rifles to their shoulders, placing spare magazines handy, taking aim, waiting. There was an occasional stutter as a machine-gunner tested that a long belt of ammunition was feeding into his Maxim properly. More belts were wound up in coils alongside the guns.

From the Australian position, at least 75 men of the first line, some of them carrying ladders and planks, had crawled out from the saps under cover on the left and lay still, 10 metres in front, awaiting the order to charge. Others of the first line in the deep trench to the right had their feet in the fire steps carved by their bayonets, ready to be pushed up and over by those waiting to replace them in the second line.

'Three minutes to go,' said Colonel White, staring down at the second hand of his pocket watch. Then: 'Go!' The whistles shrilled along the line.

The colonel, his officers and men leapt up over the parapet or jumped to their feet from their positions in front of the trench. The oaths, the cries, and the cheering of the Australian light horsemen were almost immediately drowned out by a rising crescendo of noise that increased in seconds from a crackle to one continuous roar in which it was impossible to distinguish between the rattle of rifle shots and the awful barking snicker of the machine-guns.

Then came the thud of exploding bombs. Black cricket-ball bombs thrown by the Turks, homemade jam-tin bombs thrown by the running troopers, lit from the smouldering lengths of rope hanging from their belts. Then there was the whoosh and crump of petrol bombs also thrown from the Turkish parapets. Very soon their French 75s would also be hurling artillery shells into No Man's Land, ten shells a minute.

Everyone remembered the noise. 'A thousand sticks rattled across a thousand sheets of corrugated iron at the rate of a thousand revolutions a minute would hardly give a conception of what the sound of the guns was like,' said Noel Brazier.

Bean called it 'one continuous roaring tempest. One could not help an involuntary shiver – God help anyone that was out in that tornado. But one knew very well that men were out in it – the time put the meaning of it beyond all doubt.'

'The noise was appalling,' Tom Austin wrote, 'the air was filled with the venomous hissing and crackling of bullets and the swish swish of machine guns as they traversed to and fro searching for victims'.

It was just on dawn. Chaplain Merrington, over to the right with his light horsemen, heard the noise and looked back towards Walker's Ridge:

> Through the early morning mist I looked across and saw our Australian soldiers advancing on top of the cliffs above. They were part of the Third Light Horse Brigade.
>
> In the half light their forms on the skyline looked positively gigantic. Right nobly they went on – but they never reached the trench.
>
> The enemy's machine guns acted like a saw and the gallant troopers fell ...

The line seemed to suddenly go limp and sink to the earth, as if, said another eye witness, 'the men's limbs had become string'.

The machine-guns scythed their way back and forth, back and forth, through bone and flesh. The Turkish soldiers were loading and reloading their rifles as fast as they could possibly fire, the machine-gunners feeding belt after belt into the Maxims, now almost glowing red-hot.

Colonel White managed to go eight or ten paces before he fell, his body torn and riddled by bullets. Every officer in the first line to go out was killed. Only two officers in the entire regiment would remain unwounded. Many men fell back into the trench severely wounded before clearing the parapet. Others being hit when just beyond the earth wall were now crawling back, tumbling over on top of their comrades. In the yelling, screaming chaos, the men of the second line were now stepping on and over the wounded and the dying, trying to get a foot in the fire step, ready for their turn at the enemy.

The charge of the first line only lasted about 30 seconds.

Survivors later gave accounts of what had happened to them in the murderous pandemonium. One was Sergeant Cliff St Pinnock:

> We got the order to 'GIVE IT TO THEM BOYS' … well, we got over and cheered but they were waiting ready for us and simply gave us a solid wall of lead. I was in the first line to advance and we did not get ten yards. Every one fell like lumps of meat … I got mine shortly after I got over the bank and it felt like a million ton hammer falling on my shoulder … I was really awfully lucky as the bullet went in just below the shoulder blade round by my throat and came out just a tiny way from my spine low down on the back.

Stan Mack was already in the hospital in Egypt when St Pinnock and other wounded arrived: 'He does not know how he felt, like all the others I have spoken to. They just had an idea sticking in their minds that they had to get to the trench in front of them.'

Jack Dale wrote to his mother:

> All of a sudden the Turks opened up on us with murderous machine gun fire. It was something terrific and I have never heard anything like it. Those of us who got over the very slight rise of ground were simply mown down.
>
> I was one of three who were carrying a big plank which we had to throw over any entanglements and then the trenches when we got there.

212

We got pretty close up and were lucky to get behind a slight rise in the ground. We had to lie flat on our stomachs. We were fairly safe from the bullets although some were landing very close. Bombs were bursting not five yards from where I was.

Wounded fellows were crawling past us, some with terrible wounds caused by bombs. All you could do was to make way and help them past. I was expecting a bomb any minute.

The round, black cricket-ball bombs were rolling, bouncing and exploding everywhere. Ernie Mack had a 'marvellous escape' when a bomb exploded close to his leg and 'the concussion was so great that it turned me completely over and the only thing I had to show for it was a few ragged tears in my uniform'.

Some of the machine-gunners were aiming and traversing low, chattering more death, and concentrating on the parapet. Carew Reynell watching with other officers of the 9th in reserve, said, 'some men's legs were completely severed by this fire'.

Lionel Simpson, the last living survivor of the charge, recalled in a television interview in 1988:

> I was holding one end of this plank and my cobber was holding the other end. I pulled away and wondered why it was so heavy. He (the cobber) got shot in the leg; in fact it was the knee. I could see the knee coming out with the machine gun bullets.
>
> I was going along when a bullet hit me in the left shoulder – it didn't stop me, because it went in and bounced out. The men seemed to be falling behind me … I was in the front and I could see a chap about three yards in front of me. He fell down and I thought 'It's time to get out'.

Simpson said he 'ambled' back to the trench.

It was not only Colonel White who had gone to his death with great and unhesitating gallantry. Lionel Simpson had witnessed the death of his own officer, Lieutenant Eliot Wilson, the young grazier from Warrnambool known as 'Ted', who had once helped the Macks with their horses – another time and another world away.

Simpson said Wilson was among the first to go over. The troop leader was seen sitting with his back to the enemy's parapet, brandishing a revolver, beckoning for his men to come to him and shouting: 'Come on, boys, for God's sake, come on!' Then he was shot. He tried to stagger to his feet until a bomb exploded near him and he collapsed. There was another explosion, as if his revolver had gone off underneath him.

Seven years after the charge, after some considerable correspondence, the army forwarded to Wilson's mother a tiny silver laurel wreath to 'indicate that this officer was Mentioned in Despatches to be attached to the riband of the Victory Medal'.

Major Tom Redford had died bravely, too. Corporal McGrath wrote a warm, generous epitaph in Redford's own diary:

> Our gallant major whilst lying facing the enemy's trench 10 yards away in the front of his men received a bullet through his brain as he raised his head slightly to observe. He died with a soft sigh and laid his head gently on his hands as if tired. A braver and more honourable man never donned uniform.

Lieutenant Cyril Marsh, just 22 years of age, seemed to have made the most ground before being killed. His body was sighted resting on the Turkish parapet.

'Of Mr Henty and Mr Borthwick,' McGrath wrote again, 'no one knows anything and time alone will tell of them.'

Lex Borthwick wanted to go out to find his younger, officer brother Keith that very next night. He was soon dissuaded as the Turkish machine-guns started up again directly as soon as a head appeared above the trench in the moonlight. And so Keith's body was never found.

But on the dawn of 7 August, Lex Borthwick had had his own miraculous escape. Not knowing that his brother had charged to his death, this trooper would go out with the second line just minutes later:

> My troop had a small slope to go up before the machine guns could get at them which is the reason we were not annihilated. I was lying on the top of the slope at the ridge and every man round me was dead before the order came along to retire.
>
> Bruce Kinnaird, a clerk in the Savings Bank, was lying alongside me and an explosive bullet hit him on the neck killing him instantly.
>
> Part of the bullet hit me on the buttocks and I think it is still there. It hurt for a moment but I thought to myself, I am wounded and have a good excuse to retire, but finding it was nothing I had to continue to lie there while the Turks from their trenches ten yards away were throwing bombs onto the top of my ridge.
>
> How I escaped being killed I don't know. The bombs are round like a cricket ball and one rolled over my neck, bumped alongside my body and bust a little lower down the hill. The bombs killed a lot of men that day. They make frightful, ghastly wounds.

I shall never forget the horrors of that charge which came to nothing.

Over on the right, Sergeant Roger Ebden Harcourt Palmer – former head prefect, former captain of the First XI, winner of the Fortis and Fidelis prize at King Alfred's College, Taunton – had made a dash that should have won him a posthumous Victoria Cross. Ignoring the existing shrapnel wound in his thigh, Palmer, carrying a yellow-and-red marker flag about a foot square, had reached the Turkish front trench.

There could have been three or four other troopers with him. Those mentioned by survivors are: Sergeant Major Colin Cameron, the old Scotch College boy, who before the attack had left a final letter with William McGrath; Trooper William Hind, the young monotype operator from *The Hamilton Spectator*; Trooper James Cameron, an engine driver from Orbost; and Signaller Geoffrey Grant, who had been a clerk in the Sunshine Harvester works.

A Turkish prisoner who was in the front enemy trench at the time would tell later that while he knew nothing of any Australians entering it alive, three men had succeeded in reaching the Turkish trenches, falling dead over the parapet into the bottom of the first ditch.

At least two witnesses vouched that Palmer reached the Turkish line.

The first was Trooper Preston Younger. He told Palmer's sister, Maude, after the war that he had been beside Roger Palmer and had seen him get into the Turkish trenches just as he (Preston) was knocked over by a bullet.

The other witness was Lance Corporal Don Oliver, observing keenly as Jack Mack fired their howitzer mortar with its 4-pound shells into the Turkish trenches. Oliver wrote to Charles Bean on 30 March 1924, from his club, The Warrigal:

> I am glad to say I am in a position to absolutely confirm the suggestion that a red and yellow flag was raised in the Turkish trenches during our attack on their lines.
>
> It was my duty that day to watch carefully for these flags, as I was to hurry our trench mortars across as soon as the Turks had been driven out of the first line.
>
> I am almost sure that I am the only one who saw the flag raised as it was only by careful watching that I could see it owing to the dense cloud of dust that was raised by the enemies [sic] machine gun fire immediately after the first line of our fellows went out.
>
> I would like to say also that I am very nearly certain that Sergeant Roger Palmer was the only man of ours that reached the Turkish lines.

215

He was a man of splendid physique and rather stood out among the others and I am pretty sure that it was he whom I saw drop into the enemies trench.

I am absolutely certain that the flag was raised and I am just as certain that one of our fellows did get into the Turkish line and it was after he got in that the flag was waved.

The Turks seemed to be very thick in the front line trench and I could see their bayonets shining and they seemed very close together.

I will be very pleased if I can be of any further use to you regarding any information that you may require as I was in a very good position to observe anything that happened on the day in question.

But for how long the flag fluttered behind the Turkish parapet is still open to question. A few days after the charge, Schuler and Bean were trying to reconstruct what had happened. In his first report from the battlefield, the wounded Bean said it flew for ten minutes. In his next report he said it was for only two minutes. In his *Official History* he returned to his original ten minutes, before adding that 'some unseen agency tore it down'.

Phillip Schuler, however, in his original reporting, said, 'ten minutes had scarcely gone by' when the feat was accomplished; and later, in his book, he wrote: 'The flag in the enemy's trench soon disappeared.'

Whichever of the times is correct, it flew long enough for a later fatal decision to be made, even if this was to be denied afterwards by the man who made it.

The few men who had managed to get well forward were now lying dead or wounded some 10 metres from the Turkish front trench. The vast majority lay dead or wounded no more than 5 metres from the Australian parapet. And there were others who had taken cover in the few shallow holes and dips in the ground, especially on the left, and were hugging the earth as the machine guns continued to spray death above them.

The parapet was covered with dead and dying. Stretcher-bearers were trying to reach up and drag them down into the trenches. At the same time a fresh wave of men were taking their place on the fire steps. Many times they couldn't help stepping on their wounded cobbers as they readied to go over.

As the red-and-yellow flag waved, the whistles shrilled again. The machine-gun and rifle fire, which had faded away briefly to a dull mutter, began to bark and chatter into the dreadful cacophony of death once again.

Exactly two minutes after the first 150 men of the 8th Light Horse had charged into near annihilation, the second line of 150 men jumped out without the slightest hesitation and followed them.

The commanding officer of the 8th Light Horse Regiment, Colonel White, was dead.

And nobody else tried to stop the second line.

Chapter 15

Nothing But Bloody Murder

Captain Leslie Fraser Standish 'George' Hore, born in India, educated in the UK at Wellington College and Corpus Christi College, Oxford, a barrister and solicitor, led the right wing of the second line as it charged. Under him were three subalterns and, he estimated, 175 men.

Captain Hore was one of the very few of the second line to survive. He wrote to his mother from a hospital ship afterwards, with a bullet wound through the bone of his right foot and another through his right shoulder. He said he had been through 'the valley of the shadow of death'. As soon as his men had heard the noise that greeted the first line, 'we knew we were doomed'.

He estimated that with the Turkish machine-gunners firing 600 rounds a minute and their riflemen 15 rounds a minute, there were at least 5,000 rounds a minute being poured into them on this tiny battlefield the size of three tennis courts. As the crackle of fire grew into a roar again, he said he had never heard such an awful sound.

> We saw our fate in front of us but we were pledged to go and to their eternal credit, the word being given, not a man in the second line stayed in his trench.
>
> As I jumped out I looked down the line and they were rising over the parapet.
>
> We bent low and ran as hard as we could.
>
> Ahead we could see the trench aflame with rifle fire. All round were smoke and dust kicked up by the bullets.
>
> I felt a sting on my shoulder and remember thinking it could not be a hit or it would hurt more. It bled a lot I found afterwards but it was only a flesh wound.
>
> I passed our first line all dead or dying it seemed and went on a bit further and flung myself down about forty yards from the Turkish

trenches. I was a bit ahead of my men having got a good start and travelling lighter.

I looked round and saw them all down, mostly hit. I did not know what to do, the dirt was spurting up all around like rain from a pavement in a thunderstorm. Some bigger spurts were either bombs or pom poms. I could notice they were much bigger.

The trench ahead was a living flame, the roar of musketry not a bit diminished.

I was protected by a little, a very little fold in the ground and by a dead Turk, dead about six weeks. I looked around again and reckoned I could get about six men to follow and it would have been murder to take them on ...

So More decided to lie there a while and await developments. Trooper Alexander Meldrum also wrote to his mother, from hospital in Egypt:

I only got about five yards when I felt a bullet go through my hat and it knocked me out. I seemed to be there a terribly long time but it could only have been a few seconds.

I put my hand to my head and felt the blood, but it had ploughed along the bone.

I heard our chaps still cheering as they charged so I jumped up and went on again.

I got about ten yards when another bullet took a piece of skin off my right eye.

I dropped down again as there didn't seem to be any of our chaps left.

Another bullet went through my boot, just nicking the corner of my heel and sock.

I was also bleeding at the right shoulder, so I left my rifle and crawled back.

We struck a terrible lot of bombs and they used petrol bombs which explode and burn anything near ...

To add to the horror of the barking machine-guns, the uneven rippling crack of the rifle fire, and the whoomp and crump of the bombs, death was also raining down from another direction. Two Turkish 75-millimetre field guns had the range and were now bursting their shrapnel low over No Man's Land, as fast as they could be loaded and fired.

The air reeked with the smell of cordite, as a result. And, even worse, the bullets were ripping into and opening up the sun-dried bodies of the

Turkish soldiers that had been lying out here in the open since the ill-fated attack on 29 June. The stench blended with the sweetness of freshly spilled blood, and the screams and yells of the wounded and dying only added to the unimaginable terror of those who found themselves still alive.

Major Arthur Deeble, the schoolteacher from Essendon, was in overall charge of the second line. The men apparently nicknamed him 'Annie' Deeble, good-naturedly, because soon after arriving in the trenches of Walker's Ridge, he had used particularly strong cologne in a personal effort to try to overcome the stench of the dead. With the death of Colonel White, Deeble was now also in command of the regiment. And like the beloved colonel, he was leading his men from the centre of the line.

Despite this, Deeble was unable to prevent the second line going over the top, as Major Bourne did over at Quinn's Post. The Queenslanders' commander, having seen all but one of the men in his first line mown down within seconds, held back the next line. He then spoke to his immediate superior and stopped the attack – an action that was later endorsed by his brigade commander, Brigadier General Harry Chauvel. One can only speculate in horror at how many of the 200 men in the 2nd Light Horse would have been sacrificed had Bourne not intervened.

But on The Nek, the charge had its own ghastly momentum. Deeble, at best, would have had only seconds to make such a decision, with the second line following so hard on the heels of the first. It may well have been impossible to relay an order down the line in time to prevent it going out. And in the confusion, he may not have even realised the extent of the slaughter of the first line until he cleared the parapet himself.

The moment obviously haunted Arthur Deeble for the rest of his life. A family history records that in the 1930s, when he was farming at Donald, he 'threw his Turkish hand gun into the dam in frustration of his war memories'. It was the revolver that he had souvenired from a body after the Turks had charged at The Nek in June.

Antill would later insist: 'After the zero whistle had blown, no further orders were issued until the attack had been abandoned. The Brigadier [Hughes] was on the spot himself, and if such an order were given, or to be given, it was he, and he alone competent to give it. But no such or any order was given.'

But the brigadier general was *not* on the spot. At this critical time, as the second line went over the top, and with two of his regimental commanders dead – Miell having been shot when he showed his head over the parapet to observe – Hughes had decided to leave his brigade command post. In an apparent effort to observe what was going on from another safe position, he possibly joined Jack Mack and Lance Corporal Don Oliver in their trench-mortar position, over on the right, and cautiously raised a periscope.

The Bullant remained at the command post behind the front line – he was the one really in charge now. He was in his dugout, the man 'on the spot' and making the decisions.

The men of the second line rose up cheering, then cursed and fell as the bullets scythed them down. Some of the living, like Captain Hore, promptly stayed down and abandoned the charge altogether.

After clearing the parapet, Major Deeble, as brave a man as any who faced the Turks that morning, went to ground. He would spend the next hour and a half prudently hugging the earth as the lead and the shrapnel fizzed above him. With Mervyn Higgins, Deeble would be one of only two officers of the 8th to emerge unscathed from the charge.

Lex Borthwick was one of those in the second line:

> When our Regiment made the charge Major Deeble was close to me lying flat on his stomach and he kept on saying: 'We will have to charge', while Colonel White, Major Redford and all the other officers were leading their men straight at the machine guns. If Annie Deeble had made us get up we would all have been killed so personally I was glad we were allowed to take cover.

The major would give his own account of his actions, a careful and tightly written entry in his diary, apparently entered soon after the charge. Deeble said that his second line had followed less than a minute after Colonel White, and that 'after carefully explaining the task and indicating an objective to each troop leader, the senior officers could only lead on the few around and carry forward those in their immediate vicinity'. He went on:

> The second line speedily overtook the first, which had been practically wiped out, as every man seemed to be dead or wounded.
>
> My own line came under a most deadly hail of machine gun, bomb and rifle fire and the men fell all around me. No man hesitated yet I had none to carry further.
>
> I fell on my face and taking the cover of the nearest depression of the ground managed to get together … speak to about 8 or 10 men not yet shot. I determined to wait for the 3rd line (10th Regt) and sweep forward with them.

This line was considerably late in starting – fully 25 minutes – and scarcely left the trench before being broken, and the few men with me managed to dash a yard or two forward before falling down.

I threw myself a second time on the ground and prepared for any further lines which might come forward. Seeing one or two to my left whom I could make hear me, I told them to scratch a little cover and wait for the next line. This was on our left. Probably little could be done and no assaulting party could have been formed from there, and any further lines would I think have met the same fate as ours.

At 6.05 I received word to join the 10th Regt to reform. I wriggled back into the trenches and a few around me and small parties along our front who had dropped into almost imperceptible depressions at the back.

Of the 300 who took part in the assault we sustained 210 casualties including 16 officers. The CO is missing.

Our men had to face this deadly fire from the instant they leapt from the parapet and never hesitated to follow the CO and myself until the CO had fallen and I had some around me to lead.

Some time before our second line got as far forward as the first I must have been the only officer in the line except Lt Higgins whose few followers were some distance to my left. The right half of the assault line found the same fusillade as ours. They were quite hidden from my view. No officer has returned from the right.

In fact, one man, Lieutenant Andrew Crawford, did return. His brother officers, including Charles Carthew and Tom Howard, the latter in charge of the bombers, perished along with their men.

Along with Troop Sergeant George Fuzzard, Crawford hailed from the town of Tatura, a town in Victoria famous for its tomatoes. Both men survived their severe wounds to take part in Anzac Day parades when they came home.

Crawford was in one of the deepest parts of the front trench and hauled himself up and over by means of the pegs and notches carved by bayonets in the trench wall. He saw Turks, two deep, firing over each other's shoulders. Later he wrote a letter to his sister, May, that was published in his hometown paper, *The Tatura Guardian*:

The crackle was deafening and the smoke from the bombs terrific. Nearly the whole of the first line was shot down. We were only a minute or two behind the first line, and when we got up to them there wasn't a man left standing, so we lay down and took as much cover as we could.

222

'Bomb throwers to the front' was called out by someone and Ollie Donaldson [a 20-year-old trooper from St Kilda] and another bomb-thrower rushed forward and threw some bombs and that was the last that was seen of them.

I crawled forward a few yards and had a look at the Turks' trenches. The 10th regiment formed the third and fourth lines and they came out soon after us. We got up and tried to rush forward with them but it was no use. I got hit on my thigh as soon as I started to get up and was rolled right over.

My left leg was stiffened a bit with the hit but I crawled on a bit further. I got right amongst the dead and it was there I got the one in the back, and several grazes on my back and one on my head. These I did not feel. All of the bullets that hit me came from the left flank and I am thankful to say that they went right through.

After I was hit I wriggled back as far as I could under cover and lay there for some time. After a while I heard the regiment was retiring ...

Two men took his equipment off and started to drag him in. Then two other men, Trumpeter Les Lawry, a carpenter's apprentice from Geelong, and Trooper Albert Williams, a nineteen-year-old farmer from Broadmeadows, carried him to safety.

Lawry was responsible for several rescues that day. For this he was Mentioned in Despatches for his gallantry, one of the few minor awards handed out to those in the Charge at The Nek. To this honour could be added the admiration of his fellow light horsemen.

'Les Lawry, a very decent little chap from Geelong and not 19 yet, returned to our trenches and heard that Anderson our A Troop Lieutenant was seen lying wounded near the Turk trench,' wrote Stan Mack. 'He never said a word to anyone [about] what he was going to do but hopped over the parapet, walked out and brought Lieut Anderson in without getting a scratch himself.'

Leo Anderson, one of the first Duntroon graduates, was mortally wounded. Like his commanding officer and occasional bridge partner, Colonel White, Anderson hailed from Ballarat, but now the handsome twenty-year-old was in a dirty, bloodstained trench, his body riddled by machine-gun bullets. 'Lawry got him in at 7 in the morning,' Stan continued, 'but he sank and died at 4 in the afternoon.'

Anderson lies today in the Ari Burnu Cemetery. His Duntroon classmate, Lieutenant Charles Dale, the 21-year-old adjutant who went along on Sid Campbell's last swim at Anzac Cove, had also died, with Colonel White in the centre of the first line. Dale and White have no known grave; their bones, along with all the others, are mingled under the turf at The Nek. Lieutenant Colonel Alexander White was also Mentioned in Despatches, posthumously, almost as an afterthought. The certificate was posted to his widow, Myrtle, much later on.

Captain Archibald McLaurin, the vigneron from Rutherglen, and the man who had led the second advance party from Melbourne on *Anglo-Egyptian*, was another Mentioned in Despatches and would soon be promoted to major. His efforts that day, as leader of the second line's left side, included trying to get young Anderson in to safety from a hole partly covered by some bushes. McLaurin's citation reads:

> About twenty yards in front of his sap there was a slight rise and by the time he got there the first line had been mown down by a terrific rifle and machine gun fire.
>
> Maj. McLaurin exhibited the greatest coolness and courage when exposed to this rifle fire on top of the ridge. While doing this Maj. McLaurin was wounded on the forehead but nevertheless remained out front until the order was given to retire.
>
> When this order was given, Maj. McLaurin acted with great coolness and succeeded in collecting what was left of his Squadron and getting them back quickly and in a quiet and orderly manner into our trenches.
>
> He himself was the last to return to his portion of the line.

Lieutenant Wilfred Robinson, the wheat farmer on 'Murra Warra', was in command of 'C' Squadron's 'B' Troop. Through some misunderstanding, these men were late in moving up into position and had just filed into their trench when the second line charged:

> As I climbed out of the 'secret sap' on the extreme left, my hand was shattered and I was almost knocked senseless by a bursting shell or a bomb.
>
> By some means, either falling or struggling frantically I got back into the sap, where I remember trying to think what had happened and suddenly becoming aware of a terrific rifle fire and later was fully restored to my senses by a lot of men unceremoniously walking over me.

Robinson's troop sergeant, 25-year-old Charles Lyon, who had been educated at Geelong Grammar School, took over. 'Just as we got into the front sap our troop officer was shot through the hand and retired,' Sergeant Lyon later recounted. 'I was left in charge and being unable to jam past the men jumped up and ran round to the front sap calling on them to follow but just as we got out, the line fell back nearly all wounded with orders to retire.'

Lyon was writing to the mother of Lance Corporal Norm Tetley, another public school boy, from Melbourne Grammar. Tetley was one of the men who had ignored doctor's advice. He insisted on rejoining the regiment for the charge, despite having been shaken up severely and his face peppered with gravel during a shell barrage six weeks before. Norm charged out with the first line of the 8th and was now another one of those lying dying. Lyon's letter continued:

> He was keen on being with his troop and couldn't stand the idea of being left behind.
>
> As we dropped back into the sap I saw Norman lying just in front and with the assistance of others got him in and laid him on the bottom of the trench. His leg was in a fearful state; a machine gun had got onto him.
>
> Bearers were fearfully busy and we were in and out of the way and he had to lie there over two hours before it was possible to get him away. The loss of blood must have been very great.

In the front trench, the earth was now falling down in a continuous stream from the parapet so that the doctor could not treat Tetley or any of the other wounded lying there. The suffering was appalling as the injured men crawled back to the parapet, some dragging themselves by their arms, before they fell over and then waited their turn to be half carried, half dragged back down the connecting trenches to a makeshift field hospital. Tom Austin's account provides some more detail on the plight of the 8th's wounded:

> One boy hopped in, his foot hanging by a sinew, he was laughing as he fell into friendly arms and was still full of pluck.
>
> They lopped his foot off a few minutes after at the clearing station but he got home to Australia all right.
>
> Those nearer the enemy were in a terrible plight. The slightest movement of hand or foot brought a hail of fire on them and in this way many a poor wounded fellow moving in his agony suffered death.

Lance Corporal William 'Scotty' Tosh was among those fatally wounded. Tosh was a big man, born in Fifeshire, Scotland, and had been a border sheep farmer before he migrated to Australia. There, he took up a job as assistant overseer of 'Barunah' station in Victoria.

Witnesses said that he was brought to the dressing station 'absolutely shattered by machine gun fire' and that, after being taken from the trench into hospital, he had begged for morphia. Corporal Joe Davidson would recall that, when Tosh saw that the men around him thought he was on the way out, the Scotsman told them, 'No, I'm not done.' Unfortunately he was – he died on his stretcher. Later that day Corporal Davidson buried him with nine other troopers, in the same grave.

It was 4.35 am by the time that the second line had charged and been mown down. In just five minutes the 8th Light Horse Regiment, from its commanding officer to the youngest trooper, had been almost totally annihilated. Yet the murder and the madness continued.

In the bloody mayhem of the tiny maze of trenches, the Western Australians of the 10th Light Horse were now struggling past the wounded and trying not to step on the dying as they moved up from reserve positions to take their places for the next two lines of the charge. There were frequent halts to allow the stretchers and the walking wounded past. The Turks, awaiting the next offering for slaughter, eased their fire to the occasional stutter of machine-guns and the rattle of rifle fire, aimed mainly at any survivors from the first two lines, while the shrapnel from the 75s on Hill 60 still screeched overhead.

The 10th's regimental orders were for Major Tom Todd (in command of 'A' Squadron) to form the third line on the left flank, and Major Joe Scott (in command of 'B' Squadron) to occupy the trenches to the right and form the fourth line to go out. The regimental headquarters was set up at Number 5 sap, one of the fingers probing out to the Turks towards the right of the front line.

Lieutenant Colonel Noel Brazier had wisely decided, going by the book, to command his regiment from this position and not to go over the top as White had in his heroic yet vainglorious action. Brazier, bluff and tough, was a practical man who did things by regulations. He, like White, obeyed orders, but Brazier was also the only person in the whole sad affair who really tried to stop the Charge at The Nek. He said he knew the order to go was 'decidedly wrong' and would write later: 'Had Colonel White not gone with his first line – as he was wrong in doing – and watched the proceedings, as it was his real duty to do, between us we may have been able to stop what was then an absolutely impossible task.'

Brazier sent two detailed accounts of what happened that day to the official historian, Charles Bean. One was handwritten. In it he casually mentions that he was almost shot at The Nek himself that day. (His pipe was knocked out of his mouth.)

'The lyddite fumes were thick as the 10th Regiment went into the trenches,' Brazier began. 'Owing to the trenches being choked with dead and wounded, it took the 10th a little longer to take up their positions …'

The result, the lightening up of enemy fire at the Australians' forward trenches, made it just possible for Brazier to raise a periscope and peer over at the killing ground. He saw the 8th Regiment 'lying prone in front of the trench, about 10 yards away at most, waiting for a lull in the fire [at them], or killed', but no sign of a red-and-yellow flag on the Turkish trenches that would signify they had been reached.

As he looked, a young staff officer from brigade headquarters (quite possibly Hughes' nephew, Billy) appeared by his side and asked why he had not sent his men over. Brazier replied: 'In view of the scene in front of the trenches and the fire of the enemy machine guns not having been affected by our artillery I did not intend to send my men over until I had reported what I had seen and had my orders either cancelled or confirmed.'

It was 4.40 am, now daylight. Brazier hurried back from the sap to brigade headquarters, in a dugout slightly to the rear.

Old Brigadier General Hughes was still apparently away in the trench-mortar position on the right, squinting through his periscope; probably stunned by what was happening and trying to come to terms with the carnage in front of him at The Nek. He would also have been peering anxiously down the sheer cliff face to his right into Monash Valley to see what the situation was like there. Two companies of the Royal Welch Fusiliers were climbing up this valley to attack the Chessboard. This British attack, part of the complicated grand plan, was conditional on the Australians taking The Nek because the Turks there could shoot into the backs of fusiliers from close range.

Lieutenant Colonel Antill had received news at brigade headquarters that one of the red-and-yellow flags had been seen on the enemy's trench (presumably the one spied by Lieutenant Oliver, in his mortar position). This was the signal that allowed the fusiliers to proceed forward. This was just another small disaster, a sideshow in comparison. Now the Bullant had his old friend from Perth to contend with.

Brazier found Antill alone in the dugout, 'with his back to the wall'. The scene was set for an immediate confrontation between two men who loathed each other. There was no mediator and no commanding officer to step in, but unfortunately there was also no independent witness as to what was said between the two.

Brazier told the brigade major that most of the 8th Regiment had not advanced 10 metres beyond their own trenches and were possibly all killed, and that the machine-gun fire of the Turks had already cut the scrub level with the top of the trenches. Would the acting brigadier now confirm the order to advance?

According to the 10th's CO, Antill informed him of the report that he'd received – that the 8th had reached the Turkish trenches and placed a flag there – so the Western Australians were to 'push on'. Brazier then insisted that not only was there no such flag, but 'it was murder to push on', to which the Bullant 'simply roared – "Push on".'

Brazier claimed that he replied, 'Thanks, but don't forget I told you.'

Afterwards, Antill would actually deny all knowledge of 'the flag episode', telling Bean: 'Regarding the matter of a flag being seen on the Turkish parapet, it was not until after the abandonment of the attack and until light permitted that such a report could be investigated, and so far as I know, none of our men succeeded in getting into the enemy's trenches.'

This caused Major General Sir Brudenall White, one of the outstanding Anzac leaders, to explode sixteen years after the charge, in 1931, in a letter to the British official historian, Brigadier General Sir James Edmonds:

> Antill's comments are worthless; he says he never heard of a flag appearing in the Turkish trenches – actually he was the first man who, three or four days later, gave me an account of the incident! His statements are dangerously inaccurate in every respect in which I can readily check them; many of his facts seem to me to have been invented in the intervening years.

Sadly, Brazier made his way back to his own regimental headquarters at Number 5 sap.

The roar of rifle and machine-gun fire that had met the two lines of the 8th had now subsided to almost a complete silence. A small group of officers and men from the 10th Light Horse had formed, waiting anxiously for news. As their commander returned, they gathered around him. Others stood waiting in the trench. Brazier would later say how he admired their 'breeding, education, and intelligence'.

The look on the colonel's face must have told them all what they already knew. 'I am sorry lads,' he said, 'but the order is to go'.

The troopers had written their last notes to loved ones, put aside their letters and photographs, their most precious keepsakes, for others to send home. 'Very few men expected to get back and most of them said good-bye to their pals,' Brazier wrote. 'For bravery each line was braver than that which went before. Death stared them in the face and not a man wavered.'

The men of the 10th knew exactly what would be expected of them. The dead of the 8th who had gone before now formed just another obstacle and the 10th would have to climb over their bodies on the parapet above them.

'Goodbye cobber, God bless you,' said Trooper 152 Harold Rush to his neighbour as they shook hands, then gripped their rifles and bayonets, put their feet in the fire steps on the crumbly yellow trench wall, and said their last prayer together.

It was 4.45 am. The nickel-plated whistles shrilled again.

All hell erupted once more, the noise swelling in volume as the Turks opened fire again, machine-guns jumping on their tripods, rifle bolts snicking rounds from magazines as fast as they could be worked. The air became 'hazy with lead' in the words of one 10th Light Horse officer, who estimated that the fire from at least 30 machine-guns was now sweeping the 30 metres or so of No Man's Land they had to travel. In the next ten seconds, Brazier would claim, the men who had stood near him had nearly all been killed or wounded and were falling back into the trench.

The men of the 10th were said to be smiling as they went over the top, led by Major Todd, waving his revolver. 'I saw the 10th L.H. ... come cheering and even laughing as men fell in dozens,' remembered Alexander Borthwick of the 8th, lying wounded out in No Man's Land.

Charles Bean's words would capture what a terrible moment this was for Australia's western state:

> With that regiment went the flower of the youth of Western Australia, sons of the old pioneering families, youngsters – in some cases two or three from the same home – who had flocked to Perth at the outbreak of war with their own horses and saddlery in order to secure enlistment in a mounted regiment of the AIF.
>
> Men known and popular, the best loved leaders in sport and work in the West, then rushed straight to their death.

Young Wilfred Harper was seen 'running forward like a schoolboy in a foot race with all the speed he could compass'. He was the inspiration for the Archie Hamilton character in Peter Weir's film *Gallipoli*. Wilfred was cut down – along with his elder brother, Gresley, who ran to his death with him.

Corporal Maitland Hoops' account would be written from hospital:

We charged but they dropped like flies. We did not advance further than the first line. I can tell you it looked terrible to see your chums toppling over on the ground and lying in all sorts of attitude.

I dropped down and a chum put out his hand and shook hands and said 'Good-bye' as he said he was done. He was shot through the lungs and bleeding from the mouth, but he got back into the trench and is in hospital here now.

As soon as I had shaken hands with him I heard someone calling me and discovered it was Geoff Howell, a particular chum of mine.

He desired me to shoot him as he said he was settled. It was a rare sight to see the smile on his face all the time, I will never forget it. Poor fellow, he got a bullet through the head a little later.

I was lying down alongside Captain McMasters and he got two bullets through the head and I had two through my haversack which was on my back and a piece of nickel struck me full above the right eye, but it was only a scratch.

The bullets were still falling like rain and the bombs were lively, so I thought it time to get back into the trench. This I succeeded in doing and I could see Leo Roskams lying wounded just over the trench.

I took off my puttees and put a stone on the end and threw them out. Someone pulled, so I started to haul in – who should it be but Jack Linto, a Yorkite.

I was just throwing it out again when Leo, who must have become suddenly deranged, stood up for a second facing the Turkish trenches and he got one in the eye which laid the poor fellow out …

Leo Roskams had only been appointed a Second Lieutenant the day before. So had Alexander Phipps Turnbull, a 27-year-old solicitor and Rhodes scholar. Now he lay dying in No Man's Land.

Having been sent away for a rest aboard a hospital ship on 4 August, much to his annoyance, Captain Vernon Piesse was one of the sick who chose to return just before the charge. ('I'd never have been able to stand up again if I hadn't,' he'd said.) He then went over the top with the 10th, reached a small hollow with some of his men, and took cover. Piesse raised his head to see if they could advance again and was shot dead immediately.

Sergeant John Gollan's father was a retired major who had insisted his son start off in the ranks. Gollan had been sick, in a field ambulance, the day before. He begged not to be sent away and a doctor had unwillingly relented and let him come back to be with his cobbers. Gollan had been shot through the hand before starting out from the trench. Then out in No Man's Land, now crowded with his mates, dead, dying and wounded, his leg was shattered by a bomb or an exploding shell from a 75.

Somehow he got back to the trench line only to die three weeks later from his wounds.

Captain George Hore of the 8th, still crouched in No Man's Land and using the swollen body of a long-dead Turk as cover, saw two brave men of the 10th run swiftly past him, each one quite alone, making straight for the Turkish firing line. Both men continued past him for 10 metres or so, then seemed to trip and fall headlong.

Nobody else came except a single trooper, who crawled up to him and asked this officer's advice on what he should do next. Hore advised him to make his way back if possible. Then the Indian-born lawyer was hit in the foot by a bullet. He decided to edge his way back himself, inch by painful inch, to the Australian line. The other man didn't make it.

For the second time, Colonel Noel Brazier tried to stop the slaughter.

Hardly had he returned to his regimental command post from the front line than a messenger arrived with a piece of pink paper. It was from Major Tom Todd, in charge of the third line, pinned down somewhere out there on the left flank, telling Brazier that exactly what had happened in the centre of the line had also now occurred out on the left – it was a disaster. Todd was asking for further orders, as he could not go on.

The brigade headquarters dugout was only some 30 metres away from where Brazier stood, and he again decided to go and confront Antill personally. One can imagine the CO's despair and fury; as Brazier wrote later, 'nearly all my personal pals and fellow land holders and club men who, unfortunately for them were near my position' had just been killed in front of his own eyes.

Still the brigade major refused to listen, as before, simply ordering him to 'Push on!' Brazier then asked him to write those words on a message for Todd, before repeating his earlier warning, 'don't forget I told you'.

Antill apparently scribbled something on the piece of pink paper, but Major Todd never received the message. Brazier turned on his heel.

'On getting back to the trench again,' Brazier would recall, 'there was a similar message from Major Scott on the right flank [in charge of the fourth line] asking for instructions'. The colonel saw no point in returning to see Antill in his 'resort'. So he went off in search of Brigadier General Hughes. Weaving his way through the crowded trenches he found the general either in, or just leaving, his observation post, the safe emplacement with the trench mortar.

While Brazier was away looking for Hughes, others, according to Hughes after the war, had been looking for Brazier. The old general maintained:

> The time for the waves to advance was given by two staff officers on the right and centre respectively and by regimental commander on left flank.
>
> The staff officers received instructions to stop the third line, but owing to the regimental commander [Brazier] having left his post some confusion arose as the runner was unable to find anyone to deliver the orders to.
>
> That section of the third line went forward and a few seconds later it practically ceased to exist. The enemy's fire was still devastating and the advance came to an end.

But Hughes was thoroughly confused. He actually claimed later on that the only portion of the third line to have charged was a section on the left flank – while 'none of the fourth wave ever left the trenches'. This story was nailed by Major General Sir Brudenall White, who told the British war historian: 'The comments of General Hughes are incorrect. There is no question whatever that the third line and part of the fourth went out. We know the names of those killed in them and of survivors.'

At The Nek, Brazier fronted Hughes beside the trench mortar and 'informed him of the true facts of the case, of the confirmation of squadron leaders and the instruction of the Brigade Major to "Push on".' To send any more men over, said the colonel of the 10th Regiment, 'is nothing but b———y murder'.

Hughes replied enigmatically, 'Try Bully Beef Sap'.

This seemed to indicate that the general was now thinking of attacking from an entirely new direction. Bully Beef Sap ran off the right-hand side of the trenches on Russell's Top, towards the sheer wall leading down into Monash Valley.

While Brazier debated with Hughes the wisdom of such an extraordinary decision, the men of the 10th detailed for the fourth line were now moving up and into position on the fire step.

Behind them, up a slope and to the left, was a position called Turk's Point. Here was Sergeant Cliff Ashburner of the 9th Light Horse, firing bursts of eight rounds a second from his Vickers machine-gun, water-cooled from a 2-gallon can placed alongside.

Ashburner had already fired around 10,000 rounds from Turk's Point as part of the bombardment leading up to the charge, but had been ordered to cease fire at 4.30 am, when the first wave of the 8th had gone forward, in case he should hit his own men. A former professional boxer, he was now in a ringside seat himself, a witness to the whole tragedy.

He noted the ineffectual bombardment that had missed the front line of the Turk trenches. He saw also a Turkish officer peering over the front line after the charge – until the Turk was hit by a shell. Then, when he saw Turks standing on top of their parapets and with their front trench full of Turks standing chest-high, Ashburner decided to disobey orders and opened up with his machine-gun on the enemy on the right, as they mowed the Australians down.

He had watched as the first and second lines had gone out 'running – charging' then seen the third line walking, bent down, rifles on guard. The third line had got as far as a knoll where he saw there were scaling ladders, dropped by the first line of the 8th.

Ashburner noted that a long time would elapse before the last lot of troopers came out. Then they had turned around and those who could get back to the trenches were trying to do so.

As he fired his Vickers, a message came through from Major Carew Reynell, who was now in charge of the 9th after Colonel Miell had been shot dead. Reynell asked: 'Aren't you firing at our own men?'

The answer was that all the Australians were down now. Ashburner would describe seeing some survivors 'trying to drink out of bottle afterwards and raising arms but within 3 or 4 hours they seemed to be dead'.

Reynell himself wrote in his diary: 'After six weeks of influenza and dysentery I wasn't very fit when the attack started, and trusted to the excitement to keep me going.' There was no shortage of excitement at The Nek on 7 August 1915.

He too went off to find Antill. But while Brazier was rushing around frantically, first to Antill then to Hughes, to try to get the charge aborted, Reynell wanted the Bullant to *continue* the attack. The South Australian, while scathing about most aspects of the attack, hadn't given up by any means:

> [The] attack in my opinion ought to have got into part of the trenches and when it was glued [shortly after the third line charged], I felt so strongly that it could go forward that I reported to the Brigade Major that if he gave me authority to do so I would guarantee to get the trenches with the men of the 8th and 10th that were there.
>
> However an order was sent to them to rush the trenches but the officers on the spot considered it impossible and they were withdrawn.

The order to withdraw came as the few survivors were trying to crawl home. Yet more men had been sent to die in another futile act of madness. The fourth slaughter was about to begin.

The time was now about 5.15 am. Three lines of light horsemen had been all but wiped out. What followed was total confusion, leading to more unbelievable tragedy.

Brazier was making his way back to his regimental headquarters after his inconclusive encounter with Hughes. Major Joe Scott was lined up with the men of the 10th in the fourth line, waiting for orders. The troop leaders knew at this stage that their colonel was trying to get the attack stopped.

The noise of the rifles and machine-guns had again died down, but as commands could not be safely heard in the din, the leaders had arranged that the signal to advance would be a wave of the hand. Major Scott was to give the signal to his troop leaders and they would pass it on.

According to Charles Bean, just at this stage an unnamed officer appeared to the right of the line, one who had apparently heard of the first decision of brigade headquarters – Antill's famous order to 'Push on!' – and asked the men why they had not gone forward. The troopers there, it seems, took this to mean that the fourth line had been ordered off, with the result that they went forward without waiting for the designated signal.

'By God, I believe the right has gone!' Major Joe Scott cried out.

In the secret sap leading out from the front line, the nearest NCOs looked towards Captain Andrew Rowan, a 39-year-old Boer War veteran. Rowan signalled to them to go, rising himself from the trench and waving his hand – only to be shot dead and fall back down from the parapet.

His troop sergeant was William Sanderson, a New Zealander who had settled in the Perth suburb of Claremont. Now he was running for his life in the rush of the fourth line, over rhododendron bushes on top of Walker's Ridge, Gallipoli. He noticed that the machine-guns had cut the shrubs down to mere spikes that grabbed at their puttees as they ran.

Sanderson saw that the Turks were two deep in the trench ahead of him. There was at least one machine-gun chattering to his left and any number in the trenches to his right on the Chessboard. 'The men who were going out were absolutely certain that they were going to be killed and they expected to be killed straight away,' he would say. 'The thing that struck a man most was if he wasn't knocked in the first three yards.'

Trooper Fred Weston, aged 30, an orchardist from Mundaring, was on his right and fell beside him, dead, as they got out of the trench. The force of the bullets knocked him right back into the trench.

Sergeant Arthur Biggs, a 33-year-old goldminer from Kalgoorlie, who had served with the New South Wales Bushmen in the Boer War (disguising his true age of fifteen), also fell beside him, dying of his wounds three days later.

Trooper Henry Hill was running beside Sanderson until, shot through the stomach, he spun around and fell. The 27-year-old farmer from Guildford died four days later.

Sanderson saw the Turks, not far ahead now, and looked over his shoulder. Four of his men were running about 10 metres behind him; they all dropped at the same moment.

He tripped over a rhododendron bush and then fell over a dead Turk, right on the Turkish parapet. 'The Turks were then throwing round cricket-ball bombs – you could see the brown arms coming up over the trenches. The bombs were going well over – only one blew back.' It hit him slightly in the leg.

While down, he saw two dead men to the right, towards the top of the hill, lying on the Turkish parapet. They looked like the Harper brothers, Wilfred and Gresley, united together at the end of their sprint.

Sanderson now realised how badly things had gone. He got his rifle, gave it a quick clean, and slammed the first cartridge from a full magazine into the barrel. He was expecting the Turks to counterattack over him and was determined to get a few shots in if they did.

After lying there for about half an hour, Sanderson saw Captain Henry Fry, kneeling by the secret sap on the left. He waved to him and Fry recognised his sergeant.

Meanwhile, the Turks were keeping their heads low. The Royal Navy had begun to bombard their trenches again and lyddite shells were whizzing low over the parapet. They were exploding so close that they seemed to lift him off the ground, Sanderson would say, and he was worried that the first shell to fall short would finish him off.

Then he saw Major Tom Todd, who had survived the third line, crawl along beside Fry. He shouted something that sounded like: 'Retire the fourth line first.'

Sanderson looked around him. There was no one beside him except the dead. He crawled towards the secret sap. Halfway there he came across an 8th Light Horse trooper who was lying on his back, calmly smoking.

'Have a cigarette; it's too ——— hot,' said the 8th light horseman.

Sanderson told him to get back and keep low as machine-guns were firing across from the Chessboard again, cutting the bushes back low.

Then he came across a lieutenant from the 8th Light Horse (now thought to have been Ted Henty). He had been carrying some bombs in his haversack and these had exploded, blowing his entire hip away. He was still alive and as Sanderson tried to move him into the sap, the officer begged him to let him stay, the pain obviously being too much. 'I can't bloody well stand it,' he said. They were his last words as the sergeant and the 'calmly smoking' trooper from the 8th dragged him into the secret sap, where he died as they got him in.

'In front of the secret sap,' Sanderson reported, 'there were any number of the 8th – the sap itself was full of dead. There were very few wounded – the ground in front of the trenches was simply covered.'

Sanderson eased himself over and between the dead in the secret sap, where he'd begun his charge with the other men from the 10th. There he recognised the bodies of Captain Rowan, Trooper Weston and another trooper named Hill – Arthur Hill, a 22-year-old blacksmith from Mundaring. He also noticed Lieutenant Alexander Phipps Turnbull, the Rhodes scholar, just lying there, dying, in the trench in front of him.

Up to 50 metres of the front line was now empty except for the dead and wounded.

Heroic efforts were being made to bring in some of the wounded who were on the left and in some kind of cover. But as Bean wrote, it was impossible to go up onto the exposed parapet to reach the wounded there – a place where 'no man could venture and live'.

Lance Corporal Billy Hampshire made five journeys out into No Man's Land to bring in wounded, including his troop leader, Lieutenant Leslie Craig, who had one foot shot away. Billy's sergeant had to physically restrain him and order him not to go out and risk his life again.

Trooper Martin O'Donoghue, a nineteen-year-old from a little Victorian town called Kamarooka, dodged bullets to bring in a cobber moaning in agony after having been fatally wounded by a bomb. Five months later O'Donoghue himself would be dead from gangrene after his left foot had been amputated following a mine explosion.

Major Joe Scott had managed to stop some men from going out with the fourth line. Others on the left had gone forward cautiously, keeping low and not running, and had then thrown themselves down among a mixture of survivors from the 8th's two lines and the 10th's third line.

Hugo Throssell was a young Second Lieutenant with the 10th who had taken cover in a small hollow with his men. Peter Burness says he is reported to have shouted cheerfully: "A bob in and the winner shouts.'

Throssell survived – to win the Victoria Cross three weeks later in desperate fighting at Hill 60, where, despite being severely wounded, 'by his courage and example he kept up the spirits of his party'.

Back at the 10th's regimental headquarters, while all this was going on, Brazier had returned from seeing Hughes to find himself in an unbelievable situation. His fourth line was missing. Brazier thought he and his messengers were the only ones left from his entire regiment, as he later described (referring to himself in the third person):

> On returning to his position the CO 10th, upon enquiry, was informed that every one had gone over.
>
> At the same time an officer from a company of Royal Engineers came up and said he was instructed to go into the attack and what would he do. CO 10th Regiment told him he was not to proceed any further and that he, CO 10th, would accept all responsibility. Later in the morning the officer of the R.E. thanked the CO 10th for saving his men.

Brazier waited for over an hour ('a lonely sentinel watching with a periscope') and sent a written report to brigade headquarters, saying the trenches around him were empty – and needed filling urgently in case of a counterattack by the Turks. The reply was: 'Keep on observing.'

While the colonel observed the Turkish trenches opposite over the field of carnage for an hour and a half before reinforcements arrived, unknown to him, Major Todd, leader of the third line, had himself crawled back and, after conferring with other surviving officers, had set out independently to find Brigadier General Hughes, brief him on the situation and tell him that it was now impossible to proceed further.

But Hughes, ignoring the disaster at The Nek, had only one thing in mind. He'd already diverted more British soldiers, two companies from the Cheshire Regiment, to go into Monash Valley and help the Welch Fusiliers in their suicidal climb up the sheer cliff face. Now he wanted the surviving light horsemen to go into action there, too. He had obviously lost the plot completely.

Brazier at last got some relief:

> The 9th finally entered the trenches and it was not till then and after I had told the engineers who were to go over also that it was futile to

lose any more men, that I learned that both Todd and Scott had enough brains to hang on to their men as they had received no further orders from me. Todd's men were partly protected and he withdrew them and some of Scott's were killed and wounded before he stopped them.

In the meantime Todd had been told by Hughes to try Bully Beef Sap!!!

But before anything could be remotely organised for this purpose from the shattered remnants of the two light horse regiments, news came that the British attempt had failed.

The Turks had rolled bombs down the cliff face, blowing back the leading men from the fusiliers, who then fell on those climbing behind them. As they tumbled down, two machine-guns opened up on others trying to claw their way upwards in single file. Sixty-five men were killed or wounded in this latest piece of murderous folly.

Now it was 6 o'clock in the morning of that awful day, 7 August 1915. The survivors of the charge were beginning to comprehend what had happened to them all. Later, it would be the turn of war historians, such as Les Carlyon in his book *Gallipoli*:

> The scale of the tragedy of the Nek was mostly the work of two Australian incompetents, Hughes and Antill.
>
> Hughes was the brigade commander and he didn't command; Antill wasn't the brigade commander and he did.
>
> Responsibility rattled Hughes and, either consciously or unconsciously, he walked away from it. Antill behaved, as he always did, like a bull strung up on barbed wire. Antill gave orders without finding out what was happening. He could easily have justified calling the attack off; the failure of the first line proved the objective was unobtainable.

Ernie Mack also pointed the finger of blame at Jack Antill, as he later wrote to his sister, Mary:

> The only thing we are frightened of is Bull Antill who is our Brigadier and he has not one redeeming quality and will murder us again if he has the chance.
>
> Hughes our late Brigadier has got another job thank goodness as he was a very nice man but not a soldier and always gave way to Antill.
>
> It was Antill who ought to have stopped the 10th from following us over the trenches on August 7. They did not leave until five

minutes after our second line went out and anyone who was not mad could see, if he could not judge by the noise, what had happened to us.

'They knew the risk before going out as it was the maddest idea to attempt it and there was not a single shirker,' Stan Mack reported. 'They just had the idea sticking in their minds that they had to get to the trench in front of them.'

Of the 8th Light Horse, half of those who started out had been actually killed and nearly half the remainder wounded. The official historian said this meant that of the 300 who charged in two lines, twelve officers and 142 men had been killed and four officers and 76 men wounded. The 10th, the flower of Western Australia, had lost nine officers and 129 men, of whom seven officers and 73 men had been killed.

Charles Bean would state that on no other occasion during the First World War would Australian soldiers have to face the same volume of fire that had cut down those brave men, who had charged, line after line, at The Nek, with empty rifles and bare bayonets. The official historian also provided a vivid picture of the aftermath:

> During the long hours of that day the summit of The Nek could be seen crowded with their bodies.
>
> At first here and there a man raised his arm to the sky, or tried to drink from his water bottle.
>
> But as the sun of that burning day climbed higher, such movement ceased. Over the whole summit the figures lay still in the quivering heat.

Chapter 16

Afterwards

Trooper Dave McGarvie always remembered it as the hottest – and the longest – day of his life. The dairy farmer from Pomborneit had charged that day with the first line of the 8th Light Horse, his Bible in his haversack. He wrote a long letter home to his parents from hospital about what happened to him. Later on in 1915, it was printed in *The Camperdown Chronicle*.

Then, 61 years later, he sat down with his grand-daughter Christine and spoke into a tape recorder, filling in more details of that incredible day on the heights of Gallipoli. He started from when the first line moved off, from the time Lieutenant Colonel Alexander White had ordered, 'Go!':

> Out we went – no sooner were we out than they opened fire on us. Our orders were not to fire but to rush up to within 2 yards of the trench, then wait till the bomb throwers cleared the trench with bombs, then go to work and finish the job with the bayonet.
>
> I hadn't gone 10 yards when head over heels I went amongst some wire – rifle one way, helmet the other, the sling was hooked in the wire. I extracted it, put on my helmet and raced on through a hail of bullets. We were under a cross fire from machine guns.
>
> About 20 yards from their trench was a gully about 20 feet deep with fairly thick scrub. Down this I went and got up to the Turks' trench on the other side.
>
> The trench was bristling with bayonets and another trench behind the first was full of Turks. I did not happen to be a bomb thrower so I got my rifle ready.
>
> The only thing I could see worth shooting at was a Turk bayonet, 2 yards in front, so I fired and snapped it clean in two.
>
> Then the second row of Turks stood up showing heads and

240

shoulders. I got some splendid shots – altogether I fired about 10 shots and I am certain of four or five Turks.

Heads and shoulders at 10 or 12 yards was just easy shooting. Every time I fired a man went down.

Then I felt a terrible crack on the foot.

Dave slid down a bank and took cover behind a bush. He looked around him and there didn't seem to be a man standing.

Then the second line of light horsemen came out and was mown down. A wounded man crawled behind the bush alongside him, then another who was unwounded. 'I saw dozens of wounded turn back and make for our trench but never got more than a few yards, so I made up my mind to stay until dark.'

The wounded man turned out to be Sam McColl, a 22-year-old blacksmith from Mansfield, who had been shot in the arm. His brother Allan, 25, was also out there somewhere, wounded. Dave couldn't recognise the third man who had joined them.

But along the line he recognised his section leader, Lance Corporal George Hughes, the Presbyterian minister whom he'd prayed with in the tent way back at Broadmeadows. And over there, running, was Trooper Charles Wingrove, aged twenty, a Melbourne Grammar boy who'd been a jackaroo on 'Allanvale' station near Stawell. 'Wingrove got shot in the head somewhere and he stood up and put his hand up to his head and went a few yards before going over. He got shot again.'

Hughes fired a shot from his rifle, and then rolled over onto his back. Dave noticed he had a wristwatch tied to his braces. The watch shone in the sun all that long day.

'It was an awful day. Hundreds of bullets splashed us with dirt and cut twigs off the bushes at our heads all day. One bullet just cut the calf of my leg.

'For 15 hours we three lay there. I felt quite cool all along, even when I was shooting, and I could take aim just as well as on the range. I seemed to have an idea I would get through.'

They couldn't shift their position. The slightest movement brought more bullets. To make matters worse, Dave found his feet were lying across the corpse of a Turk who had been dead for a month. A stick was digging into his hip.

Time dragged on. At one stage Dave thought it must be about 4 pm in the afternoon and whispered to McColl, who had a watch, 'What time is it?' McColl replied it was only 10.45.

Dave managed to wriggle his water bottle around to get a mouthful of water. In another whispered exchange he found out that the other

241

man behind him was Trooper Angus Trewin, a nineteen-year-old dairyman from the Goulburn Valley.

After a while Dave McGarvie, the sniper, wriggled his rifle through the bushes and carefully selected a target. Trewin begged: 'Oh don't start shooting, you'll only draw fire on to ourselves.'

And that is what happened next. A Turkish rifle bullet caught Trewin in the leg. It kicked up and his trouser leg caught in the stick of a shrub. The leg swung free, Trewin had no control over it, so the Turks began firing at this new target.

'The bullets were coming in past my nose – about 200 I reckon they fired at it before they cut the stick off and then his leg dropped down.'

After the war they would find Trewin's identity disc out there in No Man's Land.

Towards dark the Turks began coming out of their trenches. One ran behind Dave's head, swooped down and grabbed Hughes' watch glinting in the setting sun.

Then a navy shell landed close to them and Dave decided it was time to move. There were two other men lying close, unwounded, and they said, 'You better start first'.

At dark he stood up, but his foot gave way immediately. 'I got down on my hands and knees and started to crawl, but the circulation. It was all numb … I couldn't get down on my hands and knees. I had to lie down on my side.

'And you know how a worm gets along – he drags himself up and then goes a bit further. Well, that's the way I got in.'

As Dave McGarvie worm-crawled towards safety, the Turks opened up with their machine-guns again on the Australian trenches and 'the bullets were flicking up all over the place.'

What was left of the 10th Light Horse was now in this section of the trench. Dave McGarvie called out and one of the troopers fired at him. He called out again. His impaired speech saved him.

There was a trooper called Andrews who had gone out with the first line of the 10th and hadn't returned. He had a harelip, too, and the two were often mistaken for each other. McGarvie called out again, trying to get them to understand that he was one of the 8th and wanted to get in.

Then somebody said, 'That's Andrews', and they stopped firing and hauled him in. The two men behind him never turned up.

In Dave's troop, 41 men had gone out. Only five wounded came back alive.

Trooper Paul 'Ginty' McGinness – the Qantas founder – was another who crawled in after dark, again narrowly avoiding being shot. A machine-gun bullet had struck his bandolier and ploughed a red line from hip to hip.

From the trenches, they were throwing out grappling irons to try to drag in the wounded and the bodies lying near the parapet. They could see Colonel White's lying just beyond the top. Sergeant Norman Gaunt and another trooper from the 9th voluntarily dashed from the trenches several times to attempt to recover the body before they were ordered to give up the attempt because it was too dangerous. But they did recover his watch, slightly blackened, its protective face shattered with a bullet hole. It was identified from the Commercial Travellers Association membership tag on the fob chain. Today it rests back home in Melbourne, a treasured family heirloom.

Ginty McGinness and five volunteers went out the next morning to try to recover the body of Major Tom Redford. They dug a trench out from the front line to within a metre of where he lay. Then the Turks opened up and four of the men were killed. Ginty managed to get the body down into the sap, where they buried it temporarily with stones and put a little wooden cross at its head. Later it would be exhumed and taken down to be buried with the other bodies recovered in the cemetery at Ari Burnu. During the next couple of nights the Turks went out into No Man's Land and set fire to some bodies, and soon they were unrecognisable and intermingled.

Chaplain Merrington climbed up Walker's Ridge that morning, 'saw evidence of the slaughter of 3rd LH Bde' and met Chaplain Makeham working among the dead in a steep mortuary below the summit. Later in the evening he went back to the mortuary and buried the dead with Padre George Green.

The wounded and the shell-shocked were another matter. Post-traumatic stress disorder hadn't been heard of in 1915 but it would take its toll then and later down the years.

By 8 am on 7 August, three-and-a-half hours after the charge, most of the 8th and 10th were back in the trenches apart from the wounded who were being treated in the rear and then carried by stretcher, on broad backs or helped to limp back from the trenches and along the long trail down Walker's Ridge to the beach.

Once again, as with the landing on 25 April, the first-aid and field hospital system couldn't cope and deteriorated into another shambles as the casualties poured down from the battlefields, from the heights at Lone Pine, The Nek, Quinn's, Pope's and elsewhere.

Stretcher-bearer George Fish wrote on 7 August: 'I have had a very busy day. Over 300 casualties being attended to. Some of the wounds were ghastly.'

On 10 August: 'Operations, amputations, wounded are laying out in the field in 100s. Cannot be brought in. Most of the men's wounds are septic owing to lack of treatment and exposure. It is a perfect hell, worse than Mons.'

The day after the Charge at The Nek an urgent message was sent by the medical control officer to Anzac headquarters: 'Please arrange naval transport to evacuate from beach here 100 per hour for next 24 hours. Very urgent as wounded are dying for want of proper rest and treatment in hospital ships. Send all available stretchers and improvise as many more as possible. The condition of the wounded on the beaches in Anzac areas is desperate.'

Lieutenant Andy Crawford had been carried down Walker's Ridge to the clearing hospital by two Western Australian brothers on 7 August. At 9 pm he was put on a lighter to go away 'but nothing came to tow us out so after three hours of bumping about in it we were taken out of it and brought back to the clearing hospital'. He stayed on the beach all the next day and family history has it he was left for dead until someone passing by noticed a limb move.

Then he was loaded onto the lighter again, bumping around all night this time, with only a few biscuits and water for sustenance during this whole time. He was transferred to a hospital ship anchored offshore the next day, then transferred again to a transport ship fitted out to carry the wounded. It was now four days after the charge. He eventually got to a military hospital in Alexandria three days later, where he found that the wound on his back had 'gone a bit septic. It swelled terribly and was very sore and all the week they have been putting fomentations on it. I felt so horrible I could not write a line.'

Lieutenant Crawford would survive the war and died peacefully in 1974, aged 86. For many years he led the Anzac Day march in Melbourne, mounted on a grey police horse. Today his sword is still used by the Crawford family to cut wedding and birthday cakes.

Dave McGarvie, who also returned to Australia to live to a peaceful old age, had a similar experience. His wounded foot, full of bomb fragments, had only a field dressing on it. By the time he got onto a hospital transport with 3,000 other men, his wound had turned septic. Amputations were being carried out on the open deck, some without anaesthetic.

A nurse just swabbed his foot with Lysol and a doctor said he couldn't do anything for him aboard ship. By the time he got to hospital in Egypt he was dangerously ill. Only his innate toughness brought him through. After a series of operations his life was saved, and so was his foot, which had been threatened with amputation. But it was eight weeks before he could even turn over in bed, and when he returned to Australia, Dave had to go to the repatriation hospital regularly for the rest of his life.

Cliff St Pinnock wrote about his voyage with the wounded, of how they stopped at sea to bury some who had died: 'My God, the ship was like a furnace and all round the poor chaps were getting delirious ... the whole trouble was that the authorities did not know where to send us and our accommodation was for 560 and we had just over 1,200 on board.'

Eventually they reached Alexandria and caught a train for Luna Hospital – 'the girls [British and Australian nurses] gave us hot soup and everything you could wish for ... they moved all who could walk down here where we are very comfortable indeed and you really don't know what it is to see a woman's face again and hear a piano.'

St Pinnock would be killed in France while crossing No Man's Land during the Battle of Fromelles. He stopped to assist a medical orderly with a wounded man when a shell landed, killing all three.

Conditions at Anzac Cove did not improve. Ernie Mack had to be evacuated on 27 August with dysentery and the effects of the Turkish bomb that had exploded near his knee during the charge. He narrowly escaped death as he lay on a stretcher at Anzac Cove.

He wrote to his sister, Mary: 'When I was on the beach leaving Anzac a sniper got to work on me and his seventh shot got me through the arm but missed the bones of the elbow by a fraction of an inch.'

Ernie Mack was now Second Lieutenant Mack, promoted from lance corporal and one of at least fourteen promotions made on the battlefield, as the 8th struggled to regroup. He was sent to the UK to recover from his wounds and rejoined the regiment the next year when, back to strength, it advanced into the Sinai, mounted on its horses again, for the desert campaign of 1916.

Major Deeble was made a temporary lieutenant colonel in charge of the regiment but six days after the Charge at The Nek he was off sick and soon on his way to Britain too, suffering from pleurisy. After recovering, he had a training command, was one of the escorts when the king opened Parliament in London, and took command of the 49th Infantry Battalion in France before returning to Australia in 1918. Back home he went on the land, became active in conservative politics and married late in life. He had one son, Professor John Deeble. Colonel Deeble died in 1958.

Mervyn Higgins – 'Buggins' – the only other unwounded officer from the 8th in the charge, was also sent away sick from Gallipoli. On 23 December the next year he was struck down by a sniper's bullet when riding near a place called Magdhaba. The very next day, Christmas Eve, Ernie Mack, taking a tea break in a wadi at the same place was shot and killed when the camp was overrun by Turks.

Jack Mack was also evacuated from Gallipoli with pleurisy. After re-occurrent sickness, he went on to ride with the light horse in Palestine, where he was shot in the left arm. He returned to Australia and managed a property he called 'Royston', named after his celebrated general, 'Galloping Jack' Royston. Jack died in 1957.

His brother, Stan, returned to 'Berry Bank, which he managed during the Second World War with the help of two other returned men from the earlier world war. He died in 1960.

'Many of the men were quite dazed and efforts were made to get them out to a ledge on the cliff face to hold a roll call,' Tom Austin wrote, of the morning of 7 August. 'The scene there was very heartrending … many of the men on the cliff face were so shaken that they were almost helpless and the evacuations during the ensuing few days from shock were heartbreaking.'

Austin gave the results of that first confused roll call as thirteen officers and 157 other ranks killed, and four officers and 81 other ranks also wounded. He continued:

> A large number had minor wounds which were never reported. One sergeant had his hair shot away straight along the top of his head, two deep bullet scars across his chest and another right across his back. These had been done by a machine gun as he lay out in the line. He was not reported wounded though he surely earned his gold strip that morning …

When a roll call had been held on 3 August, the strength of the regiment had been twenty officers and 480 other ranks. By 5 September, with further attrition due to sickness and shell-shock, the 8th would be able to muster only five officers and 30 other ranks.

On 18 September 1915, the 3rd Light Horse Brigade prepared a casualty report. It showed that of the 2,359 men who had landed on Gallipoli, it had lost 1,647 killed, wounded or missing. Its effective strength was just 712 men.

The effects of the Charge at The Nek were both short and long term. The enormous stress the survivors endured attacked them, both mentally and physically, long afterwards.

'When we got back into the trenches most of us went to pieces for a longer or shorter period, while some were hardly affected,' wrote

Lieutenant Ernie Mack. 'For myself I went about as if I were asleep as for a week or more I had been feeling pretty rotten and was very weak.'

Lieutenant Wilf Robinson said after the war: 'I tried to discuss the affair with some of the survivors of my regiment. Some seemed half stunned and dazed. One was sobbing like a lost child of three and another laughed hysterically whenever I spoke to him.' *The Horsham Times* reported in 1915 that Robinson had returned home with his wounded hand and 'big and solid though he is, he shows signs of the stress and strain of his eleven weeks in the trenches'.

Then, 40 years later, on 14 February 1956, the same newspaper reported that an elderly Riverside farmer, Wilfred Robinson, aged 73, a breeder of stud sheep, had been found dead on his property with a double-barrelled shotgun nearby. One chamber had been discharged. His brother told the coroner, Mr P.R. Biggin, that Wilfred was 'a returned soldier from Gallipoli where he was wounded and suffered shellshock but had not been receiving treatment for this'. The coroner found that the facts pointed to an accidental death. Only one shot had been fired.

Jacky Dale wrote back to his old school, Melbourne Grammar: 'Have been feeling very knocked out and worried lately; and am longing for a holiday. So cheer up and I will try and keep going.' Although he had survived The Nek unscathed, he would be badly wounded in Palestine and die from pneumonia in 1919.

The 8th struggled to keep going with a few reinforcements for the next few months on Gallipoli but it was finished as a fighting force there. The remnants of the regiment eventually returned to their base at Heliopolis on 26 December.

Tom Austin wrote: 'Of all the fine fellows who sailed away so full of cheer on the 14th of May seven months before, only one man had not been off the Peninsula.' He was Corporal Alfred Driver, a grocer from Beaufort, who died in Melbourne in 1982, aged 89. Detailed as a stretcher-bearer, Alfred had been at The Nek. When he wrote to claim his Anzac commemorative medallion at the age of 75, the old man wrote: 'I was on Anzac from May 15, 1915 till Sunday December 19-20, 1915, second last party to leave and I am still going strong!'

As Colonel Noel Brazier wrote, the remnants of his 10th Light Horse Regiment had to remain in the trenches 'alongside their dead comrades' for three weeks longer.

The remains of the light horsemen who had died lay putrefying in the heat, on the parapets and in the scrub beyond. Body parts were tangled up with smashed rifles and uniforms and webbing and haversacks sieved by machine-gun bullets. Bombs and flares continued to char the corpses. The blowflies rose in clouds and hummed over this ghastly landscape.

In these appalling conditions, the survivors' losses from sickness and exhaustion steadily mounted, while heavy sniping day and night at The Nek, combined with a daily shelling by a Turkish 75 battery, just added to the 10th's casualties, and to the absolute and total misery on Russell's Top.

Brazier was deeply bitter and resentful about what had happened, even more so when both Miell and White were posthumously Mentioned in Despatches and he was not. 'The 10th Regiment has the smell of a ghastly failure,' he wrote.

To add insult to injury, Sir Ian Hamilton made no mention of the 10th in the course of a brief message that said: 'The 8th Light Horse only accepted their repulse after losing three-fourths of that gallant band that sallied forth so bravely from Russell's Top.' Hamilton always had a way with words. 'Gallant' would soon be the catchcry taken up afterwards, as 1915's equivalent of today's spin-doctors got to work to disguise what had really happened at The Nek.

Even three months after the charge, the scene in No Man's Land was horrific. Hamilton's nephew and ADC, Lieutenant A. McGrigor, would write after a visit to Russell's Top in October: 'One can see many of the bodies lying out there in No Man's Land with packs on their backs and water bottles complete; the bodies though are now mere skeletons. One body was within 30 yards of our parapet and could never be got at.'

Meanwhile, Hughes and Antill had decided that Brazier must go. He was holding his two superior officers in open and utter contempt. After more than three weeks of tension, Brazier wrote in his diary on 24 August: 'War in our own camp. A rotten, insulting little letter was sent to BHQ saying they had relieved me and asking that I be returned to Australia.'

Three days later, as the arguing continued, fate stepped in. 'Got shrapnel bullet in left eye,' wrote Brazier. 'Good-bye to Antill and two wars.'

Brazier went to hospital and then back home, back to 'Capeldene' to his family and his horses before his eventual death in 1947.

Brigadier General Hughes did not last much longer on Russell's Top. After more bouts of sickness and the enteric he was invalided back to Australia. Charles Bean noted that General Birdwood 'had little confidence in the brigade commander, but like many generals was averse to removing his subordinate outright, although he endeavoured to do so afterwards by invaliding. For any weakness in the brigade command this too soft, but very common, course of action must be held responsible.'

Hughes moved around Melbourne, active in business and civic affairs until his death in 1944. He is commemorated today by the F.G. Hughes Reserve, a small piece of nature strip at the end of St Kilda Road. His nephew Billy went on to win a Military Cross in the Sinai and Palestine campaigns later in the First World War. He also fought in the Second World War, when he became a prisoner of the Japanese. He served in both the Victorian and Federal parliaments, and was an idiosyncratic and outspoken backbencher. He was knighted for his work in staging the 1956 Olympic Games.

When he was nearing 70, in 1965, one of his grandchildren asked him, 'Grandpop, what is a light horseman?' This led to a mounted and uniformed section of light horse veterans being a feature of the Anzac Day parade in Melbourne, and Billy Kent Hughes becoming the most-photographed old soldier. He also worked hard to get the Desert Mounted Corps Memorial dedicated in Canberra to 'the last great cavalry corps in history'.

Frederick Hughes' second-in-command, Jack Antill, now took over on Gallipoli and soldiered on as the brigade continued to lose more men from battle, sickness and fatigue. Carew Reynell of the 9th was killed at Hill 60 in late August, as was Major Joe Scott, who had taken over Brazier's command.

In November, the Bullant could crow in his diary: 'Col. Antill is now the only officer of the brigade who has remained throughout, without going sick, or going away, and there are not more than some 130 men of 1,900 landed who have seen it out.'

He was promoted to brigadier general after Gallipoli and went with the light horse to the Sinai. Here, according to Peter Burness, he again showed he lacked the ability for quick decisive action and was sent on to France to command infantry. His health broke down in winter on the Western Front and he was invalided home to Australia.

'The luck that had delivered opportunities for him to establish a good reputation in the South African War had deserted him and he retired from active service a disappointed man,' wrote Burness. Antill retired as a major general, with suitable honours, and eventually died of cancer in 1937.

There was no official inquiry into the disaster at The Nek. Les Carlyon, in his 2001 bestselling *Gallipoli*, sums up best the attitude of those in ultimate command: 'The incident at the Nek was like incest; no-one in the family wanted to talk about it. Everyone in authority felt guilt that such a thing could happen. They became a mutual protection society and offered the occasional alibi.'

Indeed, the generals, Hamilton, Godley and Birdwood, barely mentioned The Nek in their autobiographies or in their official reports afterwards, if at all. They gave out the medals – seven Victoria Crosses – for the Battle of Lone Pine, which had begun the day before. That was the victory they wanted remembered, not the failure at The Nek. Soon the whitewash would begin, applied liberally from an adjective bucket labelled 'Gallant'.

Back home in Australia in August 1915, the telegrams began to arrive, addressed to people like Myrtle White, alone with her baby at 11 Cole Street, Elsternwick. So many telegrams. So many sad calls from officers and clergymen, so many sad, handwritten letters of consolation from comrades and commanding officers.

In Hamilton, Archdeacon Harris called on Florence Henty on 19 August to tell the pregnant young wife that she was now a widow; that Ted had died on Gallipoli at a place called Walker's Ridge, twelve days before.

Ten days later Christ Church Hamilton was filled for a memorial service for Ted. The same pews had been filled for his baptism and his confirmation. Only nine months before, Archdeacon Harris had told his congregation, Ted had 'bowed his head before the altar in holy wedlock'.

Australia, said Archdeacon Harris, was proud of its men, proud of the heroism of those who had fallen. He had a list of 53 men of those at the front who had been connected directly or indirectly with Christ Church. 'Never in the world's history has the Angel of Death passed so vividly over the Empire as he is now passing,' said the minister, 'and never in the world's history has such a fierce contest between the nations been waged at such a tremendous cost.'

The Hamilton Brass Band played *The Dead March in Saul*; a bugler sounded The Last Post. Florence went back home to 'The Caves', down the track where Ted had ridden away to war.

The official censors back in Australia did their very best at first to suppress the news of the 7 August disaster. The story did not break at home until three weeks later, and then not by plan. The very first report came from the United Service Special Cable Service in a two-paragraph report from London:

LIGHT HORSE SUFFERS
TWO REGIMENTS WIPED OUT
Victorian And W. Australian

Wounded officers from the Dardanelles report that the 8th (Victoria) and the 10th (West Australia) Light Horse regiments were practically wiped out in the heavy fighting on August 7.

When the 8th Light Horse Regiment left Australia it was commanded by Lieut-Colonel A.H. White and the 10th regiment by Lieut-Colonel N.M Brazier. They formed part of the 3rd Light Horse Brigade. A regiment consists of about 536 men.

It was tucked away in the Melbourne *Herald* on 25 August 1915, under a long despatch from Charles Bean about the fighting on 6 August, culminating in the paragraph: 'I regret that personally I have been unable to follow the later details of the great attack, owing to having been slightly wounded on the morning of August 7.'

In Perth, *The Daily News* carried the same cable report, and the next day the Defence Department received a telegram from the Premier of Western Australia, John Scadden, saying he was receiving anxious enquiries. He wanted the report confirmed or denied – together with an official comment on stories that the disaster had actually been caused by Allied artillery firing on the light horsemen. The Defence Minister, Senator Pearce, scrawled angrily across the telegram: 'How did such a cable escape censorship?'

Indeed. Only two weeks before, the Deputy Chief Censor, Colonel W.H. Hall, had sent Senator Pearce his reply to complaints in the NSW Parliament that extreme censorship was being exercised over war news.

'The public may be assured,' said the colonel, 'that matter dealing with the Australian troops at Gallipoli which is at the present time withheld is small, and so far as the public is concerned, is of minor importance. Practically the whole information, so far as it has been made available in Australia, is in the hands of the Press.'

It obviously wasn't. And this was certainly not the sort of report the colonel wanted in the press. He had said, 'there is no better way of stimulating recruiting than the publication of the spirit-stirring stories, fresh and non-controversial, of the gallant lads now fighting at Gallipoli'.

Pearce sent off a message to AIF headquarters in Egypt seeking more information. He replied to Scadden that heavy casualties had been reported but there was no official news.

Two days later Pearce agreed that this reply might be published. Scadden said it would relieve the enormous anxiety in Western Australia because many people believed that official information had been received and suppressed.

On 3 September, AIF headquarters reported total casualties of the 3rd Light Horse Brigade were thirteen officers and 310 men. Of these, approximately two-thirds belonged to the 8th Light Horse Regiment and one-third to the 10th Regiment.

The Age reported this on 11 September, with the comment that 'the casualties were certainly heavy but the Defence department considers that the (early) report exaggerated the losses'.

On 19 September, *The Daily News* upped the ante. In the stop press, it reported:

> Grave news received from Gallipoli. Disaster to Light Horse. Today grave news was received by officers of the Light Horse now serving at the front. The news conveyed was that a number of officers had been killed in action. The names mentioned but not officially available yet are those of M'Masters, Jackson, Proctor, Huxham, Piesse.

The official censors were furious. They demanded to know why *The Daily News* had reported unofficial information. The newspaper replied that the loss of ten officers had been common knowledge in Perth for two or three days and the paper had carefully left out the five names it could not confirm.

The authorities then sought a legal opinion from the Crown Solicitor as to whether *The Daily News* might be prosecuted under the draconian War Precautions Act. It was decided that a charge might not stand up and after the *News* said it would not submit to a restraint that served no useful purpose, the matter was dropped, with the censor telling the newspaper to be more careful in future.

It would take Keith Murdoch to break through the censorship barrier by visiting Gallipoli himself the next month and, ignoring the authorities, exposing the true conditions on Gallipoli in his famous 8,000-word letter that led to the sacking of Sir Ian Hamilton and the eventual evacuation of the Anzacs in December.

The Melbourne papers began publishing the names of the 8th Light Horsemen in the long casualty lists, which appeared almost daily. The sharp-eyed might have noticed the list of 'missing' published in *The Argus* of 30 August included Lieutenant Colonel White and Lieutenants Borthwick, Carthew, Dale, Henty, Howard and Woods from the 8th Light Horse.

Names and units were often mixed up with no details of where the casualties had occurred. There was no mention of Gallipoli, let alone Walker's Ridge or a place called The Nek. So the next day Lieutenant Colonel White's name was listed as having 'died of wounds' along with eleven other 8th Light Horsemen – mixed up with casualties from other units such as the 4th Light Horse and the 5th and 6th Battalions.

The names trickled out; the blow was softened, at least to the general public. Now the newspapers could present those 'spirit-stirring stories' demanded by Colonel Hall, and censored accounts of the Charge began appearing in the Melbourne metropolitan press at the end of September and beginning of October.

They were so colourful indeed that they could have made an entirely new chapter for the Reverend Fitchett's bestseller, *Deeds that Won the Empire*.

The decks of headlines over the report from *The Age*'s Phillip Schuler gave the flavour of what was to come:

A Victorian Charge
Light Horse Storm Trenches
Terrific Hail Of Bullets Faced
Imperishable Glory Won

'Once again a Victorian regiment has covered itself in glory,' he began, and soon there were phrases like 'magnificent charge', 'glorious deeds' and 'stirring advance' rolling along over three columns. There were subheadings like 'The Eighth Regiment Leads' and 'The Glory Of The Dead'.

'In this way in a brief few minutes did a regiment perish but it left behind an imperishable name,' he concluded, 'yet the regiment did no more than its duty but the men did it against fearful odds, in the face of certain death because their leaders led them.

'No one may ask if the price was not too great. The main object had been achieved. The Turks were held not only here but also right along their line – tied to their trenches; crowded together, waiting to be bayoneted where they stood ...'

Charles Bean's story in *The Argus* of 28 September went for four columns under the headlines 'GALLANT AUSTRALIANS' and 'CHARGE OF LIGHT HORSE'.

'There are no Victoria Crosses, there are no Birthday Honours; but for sheer self-sacrificing heroism there was never a deed in history that surpassed the charge,' began Bean in an otherwise reasonable reconstruction, considering he had been wounded, writing from his dugout, and had not been an eyewitness to what happened in the heights above him.

But on 8 October an unnamed 'special correspondent', also in *The Argus*, really went to town (and so did his imagination) over another four-column report – especially when he came to describe what happened when the second line of the 8th charged:

> Before they had gone half way upon their course not more than twenty were on their feet but still they charged. It was heroic! It was wonderful! In a few seconds, the twenty had dwindled to a dozen, to ten, to seven, to three. Would these last survivors persist? Two dropped. One struggled to his feet again, only to sag at the knees and go down a second time. The last remaining hero looked round. His face was red, his eyes were staring, but he smiled grimly. Still he ran to tackle the enemy single-handed but the end of the race was near. He stopped as if some invisible obstacle had blocked the way. For an instant he stood still. Then he toppled backwards, holding his rifle, with the bayonet fixed, high above his head. The charge had finished.

One report said that before the charge Colonel White had told his troopers, 'Men, you have ten minutes to live!' It was hearsay and almost certainly fiction. Myrtle White scrawled in her scrapbook beside the newspaper clipping: 'He would never say a thing like that!'

Yet the saying passed into mythology, to be used even by Alan Moorehead in an eight-line reference to the charge (in which he managed not to mention The Nek at all) in his then acclaimed 1956 book *Gallipoli*. But Moorehead also said that 1,250 light horsemen charged that day and 650 were killed, with a handful reaching the Turkish trenches firing 'green and red rockets' as the signal for others to come on.

The story was taken up eagerly by the British press in 1915 and these reports were again widely reprinted in Australia. Now the charge had got the imperial imprimatur. It could pass into immortality and the fact that it was a sheer, bloody, unmitigated disaster could be glossed over, forgiven … and forgotten.

Under the headline 'Honour the Light Brigade', *The London Standard* led the way:

> There are failures more honourable than many a success – failures anticipated, almost certainly foreseen, which are yet risked by brave men and paid for by their lives, in order that comrades, perhaps far remote, may have a chance of life and victory.
>
> We of the old country can only proudly recognise that the stock bred under the Southern Cross are the true sons of the men who held the hill of Albuera and stormed the breaches of Badajoz; that the Australian Light Horse are worthy to share the title of The Light

Brigade with the immortal Six Hundred and to be honoured along with them.

In the years that are to come this deed which the men of Victoria and Western Australia did along with many another in that blood-stained zone will bear its part in keeping the people of the British name together by the common memory of glorious deeds.

Even Charles Bean, writing for *The Times*, could conclude that the Charge at The Nek had, overall, been worthwhile:

There is no question that the charge of the Light Horse pinned down to that position during its continuance and for hours afterwards every available Turkish soldier within call. Our own machine guns were able to get in some good work amongst those crowded Turks, and those who know say that their losses must have been an ample set-off to our own.

Phillip Schuler, in his book *Australia in Arms*, published in 1916, could declare confidently:

What did the brigade do but its duty? – duty in the face of over-whelming odds, in the face of certain death; and the men went because leaders led them, and they were men. What more can be said?

No one may ask if the price was not too great. The main object had been achieved.

The Turks were held there.

The 3rd Light Horse Brigade would eventually return to Australia in 1919 after taking part with more distinction in famous actions in the Sinai and Palestine, including the famous Charge of the Light Horse at Beersheba. To survive these campaigns meant that the survivors of The Nek, especially, had led a charmed life.

Some, like George Rayment, returned home to live long and fulfilling lives. George became a clerk in the railways for 50 years before dying in 1976. Others, like Redge Mathers, died prematurely from the after-effects of Gallipoli. He was only 39 and left a widow and four young children.

Still others went on to serve their country even further. Aub Callow, one of the first to enlist with the 8th, after being evacuated ill from Gallipoli, recovered to become a commissioned officer and took part in most of the major battles in the Middle East. On the outbreak of the Second World War, he stepped forward again and went off to become

Major Callow, fighting the Japanese on the Kokoda track with the 39th Battalion. Returning to Australia in 1942 he transferred to the RAAF, where he served as a squadron leader until his demobilisation in 1946. He died peacefully at Ballarat in 1977, aged 81.

Many sons and other close relatives of the men in this book, like the Mack brothers' nephew, Greg Gillespie (son of the boys' kid sister Mary), went off to join the services in the Second World War. Greg served in New Guinea as a corporal with the Royal Australian Engineers in the 3rd Division before coming home to take over the management of 'Berry Bank' from his uncle Stan. He returned home, aged 22, and to heartbreak – blackened paddocks and the old Mack homestead just demolished by bushfires. It was a matter of starting all over again.

Colonel White's baby boy Alexander – little 'button mouth' – would grow up to become a doctor, and was a PoW of the Japanese while serving with the 8th Division. One of Colonel Brazier's nine children, a son called Arthur, was in the same division and died in Burma as a PoW working on the death railway.

Sergeant Frank Cahir (Carr), the stretcher-bearer, had three boys – Patrick, Jim and Vincent. Patrick served in the Australian Army with the 2/4th Field Regiment in the 7th Division; Jim was with 466 Squadron in RAF Bomber Command, was shot down over Germany and became a PoW; while Vincent served in the Royal Australian Navy aboard HMAS *Whangpu*.

Harold Brentnall, stretcher-bearer, was wounded in France but returned home to marry his Broadmeadows sweetheart, Jessie. But his mate, Jessie's brother George Fish, would die after being severely wounded on the Western Front in 1916. His young brother Charlie who followed him into the 2nd Field Ambulance also died from wounds in 1918.

Harold and Jessie's daughter, Beryl, served in the Australian Women's Army Service in the Second World War before marrying Jim Fowler, who was a soldier in the British Army.

The 8th Regiment arrived back in Melbourne on 7 August 1919, ironically the fourth anniversary of the charge, aboard the transport *Malta*. The regiment held its last parade early in the cold morning on the windswept New Pier at Port Melbourne. A line of motorcars took them to Victoria Barracks, where they dumped their kits and walked away.

Of all the hundreds who had sailed away on that February morning in 1915, aboard *Star of Victoria* on the great adventure into the unknown, only 38 of the original men were aboard. Nine of those were now officers, promoted in the field.

The survivors of 'the Old Eighth' kept in touch with each other in an active association after the war. They held an annual reunion (sometimes at the North Melbourne Town Hall), marched on Anzac Day and published their own magazine under the regimental motto *More majorum*. But gradually, over time, their numbers slipped away, the association was disbanded, the old colours laid up. The Old Eighth just faded away with its last known survivor of The Nek, Lionel Simpson, dying in 1991, aged 100.

The 10th's last survivor was Len Hall, who died in 1999 at the age of 102. Trooper Hall, regimental number 56, had originally joined as a bugler in August 1914 aged only sixteen years and five months. Before he sailed he gave a girl he hardly knew an emu plume from his hat. In 1919, when he returned from the war, the girl stepped forward, introduced herself as Eunice Lydiate and said: 'Excuse me, may I give you back your plume?' They married two years later and were together for 74 years before she died in 1995.

Len Hall was a machine-gunner at The Nek. He remembered shortly before he died that 'we were supposed to fire over their heads, but it was impossible'.

In 1965, some 300 Anzac veterans made a pilgrimage to Gallipoli. They went to Anzac Cove and Lone Pine. But there was no mention of anyone visiting The Nek.

Then in 1981 the cobwebs that had settled over the Charge at The Nek were blown away by Peter Weir's outstanding film *Gallipoli*, which is still screened – even on the Gallipoli Peninsula itself – on Anzac Day. This haunting, fictionalised version of events, with its mesmerising musical score, culminates with the final lines of Western Australian light horsemen running to their deaths.

It is extraordinarily evocative of the times and the loss of innocence when the Anzacs passed through Egypt and reached Gallipoli. But the portrayal of the charge is inaccurate and compounds the myth, portraying it as a suicidal rush ordered by the British to sacrifice Australian lives as a diversion while the laggardly British troops take tea on the beach at Suvla after their landing.

The British may take the blame for the grand plan for the August Offensive but it was Australian officers who ordered Australian soldiers to charge – and charged with them – to their deaths in four lines at The Nek. And it was Australian officers who failed to prevent the slaughter.

The men have not been entirely forgotten, even if the Charge at The Nek itself was only one small incident in the whole tragedy of Gallipoli.

The 10th Light Horse still exists, in fact. 'A' Squadron 10th Light Horse is an Army Reserve armoured unit based in Perth and proudly remembers its regimental history.

Elsewhere the Australian light horse still retains its mystique and allure. Across the country, enthusiastic re-enactors join outfits like the Creswick Light Horse to ride again in uniform with emu plumes bobbing and spurs a-jingling. Other enthusiasts meet in the chat rooms on the Australian Light Horse Association website as they research family history or track down some elusive piece of authentic saddlery. Look around elsewhere and you can soon find pointers to the past.

In Perth you can travel down avenues of flowering gums in Kings Park and pause to read a name from the 10th marked with the black-and-yellow colours of the regiment. Near a children's playground is a granite obelisk in memory of the 10th and each year on the Sunday before Anzac Day – the 10th calls it Old Timers Day – a wreath of bound hay is placed reverently there by the youngest trooper in the squadron to also remember the horses.

At Tongala in Victoria, Michael Thompson, whose great-grandfather, David Gellion, served on Gallipoli and in France with the 13th Light Horse, almost single-handedly raised funds to erect a light horse memorial, which was unveiled in 2003. Hundreds of descendants of light horsemen poured into the town to attend. There are plans for individuals to be remembered at this shrine, as well.

Every Anzac Day for the past few years, Michael Thompson has gone to RSL Headquarters in Melbourne with Jeff Pickerd, whose grandfather, Troop Sergeant George Fuzzard, was wounded at The Nek. The two men reverently unroll the original light-blue and yellow pennant carried by the Old Eighth and march with it to the Shrine. More great-grandchildren are joining them to march behind the old battle banner each year.

There are ironies, too. Some 60,000 people of Turkish descent now live in Australia, many in Melbourne. One hundred metres from Colonel Alexander White's old home, which still stands near the seaside in Cole Street, Elsternwick, Australian-Turkish kids with names like Azize and Umit now play beach volleyball and practise surf lifesaving in the shallows.

Meanwhile, up on the Murray River, retired colonels Douglas Hunter and John Neale and other enthusiasts have established the 8/13 VMR Museum in the 4/19th Prince of Wales's light horse base at Bandiana, near Wodonga. Here are the guidons of the old light horse regiments and cabinets full of uniforms and medals – even the battered, stained sun helmet worn by Lieutenant Andy Crawford when he fell wounded at The Nek.

Each year they hold a remembrance dinner in August, close to the anniversary of the charge. The regimental chaplain of the 4/19th says an old prayer:

Lord God we offer our thanks for all those from our shores who answered the call to arms.

Those who went with songs to the battle, who were young, true of eye, steady and aglow, who were staunch to the end against odds uncounted.

Those who fell with their faces to the foe.

Bibliography

BOOKS

Unknown, *Australia in the Great War, Individual and Social Responses*, New Century Antiquarian Books, Kew, March, 2003.

Unknown, *History of the 2nd Light Horse Regiment AIF*, Northern Daily Leader, 1926.

Unknown, *The Story of the Anzacs: An Historical Account of the Part Taken by Australia and New Zealand in the Great War*, James Inoram & Son, 1917.

Adam-Smith, Patsy, *The Anzacs*, Penguin, 1991.

—— *Victorian and Edwardian Melbourne*, John Ferguson, 1979.

Ajtleck, James (Ed.), *Geelong Grammarians at the Great War*, Cliffe Books, 1999.

Arthur, Max, *Forgotten Voices of the Great War*, Ebury Press, 2002.

Ashmead-Bartlett, Ellis, *The Uncensored Dardanelles*, Hutchinson, 1928.

Austin, Ron, *Cobbers in Khaki, The History of the 8th Battalion*, Slouch Hat Publications, 1997.

Austin, Sue and Ron, *The Body Snatchers*, Slouch Hat Publications, 1995.

Australian Dictionary of Biography 1979 and 1983. Entries on John Antill (Rex Clark), Eva and Frederick Hughes (Judy Smart), Alexander White (Peter Burness)

Australian Imperial Force: Staff Regimental and Graduation List of Officers, Government Printer, Melbourne, 1914.

Bean, C.E.W., *Official History of Australia in the War of 1914-18*, Vol 1 & Vol 2, Angus 8c Robertson 1921, 1924.

—— *Gallipoli Mission*, Australian War Memorial, 1948.

Bennett, Jack, *Gallipoli*, Angus & Robertson, 1981.

Benson, Sir Irving, *The Man with the Donkey*, Hodder & Stoughton, 1965.

Blainey, Geoffrey, Shorter *History of Australia*, Heinemann, 1994.

—— *The Causes of War*, Sun Books, 1998.

—— *A Short History of the World*, Viking, 2000.

Bown, Stephen R., *Scurvy*, Viking, 2003.

Braga, Stuart, *ANZAC Doctor: The Life of Sir Neville Howse VC*, Hale & Ironmonger, 2000.

Broadbent, Harvey, *The Boys Who Came Home*, ABC Books, 1990, 2000.

Brosnahan, Tom and Yale, Pat, *Turkey*, Lonely Planet, 1999.

Bull, Stephen, *Trench Warfare*, PRC Publishing, 2003.

Burness, Peter, *The Nek, The Tragic Charge of the Light Horse at Gallipoli*, Kangaroo Press, 1996.

Butler, A.G., *Official History of Australian Army Medical Services 1914-18*, Australian War Memorial, 1938.

Cannon, Michael, *The Long Last Summer, Australia's Upper Class Before the Great War*, Nelson, 1985.

Carlyon, Les, *Gallipoli*, Macmillan, 2001.

Carlyon, Patrick, *The Gallipoli Story*, Penguin, 2003.

Carthew, Noel, *Voices From The Trenches*, New Holland, 2002.

Celik, Kenan and Kok, Ceyhan (Eds.), *The Gallipoli Campaign International Perspectives 85 Years On*, Canakkale Onsekiz Mart University, 2000.

Clapham, Marcus (Ed.), *Wordsworth Book of First World War Poetry*, Wordsworth, 1995.

Darley, T.H. (Major), *With the 9th Light Horse in the Great War*, Hassell Press, Adelaide, 1924.

Denton, Kit, *Gallipoli One Long Grave*, Time Life Books, 1986.

Dow, David M., *Melbourne Savages*, Melbourne Savage Club, 1947.

Ekins, Ashley, *A Guide to the Battlefields, Cemeteries and Memorials of the Gallipoli Peninsula*, Australian War Memorial.

Fasih, Mehmed (Lt), *Gallipoli 1915 Bloody Ridge (Lone Pine) Diary*, Denizler Kitabevi Kaptan Yayincilik, 2003, (Turkey).

Fewster, Kevin (Ed.), *Gallipoli Correspondent: The Frontline Diary of C.E.W. Bean*, Allen & Unwin, 1983.

Fewster, Kevin, Başarin, Vecihi, Başarin, Hatice Hürmüz, *Gallipoli, the Turkish Story*, Allen and Unwin, 2003 (first published 1985).

Fitchett, W.H. Rev., *Deeds That Won the Empire*, Smith Elder & Co., London, 1897.

Frame, Tom, *Shores of Gallipoli. Naval Aspects of the ANZAC Campaign*, Hale & Ironmonger, 2000.

Gammage, Bill, *The Broken Years, Australian Soldiers in the Great War*, ANU Press, 1974.

Goodchild, George, *The Blinded Soldiers and Sailors Gift Book*, Jarrold & Sons, 1916.

Guldiz, Mehmet, *Ataturk The Birth of a Nation*, Renak, Turkey, 1998.

Hamilton, Jill, *From Gallipoli to Gaza*, Simon & Schuster, 2003.

Hammond, Ernest W., *History of the Eleventh Light Horse Regiment*, William Brookes, 1942.

Hay, Ian, *The Ship of Remembrance Gallipoli – Salonica*, Hodder & Stoughton, 1926.

Hill, Anthony, *Soldier Boy*, Penguin, 2001.

Hobbes, Nicolas, *Essential Militaria*, Atlantic Books, 2003.

Howard, Frederick, *Kent Hughes: A Biography*, Macmillan, 1972.

Hutton, Geoffrey and Tanner, Les (Eds.), *125 Years of Age*, Nelson, 1979.

James, Robert Rhodes, *Gallipoli*, Pimlico, 1999.

Kenyon, Alfred S., *The Story of the Mallee 1912*, reprinted, Ian Wood, Rainbow, 1982.

Kerr, Greg, *Private Wars*, Oxford University Press, 2000.

—— *Lost Anzacs*, Oxford University Press, 1997.

Kiddle, J. Beacham (Ed.), *1914-1918 War Services of Old Melburnians*, Arbuckle, Waddell Pty Ltd., 1923.

Kiely, John and Savage, Russell, *Steam on the Lens, the Photographs of Wilf Henty*, privately published, 2000.

King, Jonathan, *Gallipoli Diaries*, Viking, 2003.

Laffin, John, *Letters from the front 1914-18*, J.M. Dent, 1973.

—— *Digging up the Digger's War*, Kangaroo Press, 1993.

—— *Damn the Dardanelles: The Agony of Gallipoli*, Sun Books, 1985.

Liber Melburniensis Centenary Edition, Melbourne Grammar School, Griffin Press, 1965.

MacDonald, Lyn, *1915: The Death of Innocence*, Headline Book Publishing, 1991.

MacIntyre, Stuart (Ed.), *Ormond College Centenary Essays*, Melbourne University Press, 1984.

Mack, Joseph J., *Chain of Ponds: A Narrative of a Victorian Pioneer*, Neptune Press, 1983.

Main, Jim and Allen, David, *Fallen The Ultimate Heroes*, Crown Content, 2002.

Maxwell, Lt Joe VC, *Hell's Bells and Mademoiselles*, Angus & Robertson, 1928.

McKenzie, Donald, *Brave Deeds of the War*, Blackie and Son Limited, c.1919.

McKernan, M, *Australians in Wartime*, Thomas Nelson, 1980.

McKinlay, Bruce (Compiler), *Young Anzacs: The Contribution of Victorian Schools to the Gallipoli Campaign*, Victorian Ministry of Education, 1990.

Moorehead, Alan, *Gallipoli*, Hamish Hamilton, 1956.

Moses, John A. and Pugsley, Christopher (Eds), *The German Empire and Britain's Pacific Dominions 1871-1919*, Regina Books, California, 2000.

Olden, Lieut-Col A.C.N., DSO, *Westralian Cavalry in the War*, Alexander McCubbin, 1921 (with supplement compiled by Neville Browning and Ian Gill, Perth, reprint, 2001).

Oldham, John & Alfred Stirling, *Victorian Visitors Book*, The Hawthorn Press, 1969.

Oman, J.R. and Lang, P.G., *Brown's Water Holes History of Lismore 1840-1980*, J.R. Oman, 1961.

Palmer, Nettie, *Henry Bourne Higgins, A Memoir*, George Harrap & Co. Ltd, 1931.

Parker, David, *Ormond College*, Dominion Press, 1980.

Pedersen, P.A., *Images of Gallipoli Photographs from the Collection of Ross J. Bastiaan*, Oxford University Press, 1988.

Pelvin, Richard (Ed.), *Anzac. An Illustrated History*, Hardie Grant, 2004.

Reid, Richard, Dr, *Gallipoli 1915*, ABC Books, 2002.

—— *North Beach Gallipoli 1915*, Department of Veteran's Affairs, 2001.

—— *A 'Duty Clear Before Us'*, Department of Veteran's Affairs, 2000.

Richardson, Lieut-Colonel J.D., *The History of the 7th Light Horse Regiment*, limited edition, Radcliffe Press, no date.

Robson, L.L., *The First AIF, A Study of its Recruitment*, Melbourne University Press, 1982.

Ryan, James Cue and Kemp, Peter, *A Soldier's Story of World War 1 Egypt-Gallipoli-Palestine*, privately printed, 2002.

Schuler, Phillip F.E., *Australia in Arms*, T. Fisher Unwin Ltd, 1916.

Simpson, Cameron, *Maygar's Boys A Biographical History of the 8th Light Horse Regiment AIF 1914-19*, Just Soldiers Military Research & Publications, 1998.

Stallworthy, Jon (Ed.), *Oxford Book of War Poetry*, Oxford University Press, 1988.

Starr, Joan, *From the Saddlebags at War*, Australian Light Horse Association Ltd, 2000.

Steele, Nigel, *The Battlefield of Gallipoli Then and Now*, Lee Cooper, London, 1990.

Stephens, Tony and Siewert, Steven, *The Last Anzacs Lest We Forget*, Fremantle Arts Press, 1996.

Stephenson, Michael (Ed.), *Battlegrounds, Geography and History of Warfare*, National Geographic Society, 2003.

Taylor, Phil and Cupper, Pam, *Gallipoli A Battlefield Guide (Revised)*, Kangaroo Press, 2000.
The ANZAC Book – 1916, Sun Books, republished 1975.
Travers, Tim, *Gallipoli 1915*, Tempus, 2001.
Trudgeon, E.M. and Johnston, G.A., *For King and Country 1914-1918*, Longman, Cheshire, 1980.
Tyquin, Michael, Dr, *Gallipoli: The Medical War*, New South Wales University Press, 1993.
Wilborn, Suzanne, *Lords of Death*, Fremantle Arts Centre Press, 1982.
Williams, John, *Anzacs, The Media and the Great War*, UNSW Press, 1999.
Wright, Tony, *Turn Right at Istanbul, A Walk on the Gallipoli Peninsula*, Allen & Unwin, 2003.
Wylie, Michael (Ed.), *Patriotic Poems an Anthology*, Jarrold, 1994.
Younger, R.M., *Keith Murdoch, Founder of a Media Empire*, HarperCollins, 2003.

AUSTRALIAN WAR MEMORIAL RECORDS

Diary Captain Harold John Mulder, 3DRL/3400(B).
Diary Chaplain E.N. Merrington, 1DRL 0496 & 3DRL 3237.
Diary Corporal George Leslie Rayment, PR 9/1042.
Diary Lieut Colonel J. Antill, 3DRL 6458 AWM 419/3/14.
Diary Lieut Colonel N. Brazier, 1DRL 0147.
Diary Major Thomas Harold Redford, PR 85/64.
Diary Sgt Cliff Pinnock, 1DRL 0547.
Diary Trooper James Cameron No.686 8LH, PR 84/298.
Diary, Records Captain Sydney James Campbell, PR 88/102.
Diary Trooper William McGregor, PR 90/137.
Embarkation Roll First World War, AWM8.
History of 8th Light Horse Regiment (unpublished, typed signed by T.S. Austin Capt. Adjt 8LH AIF 9/10/19). Series AWM224.
Routine Orders 8th Light Horse Regiment January-May 1915, AWM25.
Official History 1914-18 War Records of Charles E.W. Bean Correspondence 1926-31, AWM 38 3DRL 7953/27 Part 3, AWM 38 3DRL 606 Item 32, AWM 38 3DRL 8043 Item 25.
Unit War Diaries 1914-18 War 8th Australian Light Horse Regiment (AWM 4, Items 1 through 50).

STATE LIBRARY OF VICTORIA RECORDS

Australian Manuscripts Collection: MS 10904 MSB 331 Trooper Redge Hugh Mathers.

PRIVATE RECORDS

Lieutenant Colonel Alexander White.
Lieutenant Charles Carthew.
Lieutenant Edward Henty.
Major Arthur Deeble.
Major Carew Reynell.

Private George Fish.
Private Harold Brentnall.
Sergeant Ernest Smith.
Sergeant Frank Cahir (Carr).
Trooper Alex Borthwick.
Trooper Aub Callow.
Trooper Dave McGarvie.
Trooper Ernie Mack.
Trooper Jack Mack.
Trooper James Sheehy.
Trooper John McGlade.
Trooper Stan Mack.

FILM AND VIDEO

Australia in World War 1, AWM & National Film & Sound Archive.
AWM Gallipoli Tour 2003, produced by Douglas Brazier, (Privately issued).
Gallipoli, feature film directed by Peter Weir, 1981.
Gallipoli – The Boys Who Came Home, produced by Harvey Broadbent, ABC Video, 1992.
Gallipoli: The Fatal Shore, produced by Harvey Broadbent, ABC Video, 1992.
Heroes of Gallipoli, Australian War Memorial, Ellis Ashmead-Bartlett's surviving film on Gallipoli with titles by Charles Bean.
The Great War – Please God Send us a Victory, volume 2 of BBC Series, 1964, re-released on video, www.ddvideo.co.uk

ARTICLES

Carlyon, Les, 'The First Casualty', *Bulletin*, 7 August 2001.
Frawley, Kevin, 'Ellis Ashmead-Bartlett and the Making of the ANZAC Legend', *Journal of Australian Studies*, 10 June 1982.
Gammage, Bill, 'Anzac's Influence on Turkey and Australia', a keynote address in 1990 at the Australian War Memorial History Conference, *Wartime Magazine*, April, 1991.
Hamilton, John, 'Love for a Hero Set in Stone', *Herald Sun*, 15 June 2000.
—— 'This is for you Dad', *Herald Sun*, 29 June 2000.
—— 'The Green Box, an Anzac Story', *Herald Sun*, 19 April 2003.
—— 'Father I Never Knew You', *Herald Sun*, 21 April 2001.
Inglis, Professor Ken, 'Gallipoli Pilgrimage 1965', *Wartime Magazine*, April 1991.
—— 'The Last Horse Standing', *The Age*, 25 April 2000.
Wilson, Neil, 'Mystery From Gallipoli', *Herald Sun*, 11 November 2002.

USEFUL WEBSITES

Australian Light Horse Association – www.lighthorse.org.au
Australian War Memorial – www.awm.gov.au
Commonwealth War Graves Commission – www.cwgc.org/cwgcinternet/search.aspx
Digger History – www.diggerhistory.info
First AIF Order of Battle – www.unsw.adfa.edu.au/wrmalle/undex.html

Leaders of Anzacs – www.anzacs.org
National Archives Australia – www.naa.gov.au
Service Personnel Australia – www.coraweb.com.au/service
Ships List – www.theshipslist.com
The Anzac Landing – www.anzacsite.gov.au
The Gallipoli Association – www.gallipoli-association.org

NEWSPAPERS

Bulletin, 1 June 1916.
Castlemaine Mail, 1915.
Camperdown Chronicle, 1915.
Dunmunkle Standard and Murtoa Advertiser, 29 October 1915.
Hamilton Spectator, 1914, 1915.
Horsham Times, 15 October 1915; 15 February and 14 March 1956.
Melbourne Punch, 1915, 1915.
Myrtleford Mail, 1915.
Portland Gazette, 1915.
Tatura Guardian, 12 and 31 October, 1915.
The Age, 1914-1915.
The Argus, 1914-1915.
The Daily News, 1915.
The Herald, 1914, 1915.
The Record, 5 and 12 May 1928.
WA Trotting Magazine, 'Wes-TROT', January 1997.

MISCELLANEOUS

A Brief History of Hamilton District and Alexandria College 1871 - 1971, compiled by
    Elise Robertson.
A Short History of St Stephens Church, Portland, 1834 - 1944.
Dad's War Stuff, 'The Story of a Gippsland Lighthorseman an exhibition from the
    Auchterlone Collection.'
—— 'The Diaries', (Ed.): Gloria Auchterlone. Pazzaz Printing, Morwell, 2001.
Fear not that Ye have Died for Naught: The History of the Sale Memorial Fallen, by Ross
    Jackson, Gary McCulloch and David Thewlis.
Gallipoli Information Sheet, Commonwealth War Graves Commission.
Gallipoli Peninsula Historical National Park Guide Map.
Gallipoli Plaques, Ross Bastiaan.
Literature/Film Quarterly, (Interview Peter Weir), Vol. 9, November 1981.
Major and Mrs Holt's Battle Map of Gallipoli.
Melbourne Cricket Club Roll of Honour 1914-18, compiled by Alf Batchelder.
The Castlemaine Cenotaph, Compiled by Ken Fitzgerald.
The Campaspe Light Horse Association, incorporating the Australian Lighthorse
    Training Manual of 1910, compiled by Lindsay Gunston (Handbook).
The Corian, the journal of Geelong Grammar School.
The Hamiltonian, the journal of Hamilton College.
The Pegasus, the journal of Geelong College.
Wartime, the official magazine of The Australian War Memorial.

Acknowledgements

An extraordinary number of kind people have helped make this book. Before I try and thank as many of them as possible – and apologise in advance to anyone I may have overlooked – it might be useful to outline how it all came about.

Peter Weir, who made *Gallipoli* after visiting the peninsula in 1976, said he felt like an archaeologist after walking the battlefields, up and down the ridges and gullies, discovering a lost Australian civilisation through relics like buttons and bits of old leather belts, even an unbroken Eno's Fruit Salts bottle he found lying there. He said he was literally touching history and was so moved by the experience he went home to make his famous film. The climax was the depiction of the Charge at The Nek.

When I first visited Gallipoli in 2000 as a journalist, rumbling onto the peninsula aboard an ancient bus to cover the 85th anniversary of the landing for my paper, the *Herald Sun*, along with a party from the Australian War Memorial, I knew very little about the Dardanelles or Anzac Cove and had never even heard of a place called The Nek. Yet within a day I had found a piece of rusty bully beef tin, a spent .303 casing, and in the emptiness of the cemetery nearby on Walker's Ridge, became profoundly moved too.

I was treading in the footsteps of some other distinguished archaeologists. My old friend and colleague, Les Carlyon, was also on Gallipoli in 2000, walking the mad country with Kenan Celik, to gather material for his bestseller *Gallipoli* and Les, who had been here before as a journalist, warned me I would be affected, that something special would reach out to touch me.

That first day on the Gallipoli Peninsula, led by Senior Historian Ashley Ekins, our party visited Anzac Cove and the little cemetery at Ari Burnu. There, in the middle of the front row by the sea, was the grave of Lieutenant Edward Ellis Henty with its ringing, defiant epitaph chosen by his widow, Florence. On the headstone the weather-beaten carved words:

Glad Did I Live And Glad Did I Die
And I Laid Me Down With A Will

I was firstly intrigued by the pioneering Henty surname on the stone and, as I looked around, saw that he was united in death with so many others in the cemetery by common inscriptions – the units, the 8th and 10th Australian Light Horse and one date, 7 August 1915.

The next day Ashley took us up Walker's Ridge to The Nek and told us what had happened there on that awful day. I knew then I must find out more about Lieutenant Henty, about so many more Australians who lived, died and were buried anonymously together here under this square of springy turf on Russell's Top.

Peter Burness, Senior Curator at the Australian War Memorial, was also on the Peninsula in 2000. I found he had actually interviewed a handful of old soldiers, survivors of The Nek, in 1984, which inspired him a decade later to write the first authoritative military history of the Charge. He said there was more to discover – and still digging to be done.

That was the beginning of the search. I knew I was on the way months later when I eventually tracked down Lieutenant Henty's son, the late Edward Ellis Henty, who had been born to his mother, Florence, in 1915, just a few months after his father died high up on that lonely ridge behind Ari Burnu.

Ted Henty had become a distinguished agronomist in New Guinea before retiring to grow tropical fruit in Tully, North Queensland. After following a long trail, I had discovered him only by writing in desperation to 'Edward Ellis Henty, c/ Post Office, Tully. Qld.'. The letter was forwarded. He had moved south. Weeks later I received a courteous reply: 'Dear Mr Hamilton, I believe you are looking for me.'

It was from Victoria, inviting me to lunch. I shared a piece of fish and some boiled potatoes with the old man, now 85, in his retirement unit at San Remo on the Victorian coast. It was not long before he died, and he showed me his most treasured possession, a leather-bound book – the Hamilton College school prize for 'Memory' awarded to young Ted Henty in 1909 – the father he never knew. Suddenly, I was touching history, too.

Within a day or two I had met his son, Stephen Henty, now also sadly deceased, and he had led me to touch the family's most treasured possession, the silver salver, Lieutenant Henty's 1914 wedding present, engraved with the names of his loyal troopers who would die with him at The Nek a few months later. Later I would touch another family heirloom kept by the grandchildren of Lieutenant Colonel Alexander White – the actual pocket watch, slightly burned and with a bullet hole through its cover – which he used to count down the minutes before the Charge that he led to his death.

Here was the inspiration to continue the search and write this book, to try and find out more about who these men were and tell the story of their tragedy, wherever possible, in their own words.

So I begin by thanking the people who got me started. To Les and Denise Carlyon and also their son, Patrick, author of *The Gallipoli Story*. I thank them – for their friendship, their help, their invaluable suggestions and continual encouragement – and for allowing me to quote from their works.

I also especially thank Ashley Ekins, infectiously enthusiastic Gallipoli expert, who led me over the battlefields in 2000 and again in 2003 and who knows every trench and – almost – every tunnel and what happened there. He has been ever generous with his time and his expertise both in Gallipoli and Canberra.

I particularly thank Peter Burness for his generosity in allowing me to quote material from his book *The Nek* not available elsewhere, especially biographical details of Hughes, Antill, Brazier and White, for answering my questions and for helpfully steering me in other directions for research.

I thank all those others who have helped me at the Australian War Museum, especially its Director, Major General Steve Gower, and to Ian Kelly, Mal Booth, Jennifer Coombes, Curator of Private Records, and all the team at the Research Centre. I would also like to thank Nick Fletcher for his expert advice on everything from bayonets and trench mortars to rifles and machine-guns.

I would also like to particularly thank Nancy Taylor, Karan Oberoi and the others in the World War One section of the National Archives of Australia for their tremendous assistance in tracking and copying the service records of many of the men in this book. Jenny Turley of the army's Medals Section has also been of great help.

I also thank the staff of the State Library of Victoria, particularly those in the Herald and Weekly Times Pty. Ltd Newspaper Reading Room, where I spent many hours, and to those who helped me retrieve material from the Australian manuscripts collection in the La Trobe section. Thanks also to Bruce Davidson, Chief Librarian of the Parliament of Victoria, Kay Rowan of the Port Phillip Library Service and to the staffs of the National Library of Australia, the Alexander Turnbull Library of the National Library of New Zealand and to the library of the Herald and Weekly Times Ltd itself.

On Gallipoli, my thanks go to Kenan Çelik for explaining what happened at The Nek from the Turkish perspective and to Serap Sacic Akis, Turkish guide, for her knowledge, her translations and for leading the way up and down Walker's Ridge safely and surely, without losing me down a cliff. I also thank John Waller of Boronia Travel for organising my two visits, and for hacking through the thorn bushes one memorable day when we followed Sid Campbell's sketch map and found the 8th Light Horse bivouac site. I also thank the Australian Ambassador to Turkey, Mr Jonathan Philp, for his assistance.

In Melbourne I have received friendship and encouragement from many members of the Turkish community including the Consul General Hasan Asan, Umut Ugur, Yilmaz Gursoy, Ibrahim Dellal, Vecihi and Hatice Hurmuz Basarm, and Ramazan Altintas, president of the Turkish sub branch of the Victorian RSL. The State headquarters of the RSL has been extraordinarily supportive and I thank the state president, Major-General David McLachlan, immediate past president Bruce Ruxton, chief executive officer Brigadier John Deighton, Elizabeth Mansfield and Rob Ferguson for all their help.

Another person who was inspired by Peter Weir's film to find out more about the men on the battlefield was Cameron Simpson, then a serving soldier with the Australian Army and also later with the Scots Guards. After an extraordinary amount of research he produced in 1997 his privately printed *Maygar's Boys A Biographical History of the 8th Light Horse Regiment AIF 1914-19*. This is an invaluable research tool for anybody interested in tracing relatives or the personnel of the regiment and I thank Cam for allowing me to use material from it.

I would also like to single out Michael Thompson, of Tongala, grandson of a light horseman, amateur historian and enthusiastic re-enactor, for his enormous help and introductions. At the annual Mountain Cattlemen's muster near Mansfield, Michael set up a light horseman's camp with Corporal Jamie McLean of the 4th/19th Prince of Wales Light Horse Heritage Group, with others, and welcomed me round the campfire. I am indebted to them all for explaining equipment and saddlery and providing historical details and extracts from the old drill manual before giving a demonstration of their horsemanship in the bush.

Another as yet unpublished history of the 8th is being prepared by Jeff Pickerd, grandson of Sergeant George Fuzzard. I thank Jeff for his support and for allowing me to quote from his material and to use his

269

extraordinary deductions as to exactly where individual officers and men were during the events leading up to and including the Charge.

I have also relied on the unpublished history of the 8th held by the Australian War Memorial under the authorship of Major Tom Austin. Jeff Pickerd and others subscribe to the view that some if not all of the manuscript may have been written by Major William 'Lachie' McGrath, as extracts under his name appeared in the 8th Light Horse Association newsletters long after the war. However, the Australian War Memorial has ruled that Austin appears to have been the author as he signed the typescript lodged there. As both men were sometime adjutants they may have been co-authors. If so, I thank them both in absentia.

Like everyone who writes about Gallipoli, I acknowledge my debt and admiration to Charles Bean and the use I have made of material from the first two volumes of his *Official History of Australia in the War of 1914-18*, especially his reconstruction of the Charge, and the wealth of material that lies in the answers of some of the participants to the letters he sent seeking information after the war. I also acknowledge the work of another fine contemporary reporter, Phillip Schuler of *The Age* and his 1916 work *Australia in Arms*.

But, back to the present. This book would not have been possible without the extraordinary and generous co-operation of a large number of surviving relatives of the men who went to Gallipoli.

Lieutenant Henty's great-grandchildren now polish the silver salver and although the last Anzac has now passed on, the letters they wrote home to loved ones and the diaries they kept sometimes survive and are treasured by their families.

Among those that were discovered by accident are the letters written by the three Mack brothers of 'Berry Bank'. They were discovered, previously unknown to the family, in a cardboard box in a cedar chest of drawers after the death, late in life, of their sister, Mary.

I am deeply indebted to Mary's son, Mr Greg Gillespie, for allowing me to use the letters and to the Honorary Archivist of Geelong College, Mr R. Bruce Jameson, for making the initial introduction. This was like handing me the keys to the doors of the Mack family home and to the Western District. From that beginning Greg Gillespie and his wife, Tim, took me in hand and soon I was meeting Stan's son, Mr Bill Mack, and nephew, Mr Joe Mack. I thank them all for recollections, family history and photographs. I also thank the then owners of 'Berry Bank', John and Beverley White, for allowing me to visit the station with Greg, and to Mr Christopher Lang of neighbouring Titanga Station for regional history and advice.

In Hamilton, the McDonald family were instrumental in finding

Edward Henty. I thank them and Ian Black of the Hamilton Historical Centre; Mr Samuel Winter-Cooke; Mr Kevin Thomas; Bernie and Carol Canavan for allowing me to visit their property 'The Caves'; and Mr Ian Maclean, deputy principal of Hamilton and Alexandra College, for showing me over Ted's school and providing material from the archives. Mr Russell Savage MLA kindly supplied early photographic records.

In Portland, Denis Naphine MLA provided introductions and Mr Bernard Wallace allowed me to use his material on 'Maretimo' and the Campbell family. Mrs Anne Grant of the History Centre filled in details on a range of subjects in the district while Mrs Jan Treloar kindly showed me through 'Maretimo' and the grounds where Sid Campbell once played as a child. Mr John De Ravin, surviving nephew of the doctor, helped with family history while Mr Michael Collins Persse, Keeper of the Archives at Geelong Grammar School, tracked down his scholastic achievements. Professor Hugh Collins, Master of Ormond College, welcomed me to that institution and Ms Sara Martin provided college records and showed me where Sid once studied and taught.

I am indebted to other schools for help about past students, especially to the Principal of Melbourne Grammar School, Mr Paul Sheahan, and school archivist Gordon Sargood and to the Principal of Caulfield Grammar School, Stephen Newton, and David Thompson. Further afield, the headmaster of King's College, Taunton, Somerset, Mr Chris Ramsey and the school's head of English, Michael Rogers, unearthed valuable information on a sometime student, Trooper Roger Palmer.

I could not have written about many of the other principal characters in this book without continual help from their families and access to their records. A very special thanks:

To the grand-children of Colonel Alexander White, Mrs Marjorie McPherson and Mr Alex White; to Major Deeble's son Professor John Deeble and to his daughter-in-law, Mrs Caroline Deeble; to Aub Callow's son, Noel Callow; to Dave McGarvie's daughter, Mrs Meg McNab and grandchildren, Christine Gascoyne and David Collyer; to Colonel Brazier's grandson, Peter Brazier, and to Doug Brazier, who although in his 80s out-climbed us all on Gallipoli in 2003 as he retraced and filmed every step taken by his relative.

To Dr Dulcie Rayment and Nigel Pratt for George Rayment's records, Redge and Diana Mathers for the original Redge's archive; Chris Borthwick for allowing me to quote from the Borthwick brothers' letters and to Noel Carthew (for allowing me to use extracts from some of the Carthew brothers' letters in her book *Voices From The Trenches* as well as supplying photographs and other records). To Graeme Smith, grandson of the sergeant who set up Broadmeadows camp, for his family records and to Mrs Beryl Fowler, daughter of stretcher-bearer Harold Brentnall and niece of George Fish for allowing me access to the extraordinary First World War time capsule kept by her late mother, Jessie. As a result of research for this book, Mrs Fowler was brought in touch with Pat and Jim Cahir, the surviving sons of Sergeant Frank Cahir, also a stretcher-bearer on Gallipoli. I thank them all for their help and for their family decisions to subsequently donate all their records to the Australian War Memorial collection.

Other relatives who helped include Terry and Loretta Sheehy, John Cameron, Leonie O'Donoghue and Mr L. Anderson, whose ancestor was Bandmaster Boyle. I also specially thank an old friend and colleague, Patrick Walters of *The Australian*, who kindly supplied the diary of his great-uncle Carew Reynell and allowed me to quote from it.

Others who have helped include Tony Ford from Tatura, Gladdie Paris of Nagambie, Gloria Auchterlonie from Morwell and Lindsay and Sue Smith from the Horsham Historical Society. I also thank John Ness of the Broadmeadows Historical Society, Heather Soyer from Benalla and John Wise and Robert Taylor for their help.

Professor Geoffrey Blainey has provided both encouragement and wise counsel and has kindly allowed me to quote from his unparalleled history of Australia. Professor John Moses of the University of New England has also allowed me access to his broad knowledge of events leading to Australia's participation in the First World War. Ross Bastiaan provided details of his Gallipoli plaques.

Ross Mallett, author of excellent entries in the Australian Defence Force Academy website, has kindly allowed me to use extracts and the Royal Military College, Duntroon, through Captain Michelle Bilston, provided details and gave permission to use the record of one of its earliest graduates, Lieutenant Leo Anderson.

A number of other both serving and former army personnel have provided invaluable help and insights. I thank especially Lieutenant Colonel Howard Ward, Commanding Officer of the Defence School of Music, Lieutenant Colonel Doug Hunter of the 8/13 VMR Museum at Bandiana, Major Robert Morrison, onetime CO of the 8/13, John Deykin, a former CO of the 10th Light Horse and Sgt Lloyd Robinson, present training sergeant with the 10th.

On Gallipoli I was fortunate to share the company of Lieutenant Colonel Iain 'Jock' Stewart, a former Vietnam company commander, and as we tramped the ridges I learned and wondered, with him, how the Anzacs achieved so much.

I would also like to thank the Herald and Weekly Time Pty Ltd and Editor-in-Chief Peter Blunden for sending me to Gallipoli in the first place and to Peter for his continual friendship and support and allowing me time to complete this project. I would also especially thank my friend and photographer colleague Craig Borrow who went with me to Gallipoli in 2000 and has provided constant companionship and professional help, then and now. Robyn Macleod and Trudy Mickelburough have both been of enormous practical assistance in writing this book and my other *Herald Sun* colleagues, especially John Trevorrow, Shane Burke, Bob Hart, Russell Robinson, Dan McDonnell and Neil Wilson, have listened to me patiently and made suggestions.

Outside, my friend Dr Peter Stratmann gave me helpful consultations on conditions ranging from the effects of dehydration to the causes of Barcoo Rot. Other friends who have helped in a multitude of ways include John and Jackie Tidey, Father Michael Elligate, Rodney Davidson, Rob Lewis, Kim West, Graeme Lush and Jenny Coates.

I would like to sincerely thank Tom Gilliatt, publisher of non-fiction at Pan Macmillan for believing in the project, for his encouragement and who, with editor Julie Crisp, copy-editor Jon Gibbs and the rest of the team, transformed an unwieldy manuscript into a book.

Lastly I thank my family. To my mother, Jean, and father, Ham, who taught me to read, write and always ask questions. To my wife, Kay, who has given her love and support throughout a life of foreign corresponding and who put up with me, this time, when I went off, weekend after weekend, to cover the First World War; and to my sons, James and Matthew, for their love. They are always there for me and can be counted on at all times.

Index